DATE DUE

DEMCO 38-296

The Marshall Cavendish Illustrated History of

POPULAR MUSIC

Volume 18

1984-1985

MARSHALL CAVENDISH
NEW YORK, LONDON, TORONTO, SYDNEY

Reference Edition Published 1990

...ion

...a. Vicenza.

Reference edition produced by DPM Services.

© Orbis Publishing Ltd.MCMLXXXIX
© Marshall Cavendish Ltd.MCMLXXXIX

Set ISBN 1-85436-015-3

Library of Congress Cataloging in Publication Data

The Marshall Cavendish history of popular music.
    p.   cm.
Includes index.
ISBN 1-85435-097-8 (vol. 18)
1. Popular music – History and criticism. 2. Rock music – History
and Criticism. I. Marshall Cavendish Corporation. II. Title:
History of popular music.
ML 3470. M36 1988
784. 5' 009 – dc19   88-21076
                                  CIP
                                  MN

Editorial Staff

Editor	Ashley Brown
Executive Editors	Adrian Gilbert Michael Heatley
Consultant Editors	Richard Williams Peter Brookesmith
Editorial Director	Brian Innes

Reference Edition Staff

Reference Editor	Mark Dartford
Revision Editor	Fran Jones
Consultant Editor	Michael Heatley
Art Editor	Graham Beehag

CONTENTS

CONTRIBUTORS

CLIVE ANDERSON

Co-author of *The Soul Book* and contributor to *Encyclopedia of Rock*, he has also written for *Black Music, Black Echoes, New Kommotion* and other magazines.

STEPHEN BARNARD

Has contributed to *Atlantic Rock, Melody Maker* and the *Rock Files* series. He also lectures at the City University, London.

DICK BRADLEY

Completed his PhD thesis on *British Popular Music in the Fifties* at the Centre of Contemporary Cultural Studies in Birmingham, England, and has also written articles for *Media, Culture & Society*.

JOHN BROVEN

Author of *Walking to New Orleans* and *South of Louisiana,* he has also contributed to *Nothing but the Blues* and *Encyclopedia of Rock*. He writes for *Blues Unlimited* and has also compiled several New Orleans rhythm and blues anthologies

ROB FINNIS

Author of *The Phil Spector Story* and *The Gene Vincent Story*, he has contributed to the major rock journals and runs a specialist record shop.

SIMON FRITH

A lecturer at the University of Warwick, England, he has built up a reputation over the last 15 years as one of the leading international commentators on rock music. He has co-edited the *Rock File* series, and written *The Sociology of Rock*.

PETER GURALNIK

Author of *Feel Like Going Home, Lost Highway* and *Nighthawk Blues*, his articles on blues, country and rock have appeared in *Rolling Stone,* the *Village Voice, Country Music, Living Blues,* the *New York Times* and the *Boston Phoenix*.

BILL HARRY

Founder member of UK's *Mersey Beat*, he later became news editor of *Record Mirror* and music columnist for *Weekend*. He is currently an independent PR for such artists as Suzi Quatro and Kim Wilde.

MARTIN HAWKINS

An acknowledged expert on the Sun era of rock'n'roll (author of *The Sun Story*), he writes for *Melody Maker, Time Barrier Express* and *Country Music*

BRIAN HOGG

Publisher of *Bam Balam*, which concentrates on US and UK bands of the Sixties, he has also written for such magazines as *New York Rocker* and *Record Collector*.

PETER JONES

Was editor of UK's *Record Mirror* from 1961 to 1969. He then became UK News editor of *Billboard* in 1977 and later UK and European Editor.

ROBIN KATZ

After 10 years in the Motown Press Office, she now writes freelance for *New Sound, New Styles, International Musician* and *Smash Hits*.

JOE McEWEN

An acknowledged authority on soul music, he has written for *Rolling Stone, Phonograph Record, Black Music,* the *Boston Phoenix* and Boston's *Real Paper*.

BILL MILLAR

As a freelance journalist he writes for *Melody Maker* and other rock papers. He is the author of *The Drifters* and *The Coasters*.

DAVID MORSE

Author of *Motown*, he lectures at the School of English and American Studies at Sussex University, England.

TONY RUSSELL

Editor of *Old Time Music* from 1971, he contributes regularly to *Blues Unlimited* and *Jazz Journal* and is the author of *Blacks, Whites and Blues*.

ROBERT SHELTON

Has written about blues, country and folk for the *New York Times* , London *Times, Listener, Time Out* and *Melody Maker*.

NICK TOSCHES

Author of *Hellfire*, a biography of Jerry Lee Lewis, he also writes for *New York Times* and *Village Voice*.

MICHAEL WATTS

Writes on popular arts for *The Los Angeles Times* and London *Times* and is rock columnist for *Records and Recording Magazine*.

ADAM WHITE

Has written about Motown for *Music Week* and *Black Echoes*, and scripted a six-hour documentary about the company and its music for US radio. Also worked as managing editor of *Billboard* magazine in New York.

Anarchy In The UK

A nation watched aghast as punk reared its spiky head

By the end of 1976, Malcolm McLaren was beginning to become known for his management of the Sex Pistols, the iconoclastic group spearheading the British punk revolution. He had previously gained some notoriety for the Sex boutique on the Kings Road that he co-owned with his partner, Vivienne Westwood.

In November he spoke to *New Musical Express'* Nick Kent about the Pistols, and their first single, 'Anarchy In The UK'. 'I don't see it as a fad, because it's such a simple attitude,' he said. 'It's the same attitude, I think, that Eddie Cochran had, that any *real* rock'n'roller had. I just see it as a reaction against the last five years of stagnation. Writing a song like "Anarchy In The UK" is definitely a statement of intent – it's hard to say something constructive in rock these days. It's a call to arms to the kids who believe very strongly that rock'n'roll was taken away from them. And now it's coming back. "Anarchy In The UK" is a statement of self-rule, of independence, of do-it-yourself, ultimately.'

Punks in Chelsea, London. This British youth rebellion was a gesture aimed not just against the establishment, but also against the rising tide of monopolized and stereotyped music that evolved as the swinging and hippy Sixties faded into the mid-Seventies.

Hippies to the slaughter

As manager of the Sex Pistols, McLaren (and his henchman Bernie Rhodes, later manager of the Clash) was directing a common but unfocused mood. Much of the nation's youth had become excruciatingly tired of the chart-dominating establishment rock bands; most of these had their roots in the 'rock-as-art' pretensions of the late Sixties, an era that provided ample cause for them to be dismissed as dope-soaked hippies and 'Boring Old Farts'.

It would be untrue to suggest that the dinosaur rock acts of the time had been allowed to roam free, totally unchallenged; pub-rock, which flourished in the early Seventies, had been one attempt at an antidote. Capable of being a drab, dispiriting affair, pub-rock often appeared to consist of little more than the attempts of assorted hostelries to act as a chain of rest homes for failed Sixties musicians. Yet the genre did have within it the seeds of much of the musical change that was to occur in 1976 and 1977. John Lydon had been a frequent

figure at the shows of Kilburn and the High Roads and the microphone mannerisms and posturings of Ian Dury, like Laurence Olivier playing Richard III, would be refined and developed into the distinctive on-stage style of Johnny Rotten.

Moreover, Joe Strummer (then known as Woody) served a rigorous musical apprenticeship in an obsessively hard-working R&B combo, the 101ers. Meanwhile, one Jake Riviera, manager of hoedown specialists Chilli Willi and the Red Hot Peppers, was familiarising himself with a scene whose true talents he was to re-mould and immortalise with the first releases on Stiff Records, the spiritual forerunner of the entire independent label movement that subsequently swept the UK and was such an important part of the punk boom.

Rats and stupidity

Stiff, indeed, was started with a loan from Dr Feelgood, whose stunning re-interpretations of R&B made them the only group to break out of the pub circuit to any great success. In fact, the short-haired, besuited Feelgoods – though derided at the time by the busily self-publicising punk musicians – bridged a vital gap between a British rock scene of intolerable complacency and *ennui* and one whose vitality made it the most exciting era to live in since the mid-Sixties Mod days. It was an important watershed when the Feelgoods' *Stupidity* album reached the top of the LP charts in the spring of 1976. In the wake of this success, record company A&R men began seizing upon other non-establishment groups – United Artists, to whom the Feelgoods were signed, quickly added the Stranglers to their roster, and in the early autumn their *Rattus Norvegicus* LP itself topped the album charts.

Punk purists, however, didn't consider the Stranglers to be true punks at all; as a style based largely on the dress and attitudes adopted by a set of Parisian poseurs who had modelled themselves on such American heroes as Lou Reed, Iggy Pop and the New York Dolls, punk had been a small élitist fashion in London since early 1974.

Above left and above right: The look of punk – do-it-yourself was the order of the day. Above: Down at the Roxy club, young punks do the pogo, the bouncing dance pioneered by Sid Vicious. Right: Malcolm McLaren lashes out at the Nashville as the Sex Pistols play on. Left: The press reacts to punk's 'outrage'. Below left: The Clash against the rails. Below: The Buzzcocks.

Bring on the spiky-tops

Throughout the first half of 1976, the Sex Pistols played regularly in London. But although controversy surrounded the group's appearance and the rumours of violence at their gigs, the real interest, contrary to what McLaren was to claim later, centred on the Pistols' music, a passionate blend of basic rock'n'roll and angry, satirical lyrics.

That same sense of savage humour, together with a determined effort to debunk the false and phoney, also dominated the lyrics of the Clash, who began playing in London in the spring of 1976. The punk scene mushroomed throughout the first half of the year, reaching some kind of first climax that September, when a punk festival, featuring the Sex Pistols, the Clash and others, was held at the 100 Club in London's Oxford Street.

'When we played the 100 Club,' Malcolm McLaren later recalled, 'half the audience we were attracting were kids who normally would've been down the road at the Crackers disco. These were young kids – mostly in the 16-17-18 bracket – who'd been into Bowie and Roxy Music but who'd been left behind . . . who'd left *them* behind because those acts just got too big, too distant . . . The Pistols don't play great and, as such, a kid in the audience can relate to that . . . he can visualise himself being up there on stage . . .'

In November 1976, the Clash signed to CBS Records. At the end of that month, the Sex Pistols' first single, 'Anarchy In The UK', was released on EMI Records. To promote it they appeared on the TV magazine programme 'Today'. Their interviewer, Bill Grundy, plainly disliked the group and the item quickly degenerated into a torrent of abuse and swearing from the Pistols. Grundy quickly wound up the feature.

The next morning the Sex Pistols were all over the front pages of the British tabloids, a position they maintained throughout the week. They had succeeded in becoming the most (in)famous group in the country, spearheading the punk movement that was to storm the UK in 1977.

CHRIS SALEWICZ

SeX PisTOLs

Was this the obituary of rock 'n' roll?

As THE EIGHTIES PROGRESSED, the most continually visible and successful survivor of the Sex Pistols phenomenon was their manager-turned-pop star Malcolm McLaren. This, along with other 'clues' dropped along the way as the most fascinating rock fable of the Seventies unfolded, makes it manifest that without McLaren there would have been neither a Sex Pistols (even the name was his) nor a punk-rock explosion.

That the time was ripe for some sort of change by 1976 goes without argument. The teenybop end of the glitter-rock boom had faded from the charts and had found no definite inheritors. Similarly, there was little or no chart action for the predominantly wizened performers on the London pub and small club circuit. The rock scene was stagnant, and a new focus had to be found.

The answer was being nurtured at the seedy, low-rent extremity of London's King's Road. Here, McLaren and a handful of key assistants were building a Frankenstein's monster of a rock group from a variety of cultural and artistic images and devices; a scheme calculated to shake the very foundations of the music business and all its attendant subcultures.

Let it rock

Like many a rock'n'roll Czar before him, McLaren had trodden the classic UK popster trail through art school (where his political leanings earned him the nickname 'Red Malcolm'). As a music consumer, however, McLaren's heart remained in the tough black leather and motorcycle heaven of the Fifties. Apt then that his first business venture – already his collaborator was the future star designer Vivienne Westwood – should be a shop specialising in the drape jackets, leathers and brothel-creeper shoes of Britain's first and longest-surviving pop cult, that of the Teds.

Above left: The Pistols sign with A&M Records outside Buckingham Palace, 10 March 1977. Left: Rotten cowers on stage.

It was as customers in his shop that McLaren first met the American group the New York Dolls. Having received an initial mighty push from their record company (Mercury), the Dolls had failed to match their flair for publicity with record sales. So it was that, with their two albums destined for the bargain bins, McLaren went to the US in a last brave attempt to save the group from total oblivion.

When McLaren dressed the Dolls in red leather and had them play stages bedecked with Russian flags, however, there was little response that was not negative. Rednecks saw red, cynics saw a new gimmick from a group that had always been the epitome of low camp. This, plus the self-destructive impetus which seemed to be the Dolls' major energy force towards the end, combined to bring the curtain down in an all-but-empty theatre.

Still, McLaren must have learned some valuable lessons, as well as passing through New York at just the right time to steal a few fresh ideas from the same clubland from which the Dolls had first emerged. (It was Television bass-player Richard Hell, for example, who originated the torn T-shirts and hacked haircut which would become the stereotype punk image – though, to be fair to McLaren, he did attempt to bring Hell to England to front a group.)

Meanwhile in London the beginnings of the Sex Pistols proper began to take shape at McLaren and Westwood's shop, Let It Rock. The shop was the hangout of two schoolfriends, Paul Cook (born 27 July 1956) and Steve Jones (born 3 May 1955) who, together with an older friend named Wally, were attempting to form a pop group. At McLaren's suggestion the combo – temporarily known as the Swankers – recruited Glen Matlock (born 27 August 1956), an assistant in Malcolm's shop. With Wally's disappearance (he was married with a kid and kept missing rehearsals), the last piece of the puzzle arrived in the form of a green-haired North London youth named John Lydon (born 31 January 1956). In the best documentary record of their history to date, Fred and Judy Vermorel's *The Sex Pistols* (1978), it was revealed that Rotten couldn't actually sing. 'But that wasn't really important, we

were all still learning our instruments at the time,' said Matlock. 'It's just that he had the right look, he fitted the image of ourselves that we must have had at the back of our minds.'

Cook and Jones' trainee repertoire of old Who and Small Faces numbers were gradually joined by a number of original items from the new group, now dubbed the Sex Pistols by McLaren. They began to appear sporadically at college gigs, sometimes legitimately, sometimes, according to legend, simply jumping on-stage uninvited.

That Johnny Rotten was a gem of a frontman was clear from the start. Many of the early concerts consisted more of Rotten's haranguing the audiences than of actual music. At this he was a master: 'You're all completely boring!' he would tell a packed Nashville, idly squeezing a spot on his chin. 'You make me bloody sick!' The voice was a nasal whine that melded the gay accent of a Kenneth Williams character with the weary petulance of Mick Jagger's Turner in *Performance*.

'We're into chaos'

The music press was initially divided as to the group's merits, but the papers eventually realised that there was good copy to be had from this oddly-attired quartet – dressed mostly from the racks of McLaren/Westwood's shop, which was now renamed Sex and was peddling bondage gear, pornographic T-shirts and similar fineries – who stumbled through a revised version of the Small Faces' 'Whatcha Gonna Do About It?' that declared: 'I want you to know that I *hate* you baby/I want you to know I don't caaare!' Their first review appeared in *NME* in February 1976 and included the classic quote, 'We're not into music . . . we're into chaos!'

In the next few months a new visual and verbal language appeared that would ultimately re-open the generation gap; in the meantime, the demarcation lines of what was hip and unhip were being rewritten.

In fact, McLaren and the Pistols weren't the first people to bring the terms 'anarchy' and 'chaos' into the dialectics of rock – Jim Morrison had used exactly the same terminologies a decade before. But for the generation that fell in line with the new wave, it must have seemed as if a new world was being created. Suddenly tight trousers replaced flares, the latter being a sign of a hippie.

McLaren's original plan to develop a stable of groups in the manner of the pop manager/impresarios of the early Sixties failed to develop into anything. Nevertheless, as 1976 rushed past and the punk virus spread, a whole crop of new groups sprang up in the Pistols' shadow. Some, like the Damned (whose 'New Rose' would be the first nationally-distributed punk record) contained former Pistols entourage members; others, like the Clash and the Banshees, were managed by Bernie Rhodes and Nils Stevenson, who had cut their teeth as McLaren aides and collaborators.

Filth and anarchy

As the year wore on, it became clear that the music of the Pistols and those that followed behind was not really as original as it at first pretended to be. Basically, punk was the old three-chord trick with a new face, a sharper pace and an English accent. Closer examination of the Pistols on disc would reveal more than a passing similarity between the phrasing of John Rotten and that of David Johansen of the now-defunct New York Dolls.

And although the punks claimed they were out to destroy the established music industry, when the Pistols finally did sign a record deal, it was not with one of the new breed of small independents but with a 'reactionary' major, EMI. Pen met paper in October 1976, with the Pistols being signed to a two-year contract in exchange for a healthy £40,000 advance. The group's debut single would be 'Anarchy In The UK', one of their big stage favourites and a rattling chunk of fairly classic rock. Of course, with such a 'controversial' group, things couldn't possibly proceed in the

standard way: the proposed sleeve design for the single was a portrait of the Queen with her face partly obliterated by the Pistols logo. EMI vetoed *that* idea immediately.

Meanwhile, the Pistols were causing more immediate outrage. In late November, the Anarchy tour of the nation – on which they were to be joined by the Clash, the Damned and the Heartbreakers – turned to farce with one council ban after another, all of which bounced backwards and forwards in the national press. Then, on 1 December, they became front-page news as a result of the notorious interview with Bill Grundy on TV's 'Today' programme. With everyone obviously a little the worse for drink, what started as a routine chat-show conversation quickly degenerated into a full-scale verbal orgy as, egged on by a smug Grundy, the lads filled the nation's homes with a sprawl of 'filth'. 'Go on. You've got another five seconds. Say something outrageous,' coaxed Grundy. 'You dirty bastard,' complied Jones. 'What a clever boy.' What a f----- rotter.'

The papers hadn't had so much fun with a pop group since the Stones urinated against a garage wall or John Lennon claimed that the Beatles were bigger than Jesus. Reports came in of honest working men who had kicked in their TV sets, of elderly ladies who had had strokes and everyone worried about how this outrage would corrupt the tender young children viewing the early-evening programme who had been exposed to – as the *Daily Mail* put it – 'some of the dirtiest language ever heard on television.' Grundy was suspended by Thames Television, EMI were extremely apologetic and everyone in the Pistols camp thought the whole thing hilariously funny. Then in mid December, with 'Anarchy In The UK' climbing the

Far left: The Pistols celebrate the Jubilee. Left: Sid with Nancy Spungen. Top: Paul Cook with original bassist Glen Matlock at the 100 Club. Above: Rotten roars.

Top Forty, staff at EMI's pressing plant threatened to strike if they had to make any more copies. It was no real surprise when, in the first week of the new year, EMI announced that they were no longer employing the Sex Pistols.

Jubilee jamboree

The Sex Pistols passed a relatively uneventful winter, if only because they were continually refused permission to play – a fact that, as McLaren obviously knew, kept the group as much in the public eye as if they *had* been playing. And early in March 1977, amid much brouhaha, the band signed with A&M. It was, as usual, to be a tragicomic farce, from the 'official' signing in front of Buckingham Palace to an abusive press reception and, finally, a handful of violent squabbles that ended with the group being sacked once more.

In February, the group had parted with

bassist Glen Matlock, whom many believed to be the real musical strength in the band. For the record, Matlock's dismissal was 'because he wanted us to be the Beatles'. His replacement was the blatantly musically incompetent Sid Vicious (born John Beverley, 10 May 1957); what Sid did have, though, was a penchant for violent abuse. It was he who was blamed for the incident which ended with a girl losing an eye during the course of the 100 Club Punk Festival in September 1976 and it was he who caused most of the physical damage which resulted in the Sex Pistols' brief liaison with A&M coming to a speedy end.

Despite this and all its attendant 'bad' publicity, despite the front-page story in all the dailies following the group's swearing lesson for the benefit of TV interviewer Bill Grundy . . . indeed, just *because* of this very topical notoriety, there were still plenty of record companies eager to talk to the Pistols. Thus, the group's recording career proper commenced when they were signed to Virgin in the spring of 1977. Their adventures thereafter, both in the charts and elsewhere, became positively ordinary when compared to the group's own super-low standards. Their 'God Save The Queen' response to the Jubilee was the Pistols' biggest chart success (reaching Number 2 in June) despite attacks in the press and a virtual TV and radio blackout.

Who killed Bambi?

By July and the third single, 'Pretty Vacant', the group actually did the unthinkable and appeared (on video admittedly; no-one would trust them live in a studio ever again) on 'Top Of The Pops'. Once again they crashed into the Top Ten. But the winning streak took something of a nosedive in October with 'Holidays In The Sun', a disc which, in retrospect, was little more than a re-run of the best bits of their former hits. Maybe Matlock's departure had cost the Pistols more than they dared to admit. The group's only legitimate LP – virtually a 'greatest hits' compilation – appeared in October. One or two shops were fined for displaying the record – sweetly titled *Never Mind The Bollocks, Here's The Sex Pistols*.

Inside the barbed wire, things were beginning to turn a little sour. Rotten was decidedly unhappy about McLaren's novel idea of doing a Pistols movie, tentatively titled *Who Killed Bambi?*, in collaboration with high-camp American skinflick director Russ Meyer. There was a brief European tour where the band were almost murdered by local teen hoods in Stockholm, and during which Sid Vicious appeared to have grasped the rudiments of bass-playing. Sid was once more the centre of attention when the Pistols finally crossed the Atlantic in January 1978. It was he who played covered in his and his fans' blood as the Pistols mashed their way through Texas.

But by the end of the tour Rotten had thrown in the towel. McLaren planned for the group to go directly to South America where, in another cheeky-sick master-stroke, they would record with escaped Great Train Robber Ronnie Biggs. In the event only Cook and Jones were on hand to back 'The Biggest Blow (A Punk Prayer)' on disc and video. Biggs' half-hearted Rotten impersonation, though a minor hit, was uniquely awful. The only real success after Rotten's departure would be Sid Vicious' hilarious mangling of the Frank Sinatra hit 'My Way'.

This last was featured on the soundtrack of *The Great Rock'n'Roll Swindle*, the movie (directed not by Meyer but by the young Julien Temple) that finally emerged from all the haggles and rewrites in 1978. In fact, the movie was less of a Pistols' project than a vehicle for McLaren as, helped by live, animated and some 'acting' footage, he revealed how to get rich by conning the record companies.

Goodbye to all that

The last nail in the coffin came with the death of Sid Vicious on 2 February 1979. The previous autumn, he had moved into New York's Chelsea Hotel with his girl-friend Nancy Spungen. Days after their arrival, Nancy was found stabbed to death, Sid was charged with her murder and con-fined to Ryker's Island prison, where he attempted suicide by slashing his wrists with a broken light bulb. Later, out on bail, he took his fatal dose of heroin.

Cook and Jones, meanwhile, rattled on as best they could, eventually changing their name to the Professionals for a flop album. Rotten would revert to his real sur-name and reappear at the helm of Public Image Ltd, a band with a shifting line-up and a quirky mixture of put-on, art-rock and serious experimentation. The combo's debut single 'Public Image', featuring Clash founder member Keith Levene on stinging guitars, Jah Wobble on booming, reggae-style bass and Lydon droning ''ello! 'ello! ... goodBYE!' in his customary, irreverent style was a remarkable and original record. It made Number 9 in the UK charts in November 1978, while their second album, *Metal Box* (1979), was to remain their most intriguing manifesto. After that, product became sporadic, although they enjoyed a UK Number 5 hit with 'This Is Not A Love Song' in 1983.

Together, McLaren and the Sex Pistols created some excellent, energetic music on record and stage. More importantly, they helped to develop the look of punk, the way of dressing, behaving and maybe even thinking. In some ways, however, the Sex Pistols were perhaps not rock's greatest success but its greatest failure. For, having built their name on controversy and out-rage, they took things too far; they allowed themselves to be carried away by their own image and, in doing so, destroyed them-selves. The tragic part is that in Sid Vicious' case, the destruction was a literal one – he was much too young to die just for the sake of an image.   GIOVANNI DADOMO

Right: A blood-splattered Sid in America.

SEX PISTOLS
Discography

Singles
Anarchy In The UK/I Wanna Be Me (EMI 2566, 1976); God Save The Queen/Did You No Wrong (Virgin VS181, 1977); Pretty Vacant/No Fun (Virgin VS184, 1977); Holidays In The Sun/Satellite (Virgin VS191, 1977); My Way/No One Is Innocent (A Punk Prayer) (Virgin VS220, 1978); Something Else/Friggin' In The Riggin' (Virgin VS240, 1979); Silly Thing/Who Killed Bambi (Virgin VS256, 1979); C'mon Everybody/God Save The Queen Symphony: Watcha Gonna Do About It (Virgin VS272, 1979); The Great Rock'n'Roll Swindle/Rock Around The Clock (Virgin VS290, 1979); I'm Not Your Stepping Stone/Pistols Propaganda (Virgin VS339, 1980).

Albums
Never Mind The Bollocks, Here's The Sex Pistols (Virgin V2086, 1977); *The Great Rock'n'Roll Swindle* (Virgin VD2510, 1979); *Some Product–Carri On Sex Pistols* (Virgin VR2, 1979); *Flogging A Dead Horse* (Virgin V2142, 1980); *The Great Rock'n'Roll Swindle* (Film) (Virgin V 2168, 1980).

THE GREAT ROCK'N'ROLL SWINDLE

How Malcolm McLaren made cash from chaos

THERE IS A CERTAIN type of rock manager whose clients become the means to express his own artistic vision: in the late Fifties, Larry Parnes groomed his stars and gave them names which were supposedly descriptive of their characters, such as Steele, Wilde, Gentle, Fury, Power, Eager; in the early Sixties Andrew Loog Oldham manufactured the Rolling Stones' bad-boy image; and Pete Meaden discovered Mod in the early Sixties and set up the Who as a focal point for that particular branch of youth subculture.

Malcolm McLaren's entrepreneurial

of all three. Like Parnes, he gave new names to his protégés – Sex Pistols, Rotten, Vicious; like Oldham, he assiduously played up the 'them and us' conflict of the generation gap and staged outrageous publicity stunts to ensure his group, the Sex Pistols, maximum media coverage;

Above: The pixie-faced, fun-loving Malcolm McLaren scratches a living as a

and like Meaden, he made the Pistols the focus for a gathering youth movement – punk. He provided figureheads for an inarticulate revolt.

At one time McLaren considered singing with Cook, Jones and Matlock and becoming a Sex Pistol himself; this ambition reflected the extent of his involvement with the band. He projected his ideas through his group, encouraged their rebelliousness and turned them into provocative caricatures of 'degenerate' youth. He saw himself more as an artist than as a manager. 'Instead of using the canvas,' he said, 'I have

Quest for fire

Born Malcolm Robert Andrew McLaren in 1947 to a Scottish father and a mother of Portuguese-Jewish ancestry, he was raised by his maternal grandmother in Clissold Park, Stoke Newington, then a middle-class area of London. Legend has it that his father was a burglar who disappeared when Malcolm was two years old, and that McLaren is related, on his mother's side, to both agony columnist Marjorie Proops and actor Danny Kaye.

He left grammar school with two GCE 'O' levels and took his first job as a trainee wine-taster. He then spent eight years as a student, studying fine art at Goldsmiths College, Harrow School of Art and Croydon School of Art.

McLaren's expectations of music were formed from childhood exposure to American rock'n'roll. He saw both Eddie Cochran and Buddy Holly on tour before he was in his teens, visited that incubator of skiffle the 2 Is coffee-bar in Soho and, while a student, began a film on Billy Fury, whom apart from Johnny Kidd, he considered the only true British rocker.

He has often spoken of the potency of rock'n'roll, believing it to be essentially anti-Christian, pagan, tribal and magic. Rock'n'roll, McLaren believed, should be a 'stepping out' from society's norms, a voluntary exile, an establishing of individual style. The jarring energy and anarchistic spirit of the Sex Pistols exactly fitted his prescription.

Let It Rock, the King's Road clothing store he opened in 1971 with his girlfriend, designer Vivienne Westwood, continued his affair with rock'n'roll deviancy, selling drape jackets, drainpipe trousers and brothel creepers at a time of flares and platform boots. In 1973 the shop's name became Too Fast To Live, Too Young To Die and a visit to London by the New York Dolls intrigued him enough to consider music again. Typically it wasn't the band's music that aroused his interest, but 'the way they carried themselves'.

Committed to the Keith Richards school of raunch and decadence, the Dolls were a cartoon of rock'n'roll dandyism and excess. McLaren followed them to New York, where he managed them for six months in 1974, dressing them in shiny red leather, draping hammer-and-sickle flags over the stage and providing a backdrop portrait of Chairman Mao. The revolution didn't happen, though, and by 1975 he was back at work in the shop, now renamed Sex and selling a selection of bondage clothing and rubberware. Here he was to encounter the bored young shoplifters who were to become the biggest shock in rock for a decade.

His awareness that the time was right for something like punk – like his marketing of Ted gear ahead of the rockabilly revival – illustrates his remarkable intuition. He had an innate ability to 'sniff the breeze', to sense underlying changes in national mood. At the turn of the Eighties, he felt the country was ready for glamour and, for a consultancy fee, advised Adam

Ant on an image drawn from the romantic figures of pirates, highwaymen and Red Indians. He later created Bow Wow Wow, discovering teenage vocalist Annabella Lwin in a local laundrette, and started pitching to the 13- and 14-year-old audience which he rightly believed was once again going to become the most important market for pop music.

Take that situation

Yet what made McLaren significantly different from his managerial forebears was his political consciousness, which was nurtured in student sit-ins, the Paris riots of 1968 and by his involvement with a West London anarchist group called King Mob, who once invaded Selfridges dressed as Father Christmases and dispensed free gifts to the customers.

While at art college, McLaren had been introduced to the ideas of 'the Situationiste Internationale', a neo-Marxist art movement which had begun in Italy in the late Fifties. The group engineered 'situations' that exposed social repression, events designed to provoke a reaction from the usually passive bystanders or 'consumers of spectacle'. Both McLaren and Vivienne Westwood aligned themselves with Situationism. 'I intend the clothes I design to cause a confrontation,' says Westwood. 'To poke fun at the world is to provoke its collapse,' says McLaren. Asked whether punk was destructive, he once said: 'For me the very destructive nature of the idea was ultimately its most creative point. To me that was what it was all about.'

Thus the Sex Pistols came to be remembered less for their music than for the front-page headlines they made: the Grundy TV incident; the banning of 'God Save The Queen'; the Thames river-boat trip; the outraged local councillors; the offending T-shirts; the shop owner arrested for displaying the album cover; their being sacked by both EMI and A&M; the deaths of Nancy Spungen and Sid Vicious; and the association with Ronald Biggs. McLaren always insisted that the group's audience and their attitude were far more exciting than the music.

The 'situations' McLaren and his group created or took advantage of, although good for sales, were more than publicity stunts. The 'Today' TV programme wanted to parade an outrageous pop group for the titillation of the viewers at home and became outraged when the band proved to be truly outrageous. The major record companies fell over each other in their eagerness to cash in on the latest in rock 'n'roll anarchy, but couldn't handle it when the same phenomenon began taking place within their doors.

Once asked whether he wasn't in fact simply offering one more product for sale, McLaren replied: 'I think that I am, without question, but I hope that people will realise that with the spectacle there is a tremendous sense of poison that ultimately wrings the neck of society.'

Yet unfortunately there was no love and

idealism to create a new order after the demolition was over. These were considered 'hippie' virtues. The poison the Pistols released contaminated them, killing Sid Vicious, breaking up the group and eventually bringing all their anger back on themselves so that they finished, as the Beatles before them, in the High Court. McLaren remained unrepentant: 'Out of chaos,' he said, 'comes a new lease of confidence.'

An essential part of McLaren's ethos is his interest in the concept of Original Innocence, which has proved both a leading philosophical concern and a popular selling-point for art of all kinds since the eighteenth century.

He has linked the idea of the noble savage with so-called 'primitive' African rhythms to clever commercial effect in the case of Adam and the Ants and Bow Wow Wow. Very soon, however, the appearance and sound of these acts lost their shock value and became just another disposable image – jungle chic.

McLaren's work in the early Eighties with the scratchers, rappers and breakers of New York can be seen as a further attempt on his part to discover the 'untainted' expression of street people who 'think with the hip rather than the head'. He has also investigated ritual music with pre-Christian origins in South America and Africa and American hillbilly music. 'I look at a lot of primitive civilisations and the culture that stems from it,' he has said, 'because I find in it a certain purity and a certain non-clichéd understanding.' The results of his wanderings could be heard on his first solo LP, *Duck Rock* (1983), which cost over 100,000 dollars to make; it featured the 'scratch' hit Buffalo Gals'.

McLaren's next project, *Fans* (1984), was a disco version of the opera *Madam Butterfly*, while his third solo album, scheduled for 1989 release, also mixed modern and classical music, fusing waltzes with the rock of Jeff Beck and the funk of Bootsy Collins. His main preoccupation then, however, was art.

The Sex Pistols' biographer Fred Vermorel has eulogised McLaren thus: 'He has the vision of an artist, the heart of an anarchist and the imagination of a spiv.' McLaren himself is just a little less sweeping in his assessment of his own talents, saying: 'I don't ever pose solutions. I'm not able to do that. I create big puffs of smoke and great volcanoes.'   STEVE TURNER

Opposite: Scenes from the life of Malcolm, featuring (clockwise from right) a publicity portrait for his 1983 single 'Soweto'; a poster for The Great Rock'n'Roll Swindle; *McLaren with Vivienne Westwood; their shop,* Sex; *and the artist's knees.*

Malcolm McLaren Recommended Listening

Duck Rock (Charisma Records MMLP1) (Includes: Buffalo Gals, Double Dutch, Legba, Obatala, Punk It Up, Duck For The Oyster).

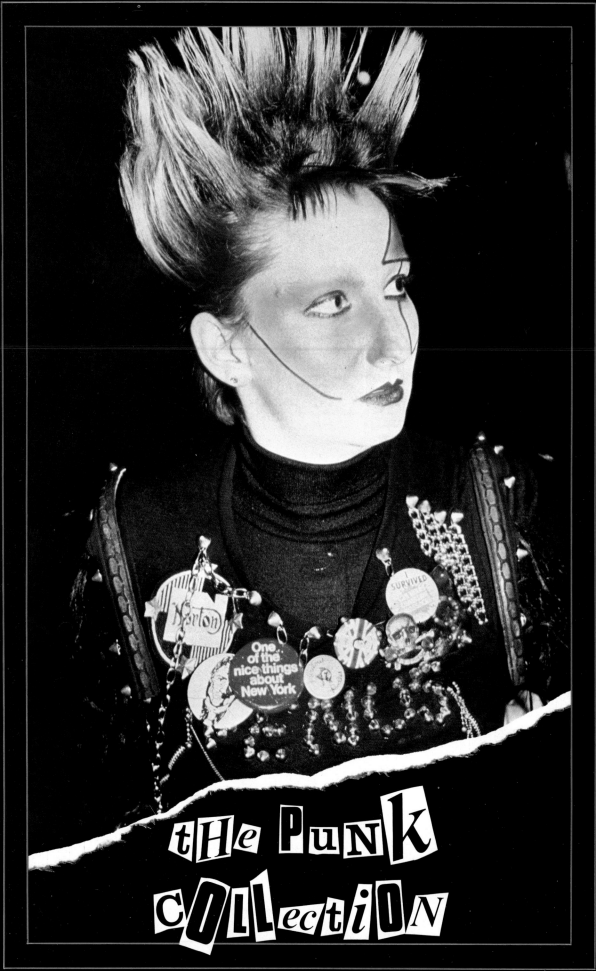

tHE PunK COllectiOn

Fear and loathing in the high street

A PUNK WANDERING down the King's Road in 1976 was every bit as startling and unexpected as the vicious sound of 'Anarchy In The UK'; long hair was still in vogue, and the sight of spiky peroxide locks and bondage straps garnered surprise if not hostility. Punk music was designed to shock and grab attention – and so were the fashions that grew up around the music.

It was, of course, the Sex Pistols who had the most direct influence: Johnny Rotten's appearance, with his spiked or gelled-up hair, ripped T-shirts, leather trousers and wristbands, inspired a host of imitators. Then there were American punks the Ramones who introduced a simpler look – leather jackets and jeans ripped at the knees (although the Ramones' hair was much too long for any self-respecting English punk). As punk's popularity began to grow, plastic sunglasses, safety-pinned jackets, painted blazers and training shoes became common wear, though these raised more laughter than indignation.

Oh bondage!

The Sex Pistols had come together at the Sex boutique in London's King's Road, run by their manager Malcolm McLaren and his clothes-designing partner Vivienne Westwood. Sex, which concentrated mainly on fetishist and Ted gear, soon became Seditionaries, selling muslin T-shirts with ridiculously long sleeves, bondage trousers with straps of various sizes stitched between the legs, kilts (bondage or conventional), parachute jackets and all the accessories of printed socks, shades and studs. With a large middle-class involvement in the early punk scene, the clothes were considered affordable – but as punk became a predominantly working-class movement, the high prices of Seditionaries were scorned and new establishments like Boy (also on the King's Road) and Stark Naked in Camden, which produced similar but cheaper goods, sprang up.

Although the McLaren/Pistols/Westwood triangle was the greatest influence on punk fashion, their more organised look was swiftly challenged by further developments. Bands like the Clash advocated a DIY approach with ripped, painted and second-hand clothes. People made their own outfits out of plastic bin liners and a sleazy world of

fashion based around sex catalogues became popular, with girls sporting holey stockings, thigh-length boots and transparent T-shirts. Poly Styrene of X-Ray Spex had a particularly individual approach – with her teeth braces, bowler hat and gaudy jumble-sale children's clothes, she was almost walking Tupperware. The bondage brigade, meanwhile, opted for leather, rubber and PVC, black remaining their favourite colour, to form their more malevolent look.

If the aim of these various approaches to self-decoration was to shock, they had

Punk chic, clockwise from right: Masked to shock; Siouxsie in S-M gear and Nazi armband; Siouxsie (second from left), Sue Catwoman (bottom) and friends show off various punk guises; bondage for sale; King's Road's Boy boutique; groovy shades for punks and Mods. Opposite: Jordan displays her hair-raising style.

exactly the right effect. The press jumped on the punk look – stories of ears and noses damaged by safety pins abounded – and those who hadn't yet heard punk music were drawn by the images with their rebellious connotations. One *genuinely* shocking development was the flaunting of swastikas by people too naïve to know better. A popular design of the day was the 'Destroy' T-shirt which depicted a swastika in flames.

Although this could be seen as a castigation of Nazism, there were some who used the frightening image for its gratuitous shock value. Siouxsie Sioux of the Banshees was seen at many of the group's early gigs sporting a swastika arm-band, Seditionaries sold swastika socks, while in the Sex Pistols film, *The Great Rock'n'Roll Swindle* (1980), Sid Vicious would be seen strolling through a Jewish quarter of Paris in a swastika T-shirt and taking bad taste to unpardonable limits. Fortunately, most performers steered well clear of such distasteful matter, while those who didn't were panned by the music press.

Tattoo vampires

A more harmless fashion 'shocker' was S-M wear, the attractions of which were impressed on London audiences by Adam Ant in particular. Adam and the Ants were often joined on stage by Seditionaries worker Jordan, whose extravagantly wild haircuts (bleached vertical spikes) and geometric designs painted on her face helped to make her a celebrity in her own right. Leather and studs were joined by lace, additional straps and harnesses, facemasks and makeup. And while this taboo and fetish scene gathered force, the Gothic look – pioneered by Damned singer Dave Vanian with his Count Dracula impersonation – gained some popularity.

Once the initial outrage caused by the look of punks had died down, the fashions slowly began to filter through to the outside world. Just as Pop Art and psychedelic clothing had been packaged for public consumption back in the Sixties, so punk apparel, suitably moderated, was marketed on a wide scale to be sold in high-street stores around the nation. Meanwhile, mail-order firms selling more 'authentic' punk gear abounded. The ready availability of inexpensive punk clothing, combined with the more slothful attitude of the later punks (why design it yourself when someone will do it for you?), helped to unify the overall image of punk.

Thus, by the time the musical fervour started to wane in 1978, those still involved had a generally uniform look: spiky hair, jeans or bondage trousers, leather jackets (adorned with band names or anarchist slogans), T-shirts, studs and

Above left: A leather-clad Sid Vicious tucks in to breakfast. Left: Gothic images from the Sex Gang Children. Below left: Punkermarket. Below centre: Super spikes. Below: Johnny Rotten.

chains – in short, the Sid Vicious clone. The clothes had become acceptable urban uniforms and the only visual developments were in styles of hair and makeup. Hardcore punks experimented with crazy-colour hair dye and eye liner, the Mohican haircut – shaven head apart from a thin, sprouting central strip – began to catch on, and facial tattoos made an impact.

By the Eighties, there was nothing 'fashionable' about punk any more and – the odd anglepoise haircut aside – there was nothing particularly noticeable about it either. The punks had become just another easily identifiable sect like skinheads, Mods or Hell's Angels.

It was in the post-punk fields of new romantic and new-wave pop that punk's original fashion ideas were to evolve, as

makeup, female lines for males, fetishism and taboos casually rolled together and erupted into new designs. The walking clothes-horse effect was taken to dandyish extremes by the Blitz crew (Steve Strange and friends); jewellery became acceptable along with studs; the leather jacket was either customised or rejected in favour of something more striking and feathery hairstyles replaced the spikes.

Among the performing trend-setters of the early Eighties were Terry Hall, of Fun Boy Three, who contributed his haircut (a basically vertical style with shaved sides above the ears), and Adam Ant whose American Indian look re-introduced colourful escapism. Vivienne Westwood tried something similar when McLaren launched his new creation Bow Wow Wow by dressing the band in 'pirate' garb. This concentration on 'noble' cultures was later adopted by new bands like Death Cult.

The Doc Marten boots, Lewis leather jackets and 12-inch spikes of the punks had given way to Kung Fu slippers, Mortici creations and vermilion fronds – 'new-wave' fashions continued to grab attention. What had once been regarded as a passing fad had blossomed; what had been regarded by some as a threat to society had become an accepted part of young people's lives.   MICK MERCER

Below left: Adam Ant and tiny fan on TV's 'Jim'll Fix It'. During punk's heyday, Adam adorned himself with S-M gear but the Eighties saw him transform himself, via face-paint and tribal fashion, into a fully-fledged pop star. Below: A punk of the Eighties – leather, studs, nose chain, face tattoos and Mohican haircut.

RIP IT UP

Fanzines proclaimed the principles of punk

IN EARLY 1976, when punk rock was brewing, the established music press hoped that, if they ignored it, it would go away. The field was clear for the punks to move in themselves; they saw the bands, they understood the music – so who better to write about it? It was also an opportunity to be involved, get free records and tickets for reviews, and actually *meet* the performers.

Fanzines were born – the bastard children of the rock press. And when the established papers *did* begin to pick up on punk, the fanzines reacted with venom: 'Certain writers in the established rags are latching on to the new bands in the same way that they change the fashion of their clothes,' wrote *Sniffin' Glue* in November 1976. 'Writing about "punk rock" is the thing to do at the moment. I hope the "fashion" soon dies out, then you'll be able to find out who really believed in the bands!'

Brash, offensive, libellous, cheap and nasty, the punk fanzines epitomised the state of the art with names like *Sniffin'*

Left and far right: Punk fanzines – 'brash, offensive, libellous, cheap and nasty.'
Below: An interview with the Damned in Jamming. *Note the glossy 'colour' picture of the interviewees.*

Glue, Kill Your Pet Puppy, Pogo Till It Hurts, Live Wire, 48 Thrills, Ripped & Torn, Jamming, Shews, Confidential and many more, all packed with enthusiasm and freshness. There was no attempt at objectivity – personal writing was the thing.

The writers were young punks, with often nothing more than a pen and access to a photocopier. As time progressed, many graduated to typewriters and local community printing presses. Eventually, shops like Better Badges and Rough Trade became involved. Photographs were usually photocopied and totally indistinguishable, but crude cartoons and drawings were often decoration enough – professionalism was never the issue. Fanzines were not rivals to *NME* or *Sounds*: they were alternatives, and, for the punks, preferred alternatives, with two fingers in the air!

Open the floodgates

The underground press had been re-born, although this was a million safety pins away from the acid-headed, self-indulgent rags of the late Sixties and early Seventies. A theme prevalent throughout the fanzines encouraged the readership to set up and do it themselves. 'Everybody start a punk fanzine and flood the market,' said *Sniffin' Glue*. 'Let's destroy all the established mags!'

The punkzines were far from negative; punk was an issue which was taken

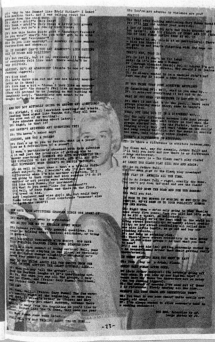

Above: 'I suppose you could call this a news page,' declares this 1978 issue of Ripped & Torn. Note the classic 'cut-out-and-stick-down' design style and the hand-lettering.

seriously by its devotees – it was more than music, it was a lifestyle. Many of the editorials showed thought and care and were intelligently written. 'People say punks are not positive,' wrote *Ripped & Torn* in March 1979. 'We know we are. Potentially, punk is the most beneficial force for productive change in society today (and the most fun). We know we've made mistakes, but we're improving, and making less while still experimenting.'

One of the main faults of fanzines, however, was their tendency to rant. Expletives and exclamation marks were often splattered about with wild abandon, while bitterness, hate and resentment oozed from the pages of some of the second-league examples. But in those days, everyone was supposed to be part of the blank generation.

The financial side of the magazines remains quite a mystery. Many were started from dole cheques or student grants, plus free donations of help or facilities. Many appeared for one issue and then sank without trace. The phenomenon was not confined to London; there was a network all over England, with several outstanding examples from Scotland (where *Ripped & Torn* originated) and Wales. These were the information rings for news that none of the 'straights' would touch.

There was little interest in organised politics, but apart from a few extremists like the racist *Chicken Shit*, the stance was generally left-wing – the Anti-Nazi League was very much in evidence at the time, getting a large following from punks by staging huge concerts and benefits. But it was personal politics that featured more strongly in the fanzines – street credibility and punk principles. 'Don't be pissed on by the people you give a living to,' said *Dirt* in July 1978. 'You do not have to be a party to their illusions of grandeur, their hypocrisy. No band is that important you can't say "get lost, I don't agree with that."

This is written for those bands who have kept their ideals and who deserve respect for that.'

Maximum speed
The main bulk of fanzine copy usually consisted of long interviews with bands, record reviews, live reviews (although these were usually months out of date), film reviews, and occasionally some bitchy gossip – all the requisites of many of the large rock journals, in fact, except that good grammar and punctuation were rejected in place of raw energy.

Punks were not the only writers of fanzines. When the Mod revival came alive in 1979, a spate of Modzines like *Maximum Speed* suddenly made an appearance. To non-Mods, however, the mag was packed with obscure references, in-jokes and silly information.

However, to be pompous about fanzines could only be condescending and patronising. It would also defeat their whole purpose; as Mark P. once said of his own *Sniffin' Glue*: 'We're thinking ahead, the early issues aren't much good anyway. For Christ's sake don't collect *SG* for the sake of it. It ain't a stamp collection you know.'

Many fanzines had no date and often articles weren't signed, adding to the immediacy and temporariness of them all. 'There ain't any credits on the writing or the pictures 'cos it's a group effort and we're not here to splash our names all over the pages,' said the creators of *The Late Clubs*. 'We're writing about other things not ourselves right?' In holding this attitude, punk fanzines could put forward a strong claim to being the purest – if most short-lived – form of rock journalism.

LINDSAY SHAPERO

The UK venues that staged a music revolution

BY DECEMBER 1976, punk had emerged from the shadows of clubs like Louise's to take the headlines by storm with tales of filth and fury. The first punk singles had appeared, but many of the bands could not find anywhere to play. To begin with, the problem had been that they were too obscure; later, they were too notorious, and councils and promoters banned them. 'I think the Sex Pistols are absolutely bloody revolting,' London councillor Bernard Brook-Partridge said in July 1977. 'We would do anything within the law to stop them ever appearing in London again.'

Initially, the first wave of punk bands played anywhere and everywhere they could. The Sex Pistols made their debut at St Martin's School of Art in November 1975; the Buzzcocks first played in public the following April, at a party for textile students at Bolton Institute of Technology; that August, the Clash gave their first performance before friends in the garage they used for rehearsals; and the Jam plugged their amps into the sockets of the Rock On record stall in Soho Market one October afternoon, startling the shoppers with their energetic R&B.

During 1976, existing establishments began to play host to this first wave of punk bands. The pub-rock boom of the mid Seventies had paved the way for punk by proving there was a substantial audience for raw, unsophisticated rock music, and the Hope and Anchor in Islington was soon putting on the Jam regularly; they played the Red Cow in Hammersmith, too, along with the Lurkers and X-Ray Spex. The other main London venues to stage punk gigs were the 100 Club in Oxford Street, the Nashville in West Kensington, the Marquee in Wardour Street and the Roundhouse in Chalk Farm.

London's burning

Of these, only the Marquee rejected this new form of music, banning punk after a Sex Pistols performance in 1976. It wasn't until the following year that they reconsidered their decision; by then, punk had become a profitable business. The Nashville played host to the Pistols and the Stranglers, while the Roundhouse staged larger, often American, bands; concerts there by the Ramones and Patti Smith had a great influence on many people then forming punk bands.

The most famous punk gig of 1976, however, was the 100 Club Festival, the English answer to the Mont de Marsan punk festival in France. For two nights in September, the 100 Club showcased the Sex Pistols, the Clash, Subway Sect, Suzie (as she was then known) and the Banshees, the Damned, Chris Spedding and the Vibrators, the Buzzcocks and the French band Stinky Toys – a gathering that has never been bettered. The festival was marred, though, when a glass thrown at

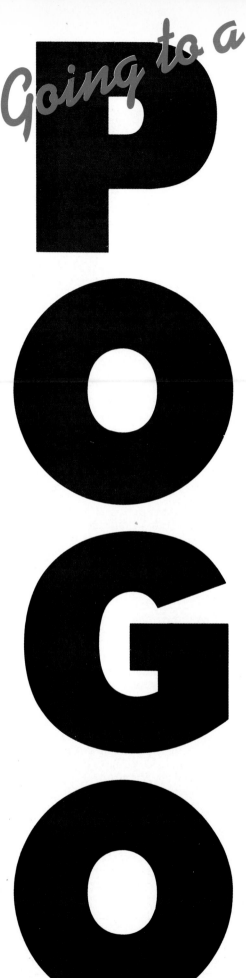

the stage during the Vibrators' set shattered against a pillar and a girl lost an eye. Banshees drummer Sid Vicious was arrested in connection with the offence, but later released, and the 100 Club placed a temporary ban on punk gigs.

The punk audience was growing rapidly, but no clubs opened to welcome the new hordes. Bands responded by taking over other buildings for the night; the Damned played in a school, the Sex Pistols at the Screen on the Green cinema in Islington and the Notre Dame Hall in Leicester Square. Punk finally got a focal point when the Roxy Club opened in Neal Street, Covent Garden in December 1976. Run by entrepreneur Andy Czezowski, the Roxy began by putting on American bands like the Heartbreakers and Wayne County and the Electric Chairs. It soon became the premier live venue for punk bands in London: the Clash, Subway Sect, X-Ray Spex, the Banshees, the Damned and the Slits all played there. The atmosphere of the club was captured on vinyl on the EMI live album *The Roxy London WC2 (Jan-Apr '77)*, which featured eight bands – not to mention the audience, who were recorded by hidden microphones.

Although the Roxy could claim a regular clientele, it was clear that the increasing audience required larger venues, and it was here that problems arose. After the Pistols' infamous Bill Grundy interview in December 1976, their Anarchy In The UK tour – on which several other punk bands, including the Clash, played – ran into serious difficulties. Several town councils decided to ban the tour 'in the public interest', and the situation was not improved by university and college social secretaries preferring to sit on the fence until the furore died down.

'A' bomb in Wardour Street

It was here that the Roundhouse came into its own. The only large venue in London open to punk at that time, its Sunday gigs regularly drew full houses. But things were improving: the Marquee reversed its exclusion policy, the Buzzcocks, X-Ray Spex, the Damned, Generation X and Adam and the Ants all enjoying successful residencies; soon, virtually every night at the Marquee was a punk night. When Andy Czezowski left the Roxy – he was later to open the Fridge in Brixton – another club opened, the Vortex in Soho's Wardour Street.

Immortalised in the Jam song '"A" Bomb In Wardour Street', it was a welcome addition to the London club scene, halfway between the Roxy and the Marquee in size. Its dubious selection policy on the door, however, caused crowds to dwindle after reaching an early peak. The Vortex also

Punks over London, clockwise from top left: Siouxsie and the Banshees at the Vortex; X-Ray Spex at the Hope and Anchor; the Jam at the Nashville; the Sex Pistols at the 100 Club; the Damned at the Roxy; Generation X at the Marquee.

produced a live album, but not of the same quality as the Roxy. A second Roxy album was released in 1978, shortly after the club closed: but it was nowhere near as good as the first.

More and more venues opened. The Music Machine in Camden (later the Camden Palace) began having punk concerts, with highly successful gigs by Siouxsie and the Banshees, Adam and the Ants and the Clash. The Sundown disco in Charing Cross Road could have been a very popular club, but it was soon closed down because the premises did not conform to the fire regulations. The Man In The Moon pub in the King's Road closed its doors to punk after a legendary residency by X-Ray Spex and Adam and the Ants. Though clubs now welcomed punk almost universally, pubs – under the wary eye of the breweries – fought shy of it, and were pleased when something less raucous like the short-lived power-pop movement of 1978 came along.

Punk and disorderly

The Rainbow was one of the first major London venues to put on punk bands; the Damned played there in the spring of 1977, supporting Marc Bolan. After a Clash gig that April, when fans tore up the seats, they hung back from punk for a few months, leaving it to the Hammersmith

Odeon to experiment, but most of their shows were reserved for visiting American outfits of the 'new wave' variety.

By 1978, London was well and truly punk-ridden, especially after the Lyceum opened its doors to punk bands. Outside London, however, things were every bit as desperate as they had been in 1976. There were a few centres of activity, however, like Eric's in Liverpool. Originally the Revolution Club, Eric's opened in Mathew Street, near the site of the famous Cavern Club, in late 1976. Although never purely a punk club, Eric's played host to such bands as Generation X and the Damned: it would later become a breeding ground for Liverpool bands like the Teardrop Explodes and Echo and the Bunnymen.

Manchester had the Band On The Wall and the Electric Circus (which produced a live album, on which Joy Division played). Together with the Rafters Club, these venues provided the focus for a vital and exciting local scene which centred around the Buzzcocks, Joy Division and the Fall. Later, Granada TV presenter Tony Wilson took one night a week at the Russell Club – a venue normally devoted to reggae – in Moss Side to put on his Factory Club, providing the basis for his successful independent label, Factory Records.

Birmingham, meanwhile, had Rebecca's

and Barbarella's, but for the most part, fans outside London had to content themselves with the large chains of dancehalls like Mecca and Top Rank. Their booking policies were conservative, though – Mecca banned punk bands from all their venues in July 1977. It wasn't until 1979 that a widespread range of venues was available to punk bands up and down the country.

By the early Eighties, punk was on the wane and the range of venues available declined once again. The 100 Club was forever banning punk after outbreaks of violence and then relenting when they thought tempers had cooled. The popularity of Sham 69 introduced an element of political violence, too, which eventually forced them to disband.

Student bodies were once again wary of booking punk bands: the Nashville closed its doors in 1980 after one firebomb attack too many, as did the Music Machine, while many venues simply banned punk altogether. Apart from the established acts which could play large venues like the Lyceum, the Hammersmith Palais or the Electric Ballroom, by 1983 punk bands were once again restricted to a few small pubs and clubs: by then, the movement's heyday was gone. MICK MERCER

Don Letts (left) and Andy Czezowski outside the defunct Roxy, 1977.

1977-Two Sevens Clash

How punk shocked the Establishment in Silver Jubilee year

As a rebel music, punk rock had close affinities with reggae. When the punk movement found a focal point and place of worship in the Roxy in Covent Garden, a former gay club that opened as a temple to punk in December 1976, it was Jamaican music – spun by the then up-and-coming film-maker Don Letts – that provided much of the entertainment between acts. Reggae, declared the hippest punks, was the only music to which they listened. Bob Marley recorded 'Punky Reggae Party', the Clash covered Junior Murvin's 'Police And Thieves' and the dominant reggae LP of the year was Culture's *Two Sevens Clash*. The title song referred to the supposed mystical significance of the year 1977 which was claimed to fore-shadow great social change.

Certainly, 1977 proved a watershed year; suddenly there were new, short-haired groups everywhere – most of whom seemed to get their names on the bill at the Roxy in the first three months of 1977. Apart from the established names like the Damned, the Buzzcocks and the Clash, there were countless others who enjoyed their 15 minutes – or more – of fame. X-Ray Spex were fronted by the engaging Poly Styrene, who made tooth-braces and chainstore kitsch fashionable. With their committed left-wing stance and the distinc-tive wail of Lora Logic's saxophone, they were responsible for some of punk's most outstanding anthems for frustrated youth – songs like 'Oh Bondage, Up Yours!', 'Identity' and 'Warrior In Woolworths'. They eventually recorded one LP, *Germ Free Adolescents*, in 1978, before Poly went solo, discovered God and reverted to her real name of Marion Ellis.

One chord wonders

Jimmy Pursey's agit-rock group Sham 69 were also notable for their political stance, and were indirectly respon-sible for the growth of Oi! later in the Seventies, while Generation X, fronted by Billy Idol – a Bromley contingent friend of the Pistols and Siouxsie – hit back at the Who with their debut single, 'Your Genera-tion'. The Adverts – 'One Chord Wonders', as one of their songs proclaimed – had a Top Twenty hit with the topical and tasteless 'Looking Through Gary Gilmore's Eyes' in August of 1977, while other regulars on the scene included Chelsea, 999, Eater – famed for their 14-year-old drummer Dee Generate – the Vibrators, the Lurkers and the Australian band the Saints. Slaughter and the Dogs and the quaintly-named Ed Banger and the Nosebleeds emerged from the Man-chester scene, while Penetration, from County Durham, had a distinctive and talented lead singer and songwriter in Pauline Murray.

Among fans, these bands caused intense polarisation, most of the arguments hingeing around whether they could or could not play. Yet this was really irrelevant, for it was the

Above: The Adverts' T.V. Smith and Gaye Advert make the most of their one chord.

groups' attitude that counted. Specifically, that attitude was one of positive iconoclasm, carried out with tongue inserted firmly in cheek. Contrary to what was claimed at the time, there was nothing negative about the essence of punk. The atmosphere was electric with excitement and full of potential.

The first major event of the year was the White Riot Tour, on which the Clash headlined, intended to promote their first CBS LP. On the tour, the Clash were subjected to constant police harrassment, Joe Strummer being arrested at one point for stealing a pillowcase from a hotel in which the group had been staying. Also on the bill were the Jam – who left halfway through the dates to headline a tour promoting *their* first album – the Slits and the Subway Sect. True to the punk ethic, both these bands consisted of unashamed beginners. The Slits – Arri Up (vocals), Tessa Pollitt (bass), Viv Albertine (guitar) and Palmolive (drums) had met at a Patti Smith gig and decided to form a band. 'If you like peace and flowers/I'm going to carry knives and chains', they sang on 'Number One Enemy', and their appearance – Arri would sport a pair of Jubilee knickers over wet-look trousers – expressed the same contempt for conventional standards of 'femininity'. Not surprisingly, their record contract was a long time in coming – it was 1979 before their reggae-influenced debut album *Cut* appeared on Island Records.

Subway Sect used to sing weird, avant-garde numbers about alienation before singer Vic Godard's preoccupation with Radio Two took them into the realm of cocktail jazz. (The band eventually parted company with Godard in 1982, and with new vocalist Dig Wayne became the JoBoxers.)

There was fierce rivalry between the various punk acts. Those like the Pistols and the Clash who had emanated from the Malcolm McLaren stable paraded their ideological principles, and were disparaging about the lack of political awareness of such groups as the Damned. Their criticisms may have been rooted in envy: the Damned were the first British punk band to have a record nationally distributed, when 'New Rose' was released on the Stiff label. For most of 1977, the Damned toured Britain at an exhausting pace with their anarchic music-hall act: their then manager, Jake Riviera, had asked them if they wanted to be rich and famous: 'We said we wanted to be famous,' recalled drummer Rat Scabies, 'because we thought if we were, we'd automatically become rich.' All they became was tired.

Although many punk acts had initially dismissed BBC-TV's 'Top Of The Pops' for its crass commercialism, many of them – the Clash excepted – willingly accepted invitations to appear

SCLE
JSIC

that it had outsold the Number 1 song, Rod Stewart's 'I Don't Want To Talk About It', and had been kept from the top slot to prevent embarrassment to Her Majesty.

Considering the other sinister events surrounding the Pistols at the time, this was not as implausible as it might seem. MP Marcus Lipton had declared that if punk rock was to be used to destroy Britain's established institutions, 'then it ought to be destroyed first'. For a while, it seemed as though a conspiracy was afoot to do just that. On Jubilee Day itself, the Sex Pistols set sail up the Thames on a boat provocatively named the *Queen Elizabeth*, a promotional event organised by Virgin Records. Midway through the group's set, a police launch ordered them to the shore and arrested members of the group and their entourage with unnecessary force on dubious charges.

The mood of paranoia surrounding the group was fuelled by Malcolm McLaren's claims that no councils would permit the Pistols to appear. Following the break-up of the group, this was discovered to have been untrue – McLaren was merely attempting to boost the band's mystique through their non-availability. Despite – or perhaps because of – the Pistols' problems, punk made massive strides. Everyone had an opinion of some sort about it. By now it was becoming apparent which acts had staying power. Groups like the Clash and new-wave singer-songwriters like Elvis Costello were impressing with the strength of their talent, and beginning to outstrip lesser artists who had optimistically taken in their flares and cropped their hair in the hope of jumping on the bandwagon.

when their records entered the charts. Partly as a result of this national exposure, the Adverts, X-Ray Spex, the Stranglers and the Jam enjoyed early success.

God save the Queen
In the heart of mainstream Britain, however, punk rock appeared to be a mere hiccup: the dominant event for most of the nation was to be the Silver Jubilee celebrations marking the 25th anniversary of the coronation of Queen Elizabeth II. To a bunch of self-styled anarchists like those pushing along the pace of punk, such an event – with all its possibilities for satire – was more than could have been dreamed of.

Again, it was the Sex Pistols who were found at the heart of this controversy. With consummate timing, 'God Save The Queen' was released at the height of the Jubilee celebrations in June, reaching Number 2 in the singles chart. Virgin Records maintained

Opposite: The Slits' Arri Up flashes her Jubilee knickers. Above: Poly Styrene of X-Ray Spex gets a lift from fans. Left: The Roxy in London's Covent Garden offered up to six hours of high-energy music for the price of a few beers. Below: Bassist Tony James and vocalist Billy Idol of Generation X.

Johnny takes the cake
Spunk, a bootleg copy of the imminently available Sex Pistols' album was on sale in certain shops by the end of September. When *Never Mind The Bollocks, Here's The Sex Pistols* finally came out a month later, an immediate furore was predictably created by the record's title. The manager of a Nottingham record shop was charged with offences under the 1889 Indecent Advertisement Act for including the record in his window display, and the LP galloped to Number 1.

The Pistols played the last official date of their British tour at Uxbridge University in West London, a chaotic, strangely sinister affair that did little credit to the group. Far finer, however, was the free show the band put on of its own accord on Christmas Day in Huddersfield as a benefit for the families of striking firemen. This was the group's last show in Britain, and concluded with some of the children present spontaneously pulling Johnny Rotten face-down into a giant Christmas cake.

A month later, the career of the Sex Pistols was over. Rotten was sacked from the group in San Francisco after the final date of their only American tour – dismissed, he claimed, for attempting to save Sid Vicious from his obviously suicidal involvement with heroin, a part of the latter's pathetic fondness for rock star 'outlaw' mystique. The Sex Pistols may have been over, but in their wake they left a host of other bands they had inspired, and a revitalised UK music scene. CHRIS SALEWICZ

ROCK '77

In 1977, British punk rock, which had been picking up momentum throughout the previous year, became an industry. While the press continued to splash punk horror stories over its pages, punk posters, fanzines and garish garb filled the shops and a plethora of pogoing acts filled the clubs. But while a number of new-wavers – including the Stranglers, the Jam, the Boomtown Rats and the Adverts – enjoyed varying degrees of chart success, established artists had little cause to feel threatened. Pink Floyd's *Animals*, Yes' *Going For The One*, Queen's *News Of The World* and Genesis' *Wind And Wuthering* all sold in massive quantities, while the singles charts continued to be dominated by acts like Rod Stewart, Leo Sayer, Showaddywaddy and Smokie.

In America, punk and the new wave had even less impact and seemed to be confined largely to the clubs of Manhattan. The pop charts remained in the grip of disco sounds; Rose Royce, KC and the Sunshine Band, Heatwave and the Commodores all weighed in with enormous hits, while the music's popularity received a further boost with the release of the hugely successful movie *Saturday Night Fever*. Fans of old-wave rock, meanwhile, welcomed Toto and Foreigner to the ranks but Elvis Costello, whose debut album *My Aim Is True* managed to dent the LP charts, showed that the American market wasn't entirely closed to the new wave.

January

9 Country-rock singer Emmylou Harris marries her producer Brian Ahern in Nova Scotia, Canada.
20 Pete Townshend attacks a photographer attempting to take pictures of the Who guitarist in conversation with Sex Pistols Paul Cook and Steve Jones, at London's Speakeasy.
22 Drummer Stewart Copeland, of recently-defunct outfit Curved Air, announces his intention to form a new-wave band called the Police.
23 Patti Smith falls off stage in Tampa, Florida, breaking her neck.
Peter Green, former guitarist of Fleetwood Mac, appears in court on charges of threatening behaviour with a rifle; he is committed to a mental hospital.

February

3 Eccentric folk artist Roy Harper is treated for toxopasmosis, a rare virus contracted while administering the kiss of life to one of his sheep.
5 The Eagles top the US charts with 'New Kid In Town', while TV actor David Soul is

at Number 1 in the UK with 'Don't Give Up On Us'. The latter goes on to become the year's biggest-selling single in Britain.
22 David Coverdale, former singer with Deep Purple, releases his first solo album, *Whitesnake*.

March

5 Bassist Glen Matlock leaves the Sex Pistols, to be replaced by Sid Vicious.
10 Having been dropped by EMI Records in January, the Pistols sign a new deal with A&M. The contract, ceremoniously signed outside Buckingham Palace, is terminated a week later.
14 Rolling Stone Keith Richards appears in court in Toronto, Canada, on charges of heroin possession.
18 Marc Bolan makes his first London appearance in nearly two years at the Rainbow, supported by the Damned.

April

8 The Damned become the first UK punk act to play in the US when they appear at New York's CBGB's.
17 The Stranglers, Cherry Vanilla and the Jam appear at London's Roundhouse. The Greater London Council stipulate, as one of the conditions for granting a concert license, that the Stranglers must refrain from 'wearing any apparel bearing any words or slogans of an offensive or abusive nature and from mouthing any such words on stage.'
23 US hard-rockers Foreigner release their first album, *Foreigner*.
30 Nicky 'Topper' Headon joins the Clash on drums.

May

7 The Dead End Kids enter the UK Top Ten for the first and only time with 'Have I The Right', a version of the Honeycombs' 1964 chart-topper.
14 The Bay City Rollers sack bass-player Pat McGlynn.
21 The Sex Pistols sign again – this time with Virgin Records.

Rod Stewart tops the UK charts with 'I Don't Want To Talk About It'/'First Cut Is The Deepest', while Stevie Wonder is Number 1 in the US with 'Sir Duke'.
28 In the High Court, Mr Justice Oliver bars RCA from distributing an album by Japanese electronic musician Tomita in Britain. The LP, *Tomita's Planets*, is based on Gustav Holst's *The Planets Suite* and the composer's daughter Imogen claims that the interpretation 'mutilates and vulgarises' her father's work.

June

12 UFO's lead guitarist Michael Schenker goes missing on the eve of a US tour. His fellow band members believe he may have joined a religious sect.
15 The Sex Pistols play at a Jubilee party aboard the Thames cruiser *Queen Elizabeth*; the boat is boarded by police, who arrest 11 people including manager Malcolm McLaren.
18 Johnny Rotten is attacked and stabbed in the arm outside Highbury's Pegasus pub; the following day, Pistols' drummer Paul Cook is assaulted by a gang at a West London train station.
22 Los Angeles' mayor Tom Bradley declares June 22 as 'Herb Alpert Day' in honour of the trumpeter's contribution to the city's commerce.

July

2 Lee Black Childers, manager of US punk outfit the Heartbreakers, is set upon by punks at London's Music Machine because he is dressed like a Teddy boy. At the same gig, singer Bob Geldof of the Boomtown Rats is punched in the face by a member of the audience.
21 The Sex Pistols appear on video on BBC-TV's 'Top Of The Pops' singing 'Pretty Vacant'.
26 Elvis Costello performs an impromptu solo set outside London's Hilton and is arrested for obstruction.
27 Led Zeppelin's US tour is halted when Robert Plant's son, Karac, dies of a mystery virus infection.
30 The Beach Boys cancel six British concerts because, they claim, they are under-rehearsed. Instead they play for an audience of celebrities at a CBS convention at London's Grosvenor Hotel.

August

13 Singapore's Ministry of Culture decide to investigate the 'punk-rock culture' by listening to records by the Sex Pistols, the Clash and the Tubes; the music of such groups is 'loud, spluttering and brutal,' concludes the committee.
16 Elvis Presley is found dead at his Gracelands mansion.
26 Ian Dury's 'Sex And Drugs And Rock And Roll' single is released.

September

3 Two weeks after his death, Elvis Presley's 'Way Down' becomes his first UK Number 1 since 1970.
6 Marc Bolan is killed when his car,

boxed set, *Consequences*, featuring the sound of their Gizmo device.
20 A charter plane flying Lynyrd Skynyrd to Baton Rouge, Louisiana, crashes near McCombe, Mississippi, killing band-members Ronnie Van Zandt and Steve and Cassie Gaines.

November
7 Alex Harvey announces his (temporary) retirement from the music business.
19 Pat Boone's daughter, Debby, reaches the top of the US charts with 'You Light Up My Life' and stays there for 10 weeks.
21 Dire Straits sign to Phonogram.

December
3 Wings' 'Mull Of Kintyre' begins its eight-week run at the top of the UK charts. Elvis Costello and the Attractions make their first UK Top Twenty appearance with 'Watching The Detectives'.
17 Teen magazines finally succumb to punk: in a feature titled 'Who's A Pretty Punk, Then?', *Oh Boy!* describe the Pistols' singer as 'Ravishing Rotten – he's so cute you can forget all those stupid spittin' and swearin' scenes the Pistols staged just to get noticed.'
30 Winifred Atwell, the West Indian pianist who notched up 11 UK Top Ten hits in the Fifties with such offerings as 'Let's Have A Party', 'Let's Have A Ding Dong' and 'Let's Have A Ball', dies in Hong Kong.

TOM HIBBERT, JENNY DAWSON

Opposite: The aptly-named Dead End Kids – one-hit-wonders in April. Above: Elvis Costello – arrested in July. Below right: The King is dead – Presley's Gracelands grave. Below: The Electric Warrior is dead – the tree where Marc Bolan met his end.

driven by girlfriend Gloria Jones, hits a tree in South London.
14 Guitarist Daevid Allen and 30 hippie friends stage a sit-in at Virgin's offices in protest at the record company's refusal to release a live Gong album.
28 Bing Crosby and David Bowie record a duet medley of 'Little Drummer Boy' and 'Peace On Earth' for a Crosby Christmas TV special.

October
8 Danny Mirror's tribute to the 'King of rock'n'roll', 'I Remember Elvis Presley', enters the UK Top Ten.
17 Lol Creme and Kevin Godley, formerly of 10CC, release a three-album

COMBAT·ROCKERS

The Clash: from revolution rags to rock riches

IF THERE WAS one band that successfully rose above punk's swift and premature decline, it was the Clash. Although historically the Sex Pistols remain the most important mid-Seventies group for their shattering effect on the complacency of the music business, it was the Clash's achievement to hone and structure punk's original wildly anarchistic intent into a more mature and durable form.

Despite occasional bouts of critical censure, the Clash survived into the Eighties with their original goals intact. Their

music changed over the years – from the stuttering riot charge of their 1977 album *The Clash* to the relative sophistication of *Combat Rock* (1982), while their lyrical concerns extended from the parochial politics of highrise/dole-queue/anti-racism that gave them their original impetus to the more potent arena of Internationalism, particularly the power of the American multi-nationals. Love affairs and revolution were only ever a track apart in the Clash's music. Like many young musicians at the time, they listened avidly to ska and bluebeat imports and were the first white group to acknowledge and mould one of punk's major influences, reggae, into their music.

Rhodes to glory

The Clash were formed in June 1976 from a nucleus of two art-school friends, guitarist Mick Jones (born 26 June 1955) and bass-player Paul Simonon (born 15 December 1955). Jones had originally formed London SS in March 1975, and among the many players who passed through that band's ranks between then and January 1976 were Simonon and drummers Terry Chimes and Nicky 'Topper' Headon (born 30 May 1955), a former office clerk who sat in for a week. Mick broke up the band to form an outfit with Simonon, and it was during this period that the pair met Joe Strummer.

Strummer (born John Mellors, 21

August 1952) had been playing with what was basically an R&B band, the 101ers, doing the familiar London pub circuit. The 101ers had already had a single – 'Keys To Your Heart' – released on the independent Chiswick label, but Strummer, in typically passionate style, had broken the band up. He'd seen the future as indicated by the Sex Pistols. 'I knew then R&B was dead,' he declared somewhat sweepingly.

By August 1976 the Clash were a five-piece, with drummer Terry Chimes (who was credited on the first album as Tory Crimes) and guitarist Keith Levine joining Strummer, Jones and Simonon. It was this line-up that, after intensive rehearsals in an abandoned Chalk Farm warehouse, was finally unveiled by manager Bernie Rhodes to a hand-picked audience of music-paper critics. Rhodes, an astute entrepreneur and an associate of Malcolm McLaren, had prepared the ground carefully, and critical acclaim was unanimous.

In the heady early days of punk, the Clash were also embroiled in what became fashionably-required scenes of destruction and devastation, even though from their earliest material they were set apart from the nihilistic stance of most of the other young bands around. Local councils were not prepared to sanction punk gigs, so that summer, Rhodes booked the 100 Club in Oxford Street himself, and staged the Punk Festival as a showcase for the band.

Cash and Clash

While the Sex Pistols' odyssey round the major record companies continued to threaten the status quo, the Clash and Rhodes signed to CBS. It was the first of a series of political contradictions the group successfully weathered. Lauded as a huge force on the alternative circuit, they had just shaken hands with one of the biggest multi-national record companies in the world. Yet over the years they managed to retain their commitment to release cheap records, never took the easy way to a hit single by appearing on 'Top Of The Pops', and were steadfast in their politics.

Meanwhile the band joined their old friends the Sex Pistols on the doomed Anarchy tour, a remarkable event given that it scarcely played one of its allotted venues. By now punk was causing the same moral outrage in Britain that the advent of rock'n'roll had caused in the United States over two decades earlier. Widely perceived as morally corrupt and an affront to decent society, it was not to be allowed a public voice.

By the time CBS released their debut album, *The Clash*, in April 1977, Keith Levine was long gone, and Terry Chimes had quit to be replaced by Jones' former London SS associate Topper Headon.

Above left: The Clash rock against racism at London's Victoria Park, 1978. Top right: The Clash of '76, from left Terry Chimes, Mick Jones, Joe Strummer and Paul Simonon. Centre: One, two, crush on you – a packed early gig. Right: Strummer sings.

*Inset: Topper Headon (left) with the band.
Above: An American dream.*

Produced by live soundman Micky Foote, *The Clash* perfectly captured the band's extraordinary urgency and their unique gift for underpinning punk's rawness with surprisingly thoughtful lyrics and references to the whole tradition of popular music: Chuck Berry's guitar riffs; pop's traditional melodic content, as on the bell-like 'Garageland'; and their homage to reggae with Lee Perry's 'Police And Thieves'.

There's a riot going on
Their second album, *Give 'Em Enough Rope*, was released in November 1978 and signalled the development of Mick Jones' musical signature: the urgent guitar semaphore of 'Tommy Gun'. The album was neither as concise nor as charged with raw energy as their debut, and suffered from a lack of instantly powerful songs. Much press criticism was levelled against producer Sandy Pearlman, whose 'traditional' methods seemed at odds with the group's spontaneous approach; but despite these critical reservations, the album quickly reached Number 2 in the charts.

By the end of 1978 the Clash were also established as a modestly successful singles band. 'White Riot', their first 45, was released in March 1977, and was followed by 'Complete Control', 'Clash City Rockers' and the ironic and affectionate '(White Man) In Hammersmith Palais', all of which reached the UK Top Forty.

'Tommy Gun', from the *Give 'Em Enough Rope* album, achieved their highest chart placing yet at Number 19.

They suffered constant business problems. Manager Bernie Rhodes' relationship with the band was both passionate and volatile. In October 1978 he was sacked amid much acrimony, which ended in Rhodes taking legal action against the Clash in the High Court. For a while they were managed by journalist Caroline Coon, later managing themselves until Bernie Rhodes was re-instated, largely at Strummer's insistence, in 1981. Relationships with their record company, CBS, were no smoother, and the band were constantly locked in bitter disagreements over marketing policies, financial arrangements and the pricing of their LPs. The song 'Complete Control' was an ironic reference to their relationship with CBS and the music business in general.

London Calling, released in 1979, was a double album that wooed the critics back to the Clash's side. Produced by the late Guy Stevens, the diamond-edged sound highlighted their development as musicians and writers. The view of the Westway from the 18th floor had enlarged to encompass other parts of the atlas and concentrate on the root of Western economic 'problems': the power of the American multi-nationals ('Koka Kola'); the recognition of peasant revolt ('Spanish Bombs'); and the new-

found street lunacy of the US seen by British eyes as the unravelling of a Hollywood scenario ('Jimmy Jazz').

'Clampdown', meanwhile, became the first song to address itself directly to the phenomenon of the young involving themselves in state power against their own age group and their own class. Amid all this came 'Lost In The Supermarket', a surprisingly pretty track that expressed the Clash's gentle identification with the confused, less macho side of the male personality while taking a shot at punk's old enemy, consumerism. The album's title track, 'London Calling', provided the band with their most successful single, reaching Number 11 in the UK charts at the beginning of 1980.

By this time, the Clash were one of the very few original punk bands to have survived. Not only that, but they had survived intact, with their pledges and commitments unsullied.

Dub and drubbed
It was to be an adventurous, often experimental album that nearly proved their downfall. Towards the end of 1980, with a series of American, British and European tours behind them, they released a triple album, self-produced in conjunction with reggae producer Mikey Dread. The disappointment of critics over *Give 'Em Enough Rope* was as nothing compared to

the savagery that greeted the 'self-indulgent' *Sandinista!* It was nevertheless a musical and ideological breakthrough for the band, introducing dub and rap to a British rock audience, and capturing the political climate of the time by focusing on the build-up of cold-war propaganda and the escalating involvement of the United States in Latin America. Ironically, given the album's implacably anti-American stance, it fared much better in the US than in the UK, where sales were severely hit by the critical drubbing.

Sandinista! was in all senses a revolutionary album, emerging at a time when British music was witnessing the rise of the new romantics and a general reversion to pop's traditional concerns of pretty melodies and dull lyrics. It reflected the influence of all things American on the band, and their involvement with black music and its cultural references placed the Clash ahead of the mainstream by well over a year.

1981 saw the band touring Europe and America, where they finally confirmed their reputation, returning victorious to Britain at the end of the year to play six sold-out nights at the London Lyceum. During each concert the enigmatically named Futura 2000, a New York street artist, spray-painted a backdrop in the course of the performance; he also did the lettering for the sleeve of their next LP.

Back in the USA
As the Lyceum appearances suggested, and their subsequent activities confirmed, the Clash had shifted their attentions full-time to the United States. This experience, together with a 1981 tour of the Far East, found full expression in *Combat Rock*. Released in 1982 and produced with the help of Glyn Johns, it pulled the threads of *Sandinista!* together and had critics hastily re-assessing their original reaction to that triple album. *Combat Rock* saw the Clash at their most seductive. The struggles of Vietnam and Latin America, the influence of the oil-rich states and US exploitation at home and abroad were combined with rap, elements of the new American jazz and a hint of traditional Eastern instrumentation. *Combat Rock* also yielded the melancholic, bitter and moving single, 'Straight To Hell'.

Relationships within the band were never easy, particularly where Strummer and Jones were concerned. A dispute between the two occurred in 1981 when Jones headed for the States with singer Ellen Foley, leaving Strummer in Britain muttering darkly about 'reaching the end of the line'. On that occasion their differences were resolved after what Strummer called: 'a simple or garden punch-up'.

Then in 1982 Strummer disappeared with no hint of warning on the eve of a UK tour. The tour was cancelled, and when the errant Strummer returned to the ranks, a dispirited Topper Headon announced *his* departure from the band. He was replaced on a temporary basis by his predecessor Terry Chimes, before auditions were held and in May 1983 Pete Howard was selected as a permanent replacement.

Finally, in September 1983 came the announcement that Strummer and Simonon had decided to 'sack' Mick Jones because 'It is felt that Jones has drifted apart from the original idea of the Clash,' although Jones bitterly contested this. Two new guitarists, Vince White and Nick Sheppard, were drafted in—though this line-up survived only one album, *Cut The Crap* (1985), before Strummer cut his losses and disbanded his group.

Mick Jones found success mixing rock and hip-hop with Big Audio Dynamite, while Strummer returned to music temporarily with folk-rockers the Pogues and more permanently via film sound-tracks for *Walker* (1988), *Straight To Hell* (1987) and *Sid & Nancy* (1986).   PENNY VALENTINE

**The Clash
Recommended Listening**

The Clash (CBS 82000) (Includes: Janie Jones, White Riot, Garageland, Hate And War, Deny, Remote Control); *London Calling* (CBS CLASH 3) (Includes: London Calling, The Guns Of Brixton, Death Or Glory, Revolution Rock, Hateful, I'm Not Down).

The new women of punk

'Some people think girls should be seen and not heard/But I think that . . . (scream) Oh Bondage, Up Yours!'

POLY STYRENE's deadly serious pronouncement that launched X-Ray Spex's 1977 single was a perfect rallying cry for a generation of young women who had previously found little excitement, relevance or opportunity in rock and pop. Shouting her head off about BO, being fat and the pressure on girls from advertising, jumping up and down in her own dayglo, thrift-store creations and shrieking through a toothbrace, she became an inspiration to girls all over the country to take to the stage themselves.

In that heady heyday of independence and rule-breaking, incompetence was incompetence, whether in a man or a woman, and now women were quick to grab microphones, basses, guitars and even drum kits. Surprisingly, drums and synthesisers were to remain very male-dominated instruments. Depeche Mode and Orchestral Manoeuvres In The Dark have had no rivals from women and only Malaria, the all-women group from Berlin, approached their territory.

Even so, since the explosion of energy that marked punk and the coincident spread of women's bands, individual female musicians have proliferated beyond anticipation. Although an all-girl line-up like the Belle Stars is rare, there have been some surprises. When Fun Boy Three appeared on BBC-TV's 'Top Of The Pops' performing 'Our Lips Are Sealed' in 1983, the three good-looking male ex-Specials sang out front, while the solid backing

Above: The Slits – wild, challenging and inspiring – rehearse in a suitably punk setting. Top left: X-Ray Spex's queen of dayglo kitsch, Poly Styrene, on stage with sax player Lora Logic.

musicians (playing everything from cello to trombone) were women from bands like the all-girl Mo-Dettes and Delta 5 (a mixed male/female group).

Of course there have always been female instrumentalists, particularly in the field of jazz. US hard-rockers Fanny matched male rock bands as early as 1970, while in 1976 Kim Fowley 'created' the Runaways in a distinctly male-oriented image (leather, suspenders, corsets). Scattered individuals have often gone unnoticed: the widely respected session bassist Carol Kaye; conga-player Bobbye Hall, notable for her Motown sessions; and Sly Stone's half-sister Rose who, together with trumpeter Cynthia Robinson, formed part of the Family Stone. The Mothers of Invention featured guitarist/vocalist Alice Stuart as early as 1965 and included keyboardist Ruth Underwood in a later line-up. Suzi Quatro tried to be a tiger in leather in 1974, while the Wilson sisters, flautist/singer Ann and guitarist Nancy, formed Heart in Canada in the same year.

Politics and passions

Despite these performers' undoubted talents, however, it was noticeable that their music lacked any specifically female perspective. Rather, they tended to be skilled players competing with men on essentially male terms.

The mid-Seventies, however, was to see a period of ferment in the UK, and politics rapidly became organically entwined with punk/new-wave music. Campaigns for relaxed abortion and squatting laws and opposing racism and sexism united men and women in a different way, while Rock Against Sexism, an offshoot from Rock Against Racism, became a focus for many new bands. *The* squatters' band of 1976, the Derelicts, featured a variable number of women on bass, electric guitar, violin and vocals. Vocalist and rhythm guitarist Barbara Gogan, later in the Passions, sang fierce political songs in a sweet schoolgirlish voice.

Jam Today represented the new strain of all-women bands, playing a fiercely feminist brand of white soul recalling (musically) the Average White Band.

London's punk haven in 1977 was the Roxy in Covent Garden. On the record immortalising that era, *The Roxy London WC2 (Jan-Apr '77)*, Poly Styrene belted out her antibondage tirade which later emerged as a comparatively polished 12-inch single. Lora Logic, then a 14-year-old schoolgirl, blew saxophone through Poly's high-pitched singing/shouting. Also on the album was the Adverts' 'Bored Teenagers', a suitably appalling anthem of the times that revealed Gaye Advert's minimal bass

technique to be plodding and rather ham-fisted. As one of the first women bassists of that period, however, she was greatly admired.

Meanwhile, at the vanguard of the punk movement, the only girl group to even re-motely challenge the male domination of the Sex Pistols and the Clash was the Slits. Less talented at the outset than their male contemporaries, and also less inhibited, they began as a wild, all-girl quartet who baffled, shocked and excited their audiences, breaking all the rules concern-ing how girls should behave on stage.

Musically, they learned fast, and by the time of their first album – *Cut*, produced by Dennis Bovell – in 1979, they had de-veloped their own very individual style, heavily rooted in reggae. Songs about boredom, new towns, shoplifting, sex and romance – especially 'Typical Girls', their ironic theme tune, were an inspiration to many other groups to leave the usual angles on relationships behind forever.

The Slits toured extensively, starting with a support slot on the Clash's White Riot tour in 1977, and exerted an impor-tant influence on many women's bands throughout the UK, among which were the Raincoats. Comprised of art school and university-educated women, the Raincoats were the honorary intellectuals of the scene. Their distinctive sound, largely due to Vicki Aspinall's haunting violin, drew heavily on the Velvet Underground, but

Above: Role reversal – women musicians back the men fronting Fun Boy Three.

they later used various folk influences while trying to free themselves from standard rock rhythms by using an embel-lished percussion section.

With most of the women's and mixed-sex bands of this time, lyrics were of para-mount importance, dealing with general political issues or, most frequently, ex-pressing frustration or anger about aspects of life for women. The Raincoats' 'Life On The Line', about being followed home by a man on the tube, was a common theme – and experience.

Poet and Pretender
Siouxsie Sue began as a punk camp fol-lower before she formed the Banshees in late 1976. Her ambiguous image, resulting from a fondness for Nazi regalia and fetish gear, polarised press and fans alike and detracted from some imaginative song-writing which, over the years, became more mystical and occultist.

Siouxsie's voice influenced many succes-sive singers, such as the Au Pairs' Lesley Wood, and changed from intoned speech to a throaty singing style, darting from high to low in rapid succession. Her influence in Germany was particularly strong, notable acolytes including the electronic group Malaria and Xmal Deutschland.

American singer Patti Smith used music to elaborate her poems. A devotee of the Velvet Underground, her sung, spoken and almost liturgical intonations in-fluenced the drawl of Pretenders' vocalist Chrissie Hynde.

While there was a common thread link-ing the performers mentioned, there were of course women from this era who emerged as individuals, incorporating personal styles or tastes from outside rock or pop. Lene Lovich's image recalled the crazed heroines of silent movies; angular and darting, her stylised clothes and singing displayed a carefully calculated theatricality. Along with Lora Logic, Lovich was one of the first women in late-Seventies pop to appear playing saxo-phone, which subsequently became a popular instrument for women.

The mistress of the vocal flutter is Kate Bush. As a late teenager, singing with the voice of a child, she first entered the charts in 1978 with 'Wuthering Heights'. Initial-ly treated as a young girl and discussed primarily in terms of her looks, she later made appearances in trade magazines, discussing digital computer synthesisers and photographed in everyday clothes, suggesting a determination to be taken more seriously by the music industry.

The music scene in the UK has changed dramatically since those heady, aban-doned years at the end of the Seventies which threatened to overturn the whole industry. In 1981 a compilation album was released called *Making Waves*, which featured 12 tracks performed by a variety of all-women bands. Although no black music was represented, the range was immense – from the leisurely jazz sound of Sisterhood of Spit Big Band's 'Hold Tight' to Rock Goddess' crushing heavy-metal workout 'Make My Night'. Amy and the Angels represented a remnant of hard-core punk with their Rotten-style chant 'I Hate Being In Love'.

If there was any common theme to be found in this collection of songs it was in the lyrics. From 'Romance', a song to Lady Diana Spencer about Prince Charles, to Androids of Mu's 'Bored Housewife' com-plete with a mock row with the kids, and Real Insects' 'In The Ruin Of Your Body', lesbian feminist erotica with Velvet Underground overtones, the lyrics were all in some way firm statements from the female point of view.

Making Waves marked the end of an era. While it was being compiled, Sheena Easton was collecting awards and heading for the Vegas circuit, Blondie's Debbie Harry was testing the waters of the film world, Tina Weymouth was organising her sisters and producing her own record away from the shadow of Talking Heads, and Joan Armatrading was finally getting recognition from as far off as West Africa. But down in the undergrowth something had stirred, and the effects of those few years in the Seventies were only just beginning to percolate through by the start of the Eighties. SUE STEWARD

BUZZCOCKS

ONE OF THE MOST refreshing things about the first wave of punk bands was its diversity. While the Clash and the Jam raged against the squalor and boredom of urban life, the Buzzcocks took fragile love songs – reminiscent at times of the early Beatles – and turned them into something new.

Another music
The Buzzcocks began to take shape in October 1975 when Pete Shelley (born Peter McNeish on 17 April 1955), an electronics student at Bolton Institute of Technology, answered an advert on the college notice-board. The advert had been placed by philosophy student Howard Devoto, and the pair began writing songs, Pete Shelley composing tunes on his guitar

Love bites and spiral scratches

for the lyrics Howard had written.

Pete had been making music since the early Seventies, when he had come up with the idea of inventing three different bands to serve as outlets for his different musical interests. The Jets of Air, who played a number of local gigs, were a pop group concentrating on covers of songs by Bowie, Roxy Music and the Velvet Underground,

Top: The original Buzzcocks, from left John Maher, Steve Diggle, Pete Shelley and Howard Devoto. Above: Steve Garvey takes Devoto's place.

together with Pete's own numbers – including the track 'Telephone Operator', which he eventually released as a solo single in 1983.

The other two 'bands' were purely hypothetical. Smash was the name he gave to the music he produced in the experimental style of groups like Can (he was later to write the sleeve notes to their 1978 compilation LP *Cannibalism*), while the name the Sky covered the Kraftwerk-inspired electronic music he made on equipment he had built himself. Each of these three kinds of music was to come to the fore at different stages of his career.

Pete Shelley and Howard Devoto decided to form a band after seeing the Sex Pistols in January 1976. They organised a gig for them in Manchester, intending to support them, but couldn't find other musicians in time. Within a fortnight, however, they had recruited 16-year-old John Maher on drums and persuaded guitarist Steve Diggle to play bass. They played two numbers at a social for the Bolton Institute of Technology textile students on 1 April, and Pete – who was now studying philosophy – gave up college to work as a trainee computer programmer to earn the money to buy sound equipment.

On 20 July, the Sex Pistols played the Lesser Free Trade Hall in Manchester, and this time the Buzzcocks supported them. By this stage, Malcolm McLaren's managerial expertise had turned the Sex Pistols' gigs into media events, and the Buzzcocks benefited from the publicity. They supported the Pistols again at the Screen on the Green in London, played local gigs at clubs like the Ranch in Manchester and appeared at the Punk Festival at London's 100 Club that September, along with the Pistols, the Damned, the Clash and the Banshees.

The Buzzcocks were then approached by Martin Hannett, who ran an agency called the Music Force. He had some free studio time left over from another project and offered to produce them. They went into Manchester's Indigo Sound Studio on 28 December 1976, and laid down the four tracks – 'Breakdown', 'Time's Up', 'Boredom' and 'Friends Of Mine' – that became the *Spiral Scratch* EP.

Shelley and Devoto borrowed £500 to put the record out on their own label, New Hormones, named after a magazine Devoto had produced at college. The first 1000 copies of *Spiral Scratch* went in a few days. It eventually sold 16,000 copies, and was re-released in 1979. In addition, Orange Juice's 1983 UK hit single 'Rip It Up' paid tribute to the EP with the line 'My favourite song is "Boredom"'.

In March 1977, with the Buzzcocks poised on the brink of success, Howard Devoto left the group, to re-emerge later that year with his new band Magazine. Pete Shelley took over lead vocals, Steve Diggle returned to playing guitar and a bassist called Garth, who had played in the Jets of Air, was recruited. The band supported the Clash on tour, and on 16 August – the day Elvis Presley died – they signed to United Artists.

In September, after playing the Croydon

Below: Slaving over a hot mixing desk, the Buzzcocks cook up another music in a different kitchen.

Greyhound, they met Martin Rushent, a United Artists A&R man who had just produced the Stranglers' first single because no established producer would touch them. The Buzzcocks recorded their first two United Artists singles, 'Orgasm Addict' (which Devoto had co-written) and 'What Do I Get?', that September, and over Christmas laid down their first LP, *Another Music In A Different Kitchen*. (Garth had left the group after 'Orgasm Addict', to be replaced by Steve Garvey.)

Rushent's production lent the Buzzcocks' sound a crystal clarity that was a startling contrast to the muddiness of many punk records. The LP also marked the beginning of his long partnership with Shelley, and a career in production that would include such successful bands as Visage and the Human League.

Sexual politics
Another Music In A Different Kitchen, released early in 1978, set the pattern for future Buzzcocks LPs. Concise, tuneful love songs like 'I Don't Mind' would be set against rambling, experimental excursions like 'Moving Away From The Pulsebeat'. Shelley tended to avoid the overtly political subject-matter of some of his punk contemporaries. A communist at 16, his

political sympathies were with bands like the Clash, although he often found their sloganising naive. Instead, he chose to write about 'the frustrated feelings of growing up', writing love songs but refusing to accept the conventional clichés about romance.

'I like to write songs that are genderless,' he said, 'so that anyone can identify with them.' Songs like 'I Don't Mind', 'Ever Fallen In Love (With Someone You Shouldn't've)' and 'You Say You Don't Love Me' could be sung just as effectively by either sex. Yet they retained their clarity through their frank, intelligent observations of human relationships: 'You insult my natural emotions/You make me feel I'm dirt, and that hurts/And if I start a commotion/I run the risk of losing you, and that's worse . . .'

'Ever Fallen In Love', from which the above lines are taken, was released in the summer of 1978 and became the Buzzcocks' biggest hit single, reaching Number 12 in the UK charts. It was taken from their second LP, *Love Bites*, which displayed the same musical schizophrenia as its predecessor. Alongside pop songs like the single, 'Just Lust' and 'Sixteen Again' was a long, experimental track, 'Late For The Train'. Steve Diggle, who had already contributed 'Fast Cars' and 'Autonomy' to the first album, wrote the ballady 'Love Is Lies', while Steve Garvey contributed the instrumental 'Walking Distance'.

The following year, Diggle wrote 'Harmony In My Head', one of the Buzzcocks' most effective singles, and contributed extensively to their third LP, *A Different Kind Of Tension* (1979). Recorded in the middle of a heavy touring schedule – which included two successful trips to the US – the album showed the Buzzcocks to be somewhat bedraggled and confused. Alongside one of Shelley's most touching and effective love songs, 'You Say You Don't Love Me', was a series of bitter little numbers like 'Money', 'Life Is A Zoo' and 'Hollow Inside', on which Shelley probed his insecurities: 'Hollow inside, I was hollow inside/But I couldn't find out what the reason was', he sang over and over again.

By now, however, the band were becoming tired and disillusioned. Beset by financial worries, they spent the whole of 1980 producing three singles, 'Are Everything', 'Running Free' and 'What Do You Know'. United Artists had been taken over by EMI, who refused to advance the band the money they needed. By now, however, Martin Rushent had built his new Genetic Studios in Reading and Shelley went down there to record some demos to take back to the band. Using Rushent's Roland Microcomposer to produce synthesised backing tracks and adding vocals and 12-string

acoustic guitar, they recorded three songs: 'Homosapien', a catchy tune from Shelley's Jets of Air days, 'Pusher Man' and 'I Generate A Feeling'. Excited by the results, they were both convinced that what they had were not demos but completed recordings.

The genetic method
By now the Buzzcocks were beginning to go their separate ways: Steve Diggle had recorded a solo single, '50 Years Of Comparative Wealth', Pete was playing with the Tiller Boys, John with a Manchester band called the Things and Steve Garvey with friends. Pete decided to leave the group, and on 6 March 1981, the Buzzcocks ceased to exist. Diggle and Maher formed Flag of Convenience, and produced one single for the Sire record label.

Pete and Martin, meanwhile, took their tapes to Island Records, having turned down offers from Virgin and EMI. 'Homosapien' was released as a single on the Island subsidiary Genetic, and though its sly innuendo – 'You and me sir, homosapien too, sir' – discouraged radio airplay, it became a massive club hit in the United States. Despite its obvious appeal to the gay club market, Pete maintains that he

intended the title to have wider connotations of shared humanity.

The album *Homosapien* (1981) was a bigger hit in the United States and Australia (where it reached Number 1 in the album charts) than in the UK, though its attractive blend of electronic and acoustic instrumentation established Shelley as a respected solo performer. On Shelley's next LP, *XL1* (1983), the sound was broadened to include Barry Adamson, bass player from the now-disbanded Magazine, and Jim Russell. 'Telephone Operator', the single off the LP, was another stomping dance number in the same mould as 'Homosapien', while tracks like 'I Just Wanna Touch' showed that Shelley's talent for tuneful, vulnerable love songs was as strong as ever. Albums like 1986's *Heaven And The Sea* showed he was likely to continue as a low-key solo performer in the Eighties.　　CHRIS SCHÜLER

**The Buzzcocks
Recommended Listening**

Singles: Going Steady (United Artists UAG 30279) (Includes: Orgasm Addict, What Do I Get, Ever Fallen In Love (With Someone You Shouldn't've)?, Everybody's Happy Nowadays, Oh Shit!, Autonomy).

*Above right: The Buzzcocks' stage manner was diffident, almost low-key in comparison to many punk bands, but their infectious songs kept up the excitement.
Right: Garth played bass with the Buzzcocks for a few months in 1977.*

JOHN PEEL

Radio's guardian of the underworld

IT IS ARGUABLE THAT the most influential figure in the British punk revolution of 1976 was a rotund balding disc jockey in his late thirties who had made his name supporting precisely the kind of music which the punks were dedicated to destroying.

John Peel was punk's mole in the media establishment. He gave it the national audience without which it might have perished in the big-city clubs. Exposure on his Radio One show became a prerequisite for credibility in the new wave. Many of his faithful listeners were bewildered when their traditional values were ousted by these raucous, undisciplined punks, claiming that Peel could only be excused on grounds of creeping senility. What they failed to realise was that he was adhering firmly to the Peel Principle – namely that the best music is always primitive and usually new.

Calling out around the world
Peel was born John Ravenscroft on 30 August 1939, not in his beloved Liverpool but across the Mersey in Heswall. His father was a prosperous industrialist in the cotton trade and at the beginning of the Fifties John was duly despatched to public school in Shrewsbury in preparation for a career in the family business. But the shy, dreamy young Ravenscroft had different ideas. He was obsessed by the glamorous broadcasters of the American Forces Network who filled the night-time airwaves with the exotic sounds of Chicago and the deep South. He tried to share his enthusiasm by joining the school jazz society, but found it too academic and escaped back to his private relationship with the wireless. When the time came to leave school, he had only one ambition: 'I wanted to play records on the radio to people who ought to share them.'

The excitement and energy of the new sound of rock'n'roll helped sustain John through the anguish of his parents' divorce and the ordeal of National Service – for which he qualified by being born just 48 hours too soon. Only his abiding passion for Liverpool Football Club was keeping him in Britain, and when his father offered to pay his passage to the States – ostensibly to help him study the American end of the cotton business – he grasped the opportunity.

His first radio broadcast was in 1961 on a local station in Dallas, Texas. Interviewed in his capacity as a young Englishman who collected blues records, he discussed the relative merits of John Lee Hooker and Sonny Boy Williamson in his impeccably

Left: On your bike, John. Inset: Super session – recording carols for the Boxing Day 1970 edition of Peel's 'Top Gear'; cast includes Marc Bolan, the Faces, Curved Air's Sonja Kristina, Soft Machine's Mike Ratledge and madcap poet Ivor Cutler.

enunciated public-school accent. After two-and-a-half years of odd-jobbing, his big break came with American Beatlemania. Suddenly any Englishman, especially one from Liverpool, was a celebrity and John made a good living as what he calls a 'pro-am Beatle expert'.

In 1965 he became a full-time DJ on radio station KOMA in Oklahoma City. By a freak of radio reception, 'The Paul And John Show', presented by Paul Miller and John Raven Croft, could be heard across 10 states and thus amassed a huge following. Next came an 18-month stint on KMEN in San Bernardino, California, where John gazed into the weird and wonderful, acid-soaked subculture of Jefferson Airplane and the Grateful Dead and became one of the first hippie DJs in California.

Under the Jolly Roger
By early 1967, he was back in Britain, his reasons for leaving the States being homesickness (Liverpool were League Champions), fear of the Draft and an extraordinarily unsatisfactory marriage. John's mother suggested he meet her next-door neighbour, who happened to work for the offshore pirate station Radio London. The prospect of employing a top American DJ so excited the company that contracts were signed without the usual formalities of demo tapes and auditions. The only problem was his name. 'We like John,' said a girl in the office, 'but Ravenscroft is too long and Raven Croft is too American. Can you think of something more English?'

So it was that John Peel sailed out into the North Sea to join those swashbucklers of the medium wave who were so successfully changing the style of British broadcasting. Peel's job was 'swing-jock' – to substitute for any regular presenter who was on shore leave or sea-sick. He brought a refreshing honesty to the daytime pop shows, avoiding the cliché-ridden and over-excited approach of so many of his colleagues and talking about the music instead of himself.

But his reputation was made in the small hours when, confident that the station's management was tucked up in bed, he abandoned the news and the playlist and launched into a celebration of rock's avant-garde fringe called 'The Perfumed Garden'. British listeners had never heard Captain Beefheart, Frank Zappa, the Misunderstood or the Velvet Underground. Within weeks, Peel was receiving more letters than the rest of the Radio London DJs put together and when his bosses finally found out, they were powerless to intervene.

It was during this period that Peel's delivery settled into the slightly nervous, jokily verbose monotone which became the model for aspiring rock-jocks. Public-school precision, a Southern drawl, dry Liverpudlian wit and West Coast cool had combined to create a unique and refreshing style.

When pirate radio was outlawed in August 1967, Peel was a natural choice for

the BBC's substitute, Radio One. They even allowed him to recreate 'The Perfumed Garden' on a weekly show called 'Night Ride', where his revelations about a visit to a VD clinic enhanced his anti-establishment notoriety. As one of the presenters of 'Top Gear' and, later, of his own programme, he exploited his role as token hippie to the full, supporting the 'underground' and 'progressive' groups of the time.

His major success was Tyrannosaurus Rex, the acoustic duo led by the pixie-faced poet and minstrel Marc Bolan. Peel plugged them incessantly and travelled the country promoting their gigs. Driving along the M1 one day in 1970 he heard that 'Ride A White Swan' had reached the Top Ten. Overcome, he pulled onto the hard shoulder in floods of tears. He even ventured into the record business with his own label, Dandelion (named after a hamster given to him by Bolan) which signed such diverse talents as Bridget St John, Principal Edward's Magic Theatre, Stack Waddy and Medicine Head, whose 'Pictures In The Sky' in 1971 was the company's only hit. Peel was too generous and too naive to

Above: Peel sports a sweater boasting of his beloved Liverpool FC's achievements.

survive as an entrepreneur, but his honest approach to the music presaged his later attitude to punk. 'If like me you're fed up with superstars, fraud, pretension and quasi-mystical hoggery,' he wrote on the sleeve of an album by Kevin Coyne's Siren, 'you'll find this record a considerable treat.'

The Pig and a pint
In spite of his reputation as a dissolute, spaced-out Bohemian, Peel was now benefiting from the twin influences of his new wife Sheila and those affable hedonists the Faces. Sheila – or 'the Pig' as Peel affectionately terms her – is a charming commonsense northerner who 'stops me feeling sorry for myself'. And it was the Faces, with their constant invitations to 'come an' 'ave a drink, you old fart' who reminded him that beer was a better energiser than dope and that rowdy rock 'n'roll was his main love.

He did stay faithful to the experimental avant-garde represented by Soft Machine and Robert Wyatt's Matching Mole. Eccentric fringe artists like Loudon Wainwright III and Ivor Cutler were still brought in for sessions, but by the mid Seventies Peel craved something new, raw and exciting to counteract the growing pomposity of the mega-bands who seemed absurdly distanced from the new generation of disillusioned and often unemployed kids. Eddie and the Hot Rods came first – loud, aggressive and stubborn. Next from America it was the Ramones – 'exciting and horrifying,' said Peel. Then, in late 1976 he found the Damned, trimmed his hair and espoused the cause of 'hooligan music'.

Keeper of the fire
John Peel's support for the punk movement was invaluable. At the time, record companies were reeling in shock and few A&R men were prepared even to visit a punk club, let alone risk investment in the music. The BBC's obligation to live musicians meant that Peel and his producer John Walters had to book bands for sessions, and instead of waiting for the industry to provide them, they went out and found new talent for themselves – sometimes in the clubs, but more often from the huge pile of home-produced demo cassettes that arrived daily at Radio One.

Getting a Peel session became the recognised way for young musicians throughout Britain to find an audience, and literally hundreds of bands, from Siouxsie and the Banshees to Altered Images and the Undertones to Joy Division, owed their early reputations to Peel's endorsement. These sessions found immortality in 1987 when Strange Fruit Records issued the first *Peel Session* EP. Featuring acts from all stages of his BBC career, these soon monopolised the indie charts.

Peel's lifestyle remains a series of impenetrable contradictions – the well-bred gentleman who seeks out the company of football hooligans, the vegetarian cyclist who owns and drives expensive sports cars, the diffident *ingénu* with the acerbic turn of phrase, the fanatical supporter of urban punk who lives in an idyllic cottage in deepest Suffolk. But his home life, apparently that of the quintessential country squire, is deceptive. Almost half the cottage is taken up by a carefully indexed record and tape library and his family – William Anfield, Alexandra Anfield, Thomas Dalglish and Florence Shankly – bear testimony to his other great loves, Liverpool FC and children.

He laughs at the idea of 'a career', but while other DJs have flashed briefly and burned out, John Peel has remained the guardian of British rock's spirit of continuous revolution. He has dedicated himself to combating the institutionalised inertia of record companies and radio programmers – and, while Radio One has the courage to employ him, British rock music is in safe hands. TREVOR DANN

Smash It Up

Mayhem and merriment from the Damned

IT IS SOMEWHAT IRONIC that the only punk group to admit from the beginning that all they wanted was fame and money should find themselves still struggling to make a decent living long after punk's initial roar had been silenced. That the Damned continued into the Eighties as one of Britain's most colourful and exciting rock acts, however, was a tribute to the band's bizarre array of talents.

Sense and sensibility

The Damned evolved from London SS, a band inspired by Iggy Pop, the New York Dolls and other punk 'godfathers'. Formed in 1975 by bassist Tony James and guitarist Mick Jones, London SS had a fluid, ever-changing line-up and among its many sometime members were guitarist Brian James and drummer Chris Miller, a former cleaner at the Fairfield Halls, Croydon. At one of the group's rehearsals, someone asked Miller why he was scratching himself so violently. 'Scabies, mate,' he replied. Just then a rat scuttled across the floor of the seedy practice room. The two images stuck and Chris Miller was re-christened Rat Scabies.

By early 1976, London SS had folded, never having played a gig; Tony James left to form Chelsea and Mick Jones would soon set up the Clash. Scabies and Brian James, meanwhile, stayed together and invited Ray Burns, an old schoolfriend of

Above: A hungry rat tucks into Scabies' bass drum. Inset: Dave Vanian takes it out on Scabies' floor tom.

Scabies, to join their new group on bass. Burns had previously been a Hell's Angel, had lived on Brighton beach for a couple of years and had worked at Fairfield Halls at the same time as Rat. He wore a dog-chain around his neck and, underneath it all, was an excellent musician with a love for early Soft Machine and Pink Floyd.

Together, these three scouted for a singer to front their putative group. One hot summer evening at the Nashville Rooms, then the heart of London's pub-rock scene, they were startled by the sight of a white-faced young man dressed as an undertaker idly propping up the bar and contemplating the stage. This was Dave

Vanian (real name Dave Letts). Although he had no musical experience, he looked the part and readily agreed to become one of the group.

So the Damned were born. Within weeks of the line-up coming together, they were invited to play at the Mont de Marsan festival in France along with the Tyla Gang, Little Bob Story, Eddie and the Hot Rods and many other bands on the border between pub-rock and punk. Despite the Damned's inexperience, the combination of James' heavy, psychedelic guitar, Scabies' demented drumming, Burns' rock-steady bass and Vanian's funereal persona went down well with the crowd and led to a contract with new independent label Stiff. (On the cross-channel ferry, another Stiff artist, Larry Wallis of the Pink Fairies, dubbed Ray Burns 'Captain Sensible'.)

The Damned's first single emerged in November 1976. Composed, as was most of their early material, by Brian James, 'New Rose' was a slice of timeless high-energy, while the B-side was a typical piece of punk irreverence – a high-speed, out-of-tune version of the Beatles' 'Help'. The record did well enough for the Damned to become the first punk group to make the front cover of *Sounds*, itself the first rock weekly to take punk seriously.

Born to be a bonehead

In keeping with punk's essential energy, the Damned's live set seethed with vitality; indeed, their early set never lasted more than about 25 minutes, including an encore. They would exhaust themselves leaping around the stage, chucking things and smashing equipment as if they were part of a speeded-up film. Unlike their contemporaries, however, the Damned were not overtly political; while others flirted with 'anarchy' and vowed that they would never 'sell out' to the established music industry, Rat Scabies would announce candidly that: 'Anyone with any honesty will admit that all they want out of this business is a colour TV and £25,000 a year.'

In keeping with such showbiz aspirations, Stiff's Jake Riviera made sure the Damned were the first British punks to play in the US. In 1977, they hit New York and Los Angeles – where the groupies reportedly said they were 'more fun than Led Zeppelin' – and on their return to the UK, they supported Marc Bolan on what turned out to be his last tour. Because of the group's less vitriolic and more humorous approach, the rock establishment accepted the Damned more readily than the other punk groups: reviewing their first album *Damned Damned Damned* (released in February 1977) in *Melody Maker*, Chris Welch compared them favourably with the early Who.

Damned Damned Damned (produced, like 'New Rose', by Nick Lowe and the first Stiff album release) remains a classic testimonial to the joys of early punk. Despite the aggression flaunted by titles like 'Born

Above: The Damned in punky pose, from left Vanian, Captain Sensible, Rat Scabies and Brian James. Below: Music for pleasure? The band make a racket on stage.

To Kill' and 'Stab Your Back', it was basically a happy record. The same could not be said for the follow-up, *Music For Pleasure*, which was produced by Pink Floyd drummer Nick Mason and released in November. The strain of success (*Damned Damned Damned* had made the UK Top Forty, the first punk album to become a hit) and living up to the punk lifestyle was proving too much for what the Captain called 'four young boneheads'. Egos had become dangerously swollen and a major policy rift developed between Brian James and the others.

James wanted another guitarist to make the sound more interesting, but the addition of Lu (Robert Edmunds) simply meant, according to Rat, that Brian played less. Scabies decided to leave, but Riviera persuaded him to stay on to record the album. Rat was no happier at the end of it: 'The only good track on it is "You Know"

with Lol Coxhill on it. So after that, I quit.' The Captain also hated *Music For Pleasure*; the idea of using a producer from a psychedelic mega-band had been a gamble, and the band were quick to admit that it hadn't paid off.

Machine gun etiquette

The loss of Scabies was a crippling blow to the Damned's fortunes. His replacement, Jon Moss (later of Culture Club), was adequate as a drummer, but a vital tension within the band had been lost. Audiences sensed the change, and *Music For Pleasure* suffered poor sales as a result. By now punk was no longer the exception, it was the rule, and punters who were disappointed by the new-look Damned had a thousand other bands to choose from.

Jake Riviera left Stiff in early 1978 to set up a new record company, Radar, and suddenly the Damned found themselves without a deal. The notoriously fickle world of show business was turning its back on them and Brian James decided to call it a day. A farewell gig at the Rainbow in April 1978 saw Scabies reunited with the others

on a second drum kit and Lol Coxhill, the legendary dome-headed saxophonist, joined them for a manic, bristling finale.

The summer of 1978 saw Captain Sensible form King, Rat Scabies form White Cats, Brian James form Tanz Der Youth and Dave Vanian joined the ailing Doctors of Madness. The winter of 1978 saw them all broke. They had over-estimated their individual drawing power, and none of them could get a record deal. There was, however, still a demand for the Damned, which their passing had in-creased. Assured of 'a couple of hundred quid' each, Sensible (switching to guitar), Vanian and Scabies joined Motorhead's Lemmy on bass for a one-off gig at London's Electric Ballroom as Les Punks. 'I learned 13 of their songs and they only learned one of mine,' complained Lemmy afterwards. But the gig was a howling success and, although Lemmy's commit-ment to Motorhead ruled him out as a permanent bass player, the other three decided to reform as the Doomed.

With Sensible's friend Henry Badowski stepping in on bass, the Doomed slogged their way around the rock dives of Britain, turning in some very dubious perform-ances but still drawing crowds. Badowski, who was really a guitarist, was replaced in early 1979 by Algy Ward, and the Doomed reverted to the Damned. The road to re-covery was completed when the band signed to Chiswick and had their first Top Twenty hit with 'Love Song' in mid 1979, following it up with 'Smash It Up', which reached Number 35.

The Damned were suddenly big business again. But this time they could handle it and were less the victims of their own life-style than they had been the first time around – except, that is, for Algy Ward who, in keeping with what he saw as the Damned's image, got through a four-week American tour on 'one meal and 30 bottles of Scotch'. Despite a superficial tendency to abuse audiences and wreck equipment whenever they visited the US, the Damned now liked to maintain a basic level of musical competence at the worst of times: this Ward was unable to do. And when Sensible found himself having to play bass

Left: Damned busters: Sensible's nursing chic, Vanian's Gothic grimace and James' guitar-hero pout on show at London's Roxy Club, 1977. Right: Chart buster: bunny has a nibble of the Captain's Number 1 smash hit, 1982.

on over half of *Machine Gun Etiquette* (1979), it was curtains for Algy.

By the time that Paul Gray had been lured from the Hot Rods to become the Damned's fourth bass player in as many years, it was apparent that the group was undergoing a profound metamorphosis. 'Love Song' had been melodic enough to chart, and melody was not something the Damned had previously been associated with. But, beneath the dye, the roots were showing through. Given the Captain's love of Pink Floyd, Electric Prunes, Brian Auger, the Left Bank, Squirming Capsule and other neglected acts of the Sixties, and Rat's penchant for Hendrix and Cream, it was perhaps hardly surprising that they should make a melodic, psychedelic heavy-metal album like *The Black Album* (1980).

On the LP, the layers of keyboards and shimmering guitars were offset by Rat's ever-pounding drums and Vanian's Gothic English growl to maintain the punk con-nection: but with 'Curtain Call', a long, rambling song punctuated with eerie key-board motifs that faded in and out of each other, the Damned finally re-invented 'pro-gressive' rock. The irony did not escape them. 'I've become what I set out to destroy,' wailed Rat. 'I'm a Boring Old Fart.'

Strawberry punks forever

Punk was now in its second wave and the Damned, 10 years older than most of their audience, had inevitably become some-thing of an institution. Their name was still painted on the back of 15-year-old punks' leather jackets, and although their records now appealed more to people twice that age, they were still marketed along with Chron-Gen, Discharge, Anti-Pasti and the Anti-Nowhere League as 'hard-core' punk for teenagers. As their music matured, however, it made less and less sense to those who preferred a hard thrash.

To escape the punk image, Captain Sensible decided to record a solo album, *Women And Captains First*, and wound up with the surprise smash hit of 1982, a synthesiser-based version of Rogers and Hammerstein's 'Happy Talk' which took him to the top of the UK charts in July. The follow-up single, 'Wot', established the Captain as a top disco act in Europe – something he had not, perhaps, antici-pated. Rat took his revenge by inciting the young hardcore punks to drench Sensible in spittle for 'being such a prissy pop star' when the Damned toured in the autumn of 1982 to promote their album *Strawberries*.

Featuring their new keyboard player Roman Jugg, *Strawberries* – their first (and last) LP for a new label, Bronze – featured electric sitar, earthy English harmonies and impregnated strawberry scent on the label. Despite some rousing uptempo tracks, particularly 'Bad Time For Bonzo', the overall feel of the album was closer to Fairport Convention than Iggy Pop – yet it proved to be the group's most successful LP so far, rising to Number 15 in the UK charts.

But the Captain's solo career was putting a strain on the band, and for two years they were without a recording contract, although they continued to gig extensive-ly. After the departure of Captain Sensible, though, they resurfaced in 1985 on MCA records with a new LP *Phantasmagoria*. Two singles, 'Grimly Fiendish' and 'Shadow Of Love', were taken from the album, and both did very well in the charts.

Though 1988 found them label-less once again, the Damned seemed likely to sur-vive as a live attraction for remaining punks, scoring the occasional novelty hit like 'Eloise', a 1986 UK Number 3.

LUTHER PAISLEY

**The Damned
Recommended Listening**

The Damned (Stiff SEEZ 1) (Includes: So Messed Up, Neat Neat Neat, Born To Kill, Stab Your Back, I Feel Alright, Feel The Pain); *The Best Of The Damned* (Chiswick/Big Beat DAM 1) (Includes: New Rose, Smash It Up, Love Song, There Ain't No Sanity Clause, Rabid (Over You), I Just Can't Be Happy Today).

Out In The Street

The simple truths of blue-collar rock rekindled the spark of Fifties rock'n'roll

IN THE HEYDAY of Elvis, Chuck Berry or the Beatles, radio was revered. It constituted rock 'n'roll's channel to the teen heart, and it struck out into the very soul of a sprawling America. Radio could reach everywhere, from the rural outlands to the inner city. Radio exposure primed the juke-boxes of diners, soda fountains and truck stops. And it was rock'n'roll radio that baptised the ears of the first folks who asserted in print that music could *matter*, as well as entertain.

In the Eighties, however, those same commentators bemoaned a supposition that radio success spelled mediocrity, banality, formulae, a mightily increased dose of plain old bribery. There was also the question of fashion. Critics have traditionally tended to disapprove of music that gained mass radio success, since they must thereby relinquish the privilege of introducing people to it. But the equation of large-scale success with a lowest common denominator has become all but entrenched in printed evaluations of music. And this prejudice was a prime factor in the creation of 'blue-collar rock'.

Collars and dollars

'Blue-collar rock' is a critical term disseminated by various rock critics who possess 'white-collar' credentials and experience. It was coined to deal with a number of American artists who were selling solidly, and had achieved somewhat heroic stature, all with 'traditional' rock songs whose lyrics featured girls, cars, rebellion and the radio. The radio provided platinum hits for three such performers – Bruce Springsteen, Tom Petty and Bob Seger.

Several supposed similarities linked these artists. They lacked 'proper' (white-collar) educations. Their smarts were street smarts, their language limited to that of the truck stop, shopping mall or suburban housing tract. They were rough and ready rockers in the guise of people's heroes – spokesmen and role models for the little guy and his girl.

It is a glib assessment at best, but one that often proceeds from an educational viewpoint which is far more cerebral and far less a matter of practical, *direct* experience than that which is common to the 'blue-collar rockers' themselves. With a few notable exceptions, the rock writer tends to have a college degree and is not likely to be the son or daughter of an assembly-line worker, waitress or small-town, small-time businessman.

Rock'n'roll, by contrast, has always renewed its vigour from raw (black) America and neither 'education' nor 'culture' has contributed much to its cyclical evolution. Its greatest pioneers have not been thinkers but poets. Traditionally, self-expression has been the poor American's religion and his passport to Somewhere.

Springsteen's Dad earned his living in a plastics factory, as a bus driver and a prison guard; Tom Petty's father (now a widower) is a disabled, retired insurance salesman. Neither endorsed their sons' attempts to escape by mastering the magic that radio had filtered into their younger lives. Yet it was to the

Below: Blue-collar heroes Bruce Springsteen (left) and Bob Seger acknowledge the acclaim of their fans. Both exhibited an identification with their audience that went beyond mere commercial considerations, while their songs of New Jersey and Detroit were directed at ordinary Americans – who bought their records in ever-increasing numbers. Inset: Asbury Park adorned Springsteen's first album.

promises beamed out by the radio that these white Americans pledged their allegiance. They remain defenders of the faith, committed to the original populism and dream of unity they recognised in the music of their youth.

'In America,' Tom Petty commented in the Eighties, 'the press still don't sell records – records sell because of the radio. And today it's real sick about what they call AOR radio – they just won't play black music. I mean, old Jimi Hendrix maybe, but they seem to think if they play Marvin Gaye people ain't gonna listen, it's gonna wreck their ratings . . . it's getting so limited and you only hear one sound, loud-guitars, pretty formulated. We've tried to ignore it but even any of our stuff with a funkier sound they won't touch.

'But I prefer the idea of buying a record because I've heard and liked it,' he asserts firmly, 'rather than because somebody told me to buy it. You know, kids may go nuts over Bruce or nuts over us but it's all the same old music, the music's always been there. We grew up hearin' all these classic American musics and our basic theory is just to take these sounds and keep on mixing 'em up and pouring 'em out and each time get a different stew.'

'What I heard in the Drifters, in all that great radio music,' Bruce Springsteen says, 'was the promise of something else. Not a politician's promise, y'know, that everything is gonna be alright . . . that would be a false promise anyway. I mean the promise of *possibilities*: the promise that the search and the struggle matter, that they affirm your life. That was the original spirit of rock'n'roll. And that's what I hope we carry on, a message that no one, *nothing* has the right to tell you you gotta forfeit your hopes and your dreams.'

Love and marriage

Petty has always couched the majority of his music in the love-song format ('it's the easiest for hooking someone in'). He has also been married for five years ('I have a good marriage now and, believe me, I haven't always') and has two children. Marriage – 'the ties which bind' – is a theme Springsteen felt ready to face only on *The River* (1980). 'When I was writing the early songs,' he demurs, 'the girl was still a part of it, she was just part of the future. But she was always there, that was always there, because it's simply a basic human need'.

'There's a hunger for that relationship,' he will say, shaking his head. 'But my characters, they're wrestling with the fact that it's so hard now to separate *traditions* of love and possession, romance and relationships, from the realities of those things today. It's a puzzle to me, because the desire to become truly involved is as strong as anything about freedom. It's a basic reality of how people are.'

Neither Petty nor Springsteen has ever cared to be more fashionable, more educated, more 'influential' outside the rock'n'roll arena. The primary attentions of each have gone to their music, their bands, their fans – and the battle to, as Petty puts it, 'evolve your own art, which is the thing you always have to do, painful or not'. Each has weathered extended legal battles to ensure maximum personal control of that evolution; just as each has endured performing and recording layoffs as a result.

All this occurred, however, at a time when rock was no longer a revolution but a distraction and a diversion. It was also a time when economic stress placed the radio listener's life at the furthest possible remove from that of the 'star'. The thing Petty, Springsteen and Seger really share is a stubborn determination to continue making music that really matters, which is not just content to reflect contemporary life, but offers a criticism of it and provides an alternative viewpoint.

Like Springsteen's songs, Petty's work places tenacity in opposition to the ever-threatening 'darkness' (meaninglessness or irrational chaos) of modernity. It supports the confused listener, promising 'You Can Still Change Your Mind', exhorting against 'A Wasted Life'. 'I know you have to feel a little used up/And no one can give you enough/Baby hold on tight/Don't have a wasted life/I love you too much/Don't have a wasted life'. And a song like Petty's 'The Same Old You' or Springsteen's 'Highway Patrolman', is addressed to nothing less than America itself.

I have a dream . . .

'Highway Patrolman' is the set-piece of Springsteen's *Nebraska* (1982), the album that symbolised his wilful independence from entrepreneurial guides such as producer Jon Landau and critic Dave Marsh, two of the numerous fan-supporters who had guided him to superstar status. *Nebraska* renders the state of American disunion more directly and effectively than anything since the era of the Vietnam War and the writing of Hendrix, Fogerty, Sly Stone, the MC5, the Band and Dylan. But it evolves, it is clear, from a struggle with that riddle central to the title track of the earlier *The River*: 'Is a dream a lie that don't come true/Or is it something worse?' What forces that issue is the central tenet of Springsteen's belief: this land is *all* our land.

The protagonists of the stark, unembellished *Nebraska* are largely losers – not just losers in love but in life. The fact that their belief remains resilient, even as traditions and natural justice fail, offers the only light at the end of a long tunnel: 'Struck me kinda funny/Funny yeah indeed/How at the end of every hard earned day/People find some reason to believe' ('Reason To Believe'). Ostensibly – particularly to British critics – 'Highway Patrolman' is simply the story of one erring brother as told by his law-abiding elder. To American listeners, scarred by the generational battles and loss of faith the Vietnam and Watergate eras initiated, and in many areas battered by recession, it has far wider connotations. The 'brotherhood' alluded to is the one Springsteen believes should be shared by all people, the same dream explicitly espoused for America 20 years before by Dr Martin Luther King.

The rock dreams of Springsteen and Petty are not new but eternal, not revivalist, just anchored in emotions which never faded, and have now been re-articulated. Like Fogerty, or Chuck Berry, or Hendrix, or Elvis himself, neither Petty nor Springsteen were born 'Fortunate Sons'. The message behind their music is a vision which wears no collar and knows no colour . . . and has never been extinguished.

CYNTHIA ROSE

HARD PROMISES

How Tom Petty kept faith with his fans

TOM PETTY first decided he wanted to be a rock'n'roll star after seeing the singing cowboy, Gene Autry, in a film and noting the guitar slung casually across his saddle. Petty (born 20 October 1951 in Gaines-ville, Florida) found his decision was con-firmed for him when Elvis Presley arrived in Florida to make a film. Petty recalls visiting the film set when he was only 11 years old: 'All I remember is a scene with thousands of people. And trailers. And Elvis in a white Cadillac. He looked great.' After persuading his mother to subsidise the purchase of a guitar, Petty made his debut in the high school band performing elementary surfing songs.

From there it was a short step to the Epics, an archetypal semi-professional bar band with a large and constantly shifting personnel and, more importantly, a van. Operating within a 500-mile radius of Gainesville, the Epics played four sets a night over the weekends mixing stan-dards by James Brown, the Animals and Sam and Dave. A week's booking in a topless bar was enough to persuade Petty that an education with the Epics in sex, drugs and drink was preferable to school, but the hedonistic side of life in the band eventually swamped the music. Petty left and went back to school, avoiding the Vietnam draft into the bargain. After school Petty joined Mudcrutch, a band which already contained future Heartbreakers Mike Campbell (lead guitar) and Benmont Tench (keyboards).

Mudcrutch quickly secured themselves a niche as the stars of Gainesville, but after a time the frustrations of a purely localised fame prompted a move. Encouraged by the example of another Gainesville native Don Felder, who had found fame and fortune in Los Angeles with the Eagles, Petty and

Heartbreaker-in-chief Tom Petty (opposite and right) rocks with drummer Stan Lynch and bassist Ron Blair (below).

2085

Mudcrutch followed suit. Petty commented at the time, 'I started writing songs so as to write my way out of Gainesville somehow, so we wouldn't be stuck there forever.' Unfortunately, reaction in LA to the demo tape that Petty hawked around was discouraging.

Petty spent the next four years in LA without tangible success, but that period enabled him to form his own band, the Heartbreakers, and to weld them into a formidable rock'n'roll unit. Apart from Campbell and Tench, the band featured Ron Blair (bass) and Stan Lynch (drums). Eventually Petty negotiated a recording contract with Denny Cordell's Shelter record label, and also got a booking as support act on the 1976 Nils Lofgren tour, which included a visit to the UK.

It was a difficult tour for the Heartbreakers. Lofgren, who was at the height of his popularity, was recording material for a live album, which entailed increased attention to technical detail for his band and less time spent on the support group. The Petty band however received consistently good notices, and ended the tour on a triumphant note, playing an extra London date in their own right.

Torpedoed!

The debut LP, *Tom Petty And The Heartbreakers*, was released in 1977 to critical acclaim which was boosted by their reception in the UK – an experience they shared with an increasing number of US bands at this time, Blondie, Television, the Ramones and Talking Heads being the most prominent. The album was a traditional mix of rock numbers and ballads, and all were executed with a dynamic and flashy swagger.

Petty also enjoyed minor UK singles successes in 1977 with the Stones-influenced 'Anything That's Rock'n'Roll', swiftly followed by the Byrds-sounding

'American Girl', but he didn't make any impression on the American singles chart until early 1978 when 'Breakdown' made a fleeting appearance in the Top Forty.

The success of the debut album was consolidated by the release of a follow-up, *You're Gonna Get It*, in 1978. But trouble loomed with the demise of Shelter and its parent company ABC. MCA, having bought out ABC, claimed the rights to Petty's contract. Petty refused to cooperate and they sued him, signalling the start of a year's wrangling during which Petty filed for bankruptcy and nearly wrecked his career. A compromise solution was finally hammered out and Petty and the Heartbreakers signed to Backstreet Records, a subsidiary of MCA. The experience may have been cathartic, as the third LP, *Damn The Torpedoes* (1979), was Petty's most consistent and confident record to date and quickly went platinum in America.

But ill-fortune was still close at hand, however; within a week of commencing his first tour to promote the album, Petty lost his voice due to tonsillitis and suffered a nerve-wracking spell in hospital before his vocal chords returned to normal. The group soon resumed touring and were one of the acts to appear at the 1979 No Nukes concerts in New York, although Petty refused to let the group appear in the subsequent film as he considered their performance to be substandard.

The long-awaited follow-up to *Damn The Torpedoes* appeared in 1981, entitled *Hard Promises*, and controversy was again at hand. Petty heard that his record company might increase the price of the US album by one dollar to nine dollars and 98 cents, and threatened to withhold the record. Petty's stand was successful.

Below: Petty pouts with Fleetwood Mac's Stevie Nicks (left) and picks with his lead guitarist Mike Campbell (right).

Duet success

Outstanding tracks on *Hard Promises* included 'The Waiting' (a US hit single), 'King's Road' and 'The Insider'. The latter was originally written for inclusion on Stevie Nicks' solo LP, *Bella Donna*, and she duetted with Petty on this version. However, it was a Nicks/Petty collaboration on another Petty composition, 'Stop Draggin' My Heart Around', that became a smash hit in the US, reaching Number 3 in 1981, his highest ever singles placing.

Petty released his fifth LP in 1982 under the title *Long After Dark*, and its polished power owed much to the understanding which Petty and co-producer Jimmy Iovine had built up over three albums together. The new LP was notable for the first personnel change in the Heartbreakers, bassist Ron Blair making way for Howie Epstein.

By 1986's overblown live *Pack Up The Plantation,* however, Petty had lost his sense of adventure—a feeling *Let Me Up I've Had Enough* (1987) reinforced.

Despite his occasional brushes with 'the business', Tom Petty retained a remarkable freshness in his approach to rock music, and at his best managed to transcend the limitations of the rock format to produce some enduring gems of muscular romanticism.

PETER CLARK

Tom Petty and the Heartbreakers Recommended Listening

Tom Petty And The Heartbreakers (Shelter ISA5014) (Includes: Luna, Breakdown, Mystery Man, American Girl, The Wild One, Forever, Hometown Blues); *Hard Promises* (MCA MCF 3098) (Includes: The Waiting, The Criminal Kind, Something Big, King's Road, Letting You Go, The Insider).

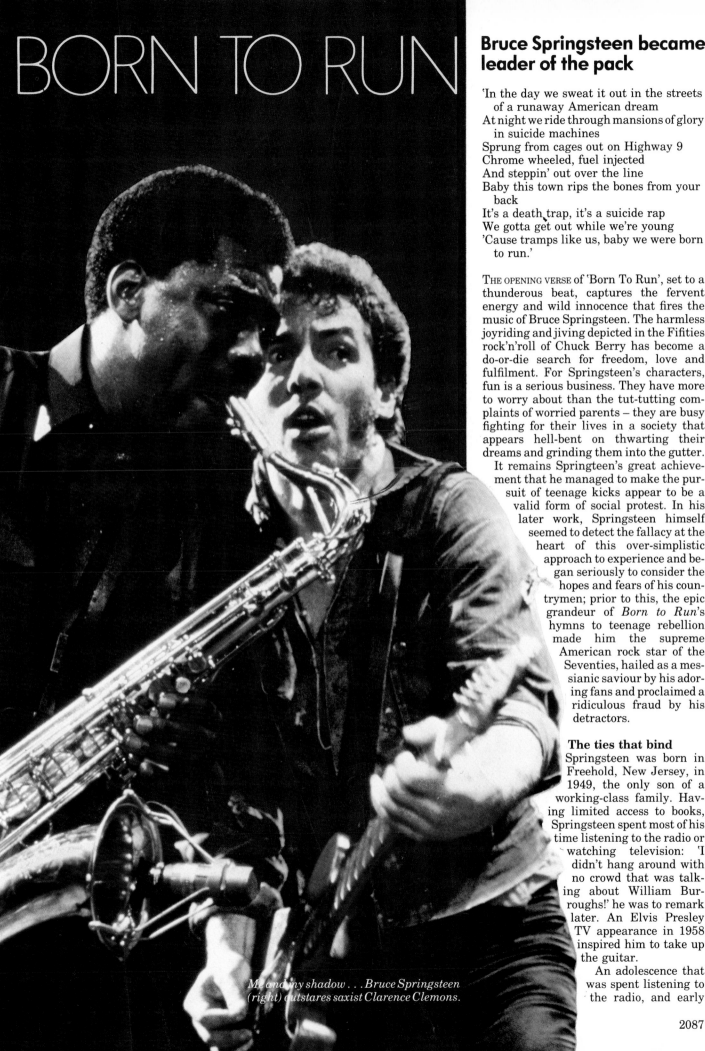

BORN TO RUN

Bruce Springsteen became leader of the pack

'In the day we sweat it out in the streets
    of a runaway American dream
At night we ride through mansions of glory
    in suicide machines
Sprung from cages out on Highway 9
Chrome wheeled, fuel injected
And steppin' out over the line
Baby this town rips the bones from your
    back
It's a death trap, it's a suicide rap
We gotta get out while we're young
'Cause tramps like us, baby we were born
    to run.'

THE OPENING VERSE of 'Born To Run', set to a thunderous beat, captures the fervent energy and wild innocence that fires the music of Bruce Springsteen. The harmless joyriding and jiving depicted in the Fifities rock'n'roll of Chuck Berry has become a do-or-die search for freedom, love and fulfilment. For Springsteen's characters, fun is a serious business. They have more to worry about than the tut-tutting complaints of worried parents – they are busy fighting for their lives in a society that appears hell-bent on thwarting their dreams and grinding them into the gutter.

It remains Springsteen's great achievement that he managed to make the pursuit of teenage kicks appear to be a valid form of social protest. In his later work, Springsteen himself seemed to detect the fallacy at the heart of this over-simplistic approach to experience and began seriously to consider the hopes and fears of his countrymen; prior to this, the epic grandeur of *Born to Run*'s hymns to teenage rebellion made him the supreme American rock star of the Seventies, hailed as a messianic saviour by his adoring fans and proclaimed a ridiculous fraud by his detractors.

The ties that bind

Springsteen was born in Freehold, New Jersey, in 1949, the only son of a working-class family. Having limited access to books, Springsteen spent most of his time listening to the radio or watching television: 'I didn't hang around with no crowd that was talking about William Burroughs!' he was to remark later. An Elvis Presley TV appearance in 1958 inspired him to take up the guitar.

An adolescence that was spent listening to the radio, and early

Me and my shadow . . . Bruce Springsteen (right) outstares saxist Clarence Clemons.

experience in several local bands, provided Bruce Springsteen with a rich and varied musical background, including Fifties rock'n'roll, R&B, electric Dylan, British beat groups and soul. He drew freely on all these influences in his later concerts and recordings.

A chance meeting with wheeler-dealer Mike Appel (who subsequently became his manager) allowed Springsteen to escape from the local Asbury Park band circuit. Appel fixed an audition for Springsteen with CBS's John Hammond, who had become a legend for having the keenest pair of ears in the business. Hammond had nurtured the careers of Benny Goodman, Bessie Smith, Robert Johnson and Bob Dylan for CBS, and swiftly included Springsteen in that illustrious company. Hammond signed Springsteen to the label (putting aside his personal antipathy towards Appel) and mentally cast him as an acoustic poet, in the same vein as early-Sixties Dylan.

Springsteen's confident debut album, *Greetings From Asbury Park NJ* (1973), defied such typecasting. Yet despite being chock full of vivid images of contemporary America, the LP almost got lost amid the plethora of recordings released by other promising singer-songwriters such as John Prine, Steve Goodman and Loudon Wainwright III. Like them, Springsteen had to endure the mixed blessing of being hailed 'the new Dylan' by the music press.

By the time of his second album, *The Wild, The Innocent And The E Street Shuffle*, later in 1973, Springsteen had honed his style, and sharpened his eye for detail, particularly with songs like 'Sandy' and 'Incident On 57th Street'. The brashness and machine-gun metaphors of his first album were replaced by a more mature style of writing; the LP also boasted a crisper production, and earmarked Springsteen as a performer with a great future.

However, it took the epic elegance of 1975's *Born To Run* to tip the scales firmly in Springsteen's favour. The album was years in the making and arrived halfway through a decade uncertain of its musical direction. It managed to hark back wistfully and enviously to rock'n'roll's past, while seeming to offer hope for its future.

Into the darkness

Ironically, *Born To Run* – which brought Springsteen to the forefront of rock music – became a millstone around his neck. His face adorned the covers of *Time* and *Newsweek* in the same week (the only non-political figure to be accorded such an accolade); CBS promoted him in absurdly pompous terms with posters featuring the legend: 'I have seen the future of rock'n'roll and its name is Bruce Springsteen'; in addition, Springsteen became involved in an acrimonious wrangle with Mike Appel which

Above: Springsteen claims the microphone from Clemons (left), bass-player Garry Tallent (second from right) and guitarist Steve Van Zandt. Opposite: Bruce bounds.

resulted in Springsteen being legally prevented from making another record for three years. In their various ways, these factors made Springsteen an easy target for the critics' jibes.

Springsteen's enforced lay-off from recording saw him establish himself as America's premier live performer. Backed by the superb E Street Band, whose regular members included Roy Bittan (piano), Clarence Clemons (saxophone), Danny Federici (organ) and Max Weinberg (drums), he played all the songs from his own three albums, he provided his adoring fans with generous slices of rock'n'roll history, performing numbers by Little Richard, Mitch Ryder, Creedence Clearwater Revival, Buddy Holly, the Crystals and Bob Dylan. With acts like Patti Smith, Southside Johnny and the Pointer Sisters achieving hits with his songs, Springsteen's name was never far from the rock-paper headlines.

By the time *Darkness On The Edge Of Town* was released in 1978, much of the impetus of Springsteen's music had been overtaken by the youthful ardour of punk rock. Yet Springsteen found his audience still devoted and his popularity untouched.

Darkness was an altogether bleaker, *adult* album. The car imagery and romanticism of *Born To Run* was still present, but tempered with a realism and integrity that implied that, yes, there *was* a 'Promised Land', but the only way to it was by way of suffering and experience.

The breadth of emotion on *Darkness* was expanded on in *The River* (1980), one of the few double albums in rock that actually merits four sides. It showed Springsteen extending his range, and consolidating his strengths. Springsteen balanced the moodier, more serious songs such as the title track, 'Independence Day' and 'Wreck On The Highway' with exuberant rockers such as 'Cadillac Ranch', 'Hungry Heart' and 'Ramrod'. The diversity of *The River* was fully reflected in Springsteen's live shows. Consequently, with only five albums to his name, Springsteen became one of rock's most widely bootlegged artists. Despite this dubious accolade – indicative of the huge public demand for Springsteen's work – he refused to be pressured into rush-releasing albums, and continued to pay scrupulous attention to every detail when it came to recording.

At the beginning of the Eighties, Springsteen was firing on all cylinders. He had joined his friend Jackson Browne at the MUSE concerts in New York, and came away the undoubted star of the subsequent film and triple album. Then, in the spring of 1981, he embarked on his first European tour. At last, audiences outside the US had the opportunity to see him perform songs stretching back to *Born To Run*, six years before, together with the composer's own versions of 'Fire' and 'Because The Night'.

At a time when rock music had become overly concerned with 'image' and gimmicks, Bruce Springsteen and his E Street Band remained true to its original power and passion. The man's overriding integrity, and enthusiasm for his craft left few in doubt about his consummate talent. His next move, however, was as audacious as any in his already controversial career.

Nebraska was released in the autumn of 1982, and came as much of a surprise to Springsteen's record company as to his fans. In place of the now familiar honking sax breaks of Clarence Clemons and the driving rhythmic pulse of the rest of the E Street Band, *Nebraska* featured the singer alone, accompanying himself on guitar and harmonica. The LP's aching, plaintive songs, were steeped in the folk and country traditions of Woody Guthrie and Hank Williams; its starkness and musical simplicity initially alienated many of Springsteen's fans, but allowed the singer to explore his perennial themes of family loyalty, guilt, redemption and honour with new seriousness and depth. It stands as one of the most iconoclastic albums ever released by a major rock star.

Springsteen's 1984 album *Born In The USA* put *Nebraska*'s concerns in the musical perspective of his earlier career. This melding of social comment and rousing rock brought him a major new audience—especially in Europe, where the album topped charts all over the continent.

Despite losing Steve Van Zandt, his trusted lieutenant (replaced by Nils Lofgren), a broken marriage (to actress Julianne Phillips) and a less than successful five-album concert set (*Live* 1975-85), 1987's country-flavoured *Tunnel Of Love* put Bruce Springsteen back where he belonged—at the top of rock.

PATRICK HUMPHRIES

BRUCE SPRINGSTEEN
Discography (UK releases to 1984)

Singles
Born To Run/Meeting Across The River (CBS 3661, 1975); Tenth Avenue Freeze-Out/She's The One (CBS 3940, 1976); Prove It All Night/Factory (CBS 6424, 1978); Badlands/Something In The Night (CBS 6532, 1978); Promised Land/Streets Of Fire (CBS 6720, 1978); Hungry Heart/Held Up Without A Gun (CBS 9309, 1980); Sherry Darling/Be True (CBS 9568, 1981); The River/Independence Day (CBS A 1179, 1981); Cadillac Ranch/Wreck On The Highway (CBS A 1557, 1981); Atlantic City/Mansion On The Hill (CBS A 2794, 1982); Open All Night/The Big Payback (CBS A 2969, 1982); Dancing In The Dark/Pink Cadillac (CBS A 4436, 1984); Cover Me/Jersey Girl (CBS A 4462, 1984); I'm On Fire/Born In The USA (CBS A 6342, 1985); Glory Days/Stand On It (CBS A 6375, 1985).

Albums
Greetings From Asbury Park, NJ (CBS 65480, 1973); The Wild, The Innocent And The E Street Shuffle (CBS 65780, 1974); Born To Run (CBS 69170, 1975); Darkness On The Edge Of Town (CBS 86061, 1978); The River (CBS 88510, 1980); Nebraska (CBS 25100, 1982); Born In The USA (CBS 86304, 1984).

'The Boss' on his home turf of New Jersey in 1973 (top left), playing with the E Street Band (above left), making his guitar 'talk' (right) and composedly contemplating new musical goals in 1980 (bottom left).

Johnny too bad

Southside Johnny: in the shadow of Springsteen?

'SOUTHSIDE' JOHNNY LYON grew up in Ocean Grove, alongside Asbury Park near the oil refinery belt of the New Jersey shore. '30 years ago it was a very big resort community,' he related in the Eighties, 'but it sort of fell by the wayside. Over the past 15 years most of the shops and the big hotels have closed down. If you walk down the main street of Asbury Park now, all you see is "out of business" signs. The only really viable business venture is a bar with a band, and they *all* have bands. I started playing in these bars when I was about 16 and up until that point there was only hit cover bands playing around the Jersey shore. We came along, younger than we should have been, and played rhythm and blues, y'know, lots of Rolling Stones-style rock'n'roll. No Beatles or anything like that, but Mitch Ryder, James Brown and the stuff people could dance to.'

Wrong side of town

Lyon started appearing at Asbury Park's Upstage Club while still at school. His obsession with Chicago blues and R&B drew him into the same social scene as other young buffs. Through the first half of the Seventies he played in a floating community of bar bands whose participants included future members of the E Street Band and the Asbury Jukes. His first serious band came together during a college semester in 1967, when he joined forces with veteran bandleader Sonny Kenn in the Sonny Kenn Blues Band. From that point onwards, it is hard to keep track of his band-hopping.

Bruce Springsteen led the exodus of bands out of New Jersey and into national and international prominence in the early Seventies. At the time, Johnny was playing in the Blackberry Booze Band with guitarist Steve Van Zandt, around the better bars/clubs such as the Stone Pony. This unit evolved into the original Southside Johnny and the Asbury Jukes around 1975, the first formation including Kenny Pentifallo (drums), Alan Berger (bass), Carlo Novi (tenor sax), Kevin Kavanaugh (keyboards) and Billy Rush (guitar).

By the end of 1975 Bruce Springsteen's face had been carried by the front cover of *Time* and *Newsweek*, and New Jersey rock was definitely flavour of the month. This sort of concentrated focus had both positive and negative repercussions for Southside Johnny and the Asbury Jukes. On one hand, Epic Records stepped in swiftly to sign them up; on the other hand The Boss himself stole away Steve Van Zandt for his E Street Band before the Jukes had even

Top left: Guitarist Billy Rush and trombonist Richie 'La Bamba' Rosenberg (in hat) lend Johnny vocal support. Above left and left: Southside solo. Opposite: The Jukes stand proud amid the peeling paint of the Asbury Park shorefront.

got into the studio to start work on their debut album entitled *I Don't Want To Go Home* (1976).

There is no doubt that Springsteen, despite his musician pilfering, was quite an asset to the growth of the Jukes. He supplied 'You Mean So Much To Me' and the single 'Fever', as well as the liner notes, in which he reminisced about his first meetings with Southside Johnny: 'He was the only white kid on the Jersey shore that you could stand to hear sing straight R&B five sets a night . . . Johnny's friendship is something that grew out of those friendships and the long summer nights when there was no particular place to go and nothing to do, except play.'

The sky's the limit
In fact, the Jukes didn't need Springsteen's endorsement. The first album was a spinetingling, hair-raising, wonderfully emotive excursion into white R&B, mixing fine originals with artfully chosen slabs of Steve Cropper, Ray Charles, Buster Brown and Solomon Burke. The cake was iced with glorious guest vocal duets by Lee Dorsey on 'How Come You Treat Me So Bad' and Ronnie Spector on 'You Mean So Much To Me'. Buoyed by ecstatic reviews and undeterred by moderate sales, Southside expanded his use of veteran R&B performers with the second of his three Miami Steve Van Zandt-produced albums, *This Time It's For Real* (1977). With vocal

contributions from re-formations of the Coasters, Five Satins and Drifters, and three more Springsteen compositions, 'Little Girl So Fine', 'Love On The Wrong Side Of Town' and 'When You Dance', this was another *tour de force*, a vibrant, brassy pot-pourri of influences welded together by Southside's gutsy vocals.

His singing reached its peak on the third and best album, *Hearts Of Stone* (1978). On the Springsteen-penned title track, an intense ballad one could easily imagine Clyde McPhatter or Sam Cooke rendering, the horns punched like guitars. Springsteen's two other songs were of exceptional quality, as was Van Zandt's 'This Time Baby's Gone For Good' – described by *Rolling Stone* as 'a pop song Leiber and Stoller could envy'.

Despite being a truly great rock'n'roll album, it barely sold a copy; after whipping out a hasty 'best of' compilation, *Having A Party* (with one unissued track) in 1979, Epic bade farewell to the band. They signed with Mercury and commenced recording *The Jukes* (1979), a dramatic departure from the style established by its three predecessors. With no Springsteen songs, production by Barry Beckett at Muscle Shoals, and an expanded role for the full horn section introduced on the previous album, this was a work that was hard to assimilate. New members Steve Becker (drums) and Joel Gramolini (rhythm guitar) contributed to the harder

edge, which gave the band their highest-charting album of all. While the public paid their dollars, however, the critics inevitably withheld much of their praise, as they later did with *Love Is A Sacrifice* (1980) and the disappointing double live set *Reach Up And Touch The Sky* (1981).

This course of events left Southside Johnny Lyon at an impasse in his career. Even when he mildly compromised he never sold *that* many records, certainly not in comparison with Springsteen, although his music was no less potent. His zeal for R&B seemed to have faded, with his fans vainly praying for a new spark of excellence, even a hint of the magic of the first three albums. In the meantime, Southside Johnny and the Asbury Jukes continued to tour: 'Don't ask me why it's important and so necessary. After 15 years I still don't know. But there's an instinctive feeling that without the audience, without the lights, the stage, the band, the music . . . the whole experience, you'd be dead.'

GLENN A BAKER

Southside Johnny and the Asbury Jukes Recommended Listening

This Time It's For Real (Epic 81909) (Includes: First Night, This Time It's For Real, Little Girl So Fine, She Got Me Where She Wants Me, When You Dance, Love On The Wrong Side Of Town); *Hearts Of Stone* (Epic EPC 82994) (Includes: This Time Baby's Gone For Good, I Played The Fool, Talk To Me, Light Don't Shine, Trapped Again, Take It Inside).

KING OF THE ROAD

Tom Waits' guide to the underworld

A WHISPER WENT AROUND the night-clubs of the West Coast in the early Seventies about a new and wonderful performer, part comedian, raconteur, torch singer and poet, called Tom Waits. As befitted a man who later professed never to spend 'more than two dollars on a meal and six dollars on a suit', Waits would take the stage looking like a late-night exhalation from a flop-house – a studied blend of bum and low-rent pimp. His jacket and trousers were plainly of uncertain vintage and dubious antecedents. He wore his hair greased back over his large, bony forehead, while his angular countenance was emphasised by a straggling goatee. A battered newsboy's cap and a necktie worn at half-mast completed his *ensemble*.

In a voice that sounded like Satchmo's dying breath, coated with nicotine, soaked in beer and pickled in bourbon, Tom Waits would then proceed to unfold his scenarios of life on the skids, vivid scenes shot through with whimsical tenderness, lingering melancholy and wild, heady exuberance.

Despite the wealth of experience that seemed to invest his work, Waits was only in his early twenties when he first came to public notice, having been born in Pomona, California, on 7 December 1949. Like his major influence, the 'King of the Beats', Jack Kerouac, Waits' background was solidly middle-class but his existence was hardly settled: 'My parents were divorced when I was 10 years old, my father's been married about three times, and my mother finally remarried a private investigator.'

In the light of these facts, it is perhaps not surprising that Waits was desperately keen to assert his independence. He found lasting inspiration in characters such as Dean Moriarty, the vagabond hero of Kerouac's novel *On The Road*, and in the anti-bourgeois stance, riotous excesses and linguistic pyrotechnics of the writers of the Beat generation of the Fifties – Kerouac, Allen Ginsberg and William Burroughs.

Waits himself chose to base his style on the original models, sharing their love for jazz, Charlie Parker and Miles Davis, and finding little in acid rock; he later described the Sixties as a decade he 'slept through'. His songs would later also evoke the atmosphere of Forties and Fifties Hollywood *film noir* and the hard-boiled, wisecracking style and world-wearied romanticism of thriller writers like Raymond Chandler, Dashiell Hammett and David Goodis.

Roadhouse blues

Having taken various odd jobs, including washer-up, cab-driver, ice-cream man and firefighter, Waits decided to concentrate on making a career as a songwriter. He was quickly snapped up by the then go-ahead Asylum Records. *Closing Time* (1973), Waits' first LP for Asylum was, with hindsight, somewhat tentative, several of the tracks having an indeterminate folk/country feel. However by the second side, Waits seemed to have hit his stride. With songs like 'Ice Cream Man', 'Little Trip To Heaven (On The Wings Of Your Love)' and the poignant instrumental 'Closing Time', there were clear signs of the spare, jazz/blues melodies and arrangements that would provide such evocative settings to his subsequent stream-of-consciousness narratives and torch ballads. Two songs from the album were to establish Waits' name – 'Martha', covered by Tim Buckley on *Sefronia* (1974) and 'Ol' 55', given a syrupy treatment by the Eagles on their platinum-selling *On The Border* (1974).

He consolidated his reputation as a writer of bluesy, carefully constructed love songs with his next LP, *The Heart Of Saturday Night* (1974). However, only the scat vocal delivery of 'Diamonds On My Windshield', set to a freewheeling upright bass and drums backing, prepared those of his fans who had not caught his stage act for the revelation of his live double set *Nighthawks At The Diner* (1975).

The record's production by Bones Howe captured perfectly the intense excitement of Waits in performance and the intimate relationship he was capable of forming with a small but enthusiastic club audience. All the tracks were brand new, with the exception of Red Sovine's masterly folk-tale of a ghostly trucker, 'Big Joe And Phantom 309'. With a private-eye's attention to detail and a poet's joy in the power and sound of words, Waits, backed by a jazz quartet, went on a nostalgic, extravagant pilgrimage through the heartlands of America – the diners and bars, the vast open spaces, the 'shy and

Opposite: Waits in his favourite character role as a booze-crazed down-and-out – a persona that evolved from his mid-Seventies 'Beat-poet' image (above).

sleepy' mid-Western towns and the big cities, seething with life. 'Well the dawn cracked hard just like a bullwhip/Cause it wasn't takin' no lip from the night before/As it shook out the streets, the stew bums showed up/Just like bounced checks, rubbin' their necks/And the sky turned the colour of Pepto-Bismol . . .'

The LP also showed what a versatile songwriter Waits could be with the achingly simple blues lament 'Nobody', the funny and moving 'Emotional Weather Report' and the bitter-sweet hobo song 'Better Off Without A Wife'.

Nighthawks represented such a spate of creative energy that it seems incredible that his next release the following year, *Small Change* (1976), should have bettered it. The mood of the record was darker, with Waits really getting under the skins of his subjects – petty criminals, hookers, drifters, boozers and losers of all kinds. *Small Change* was also stronger on melody than *Nighthawks*, with the outstanding 'Tom Traubert's Blues' and 'Invitation To The Blues' (which featured in Nicolas Roeg's 1980 film *Bad Timing*). In addition, the raps were wilder, crazier and punchier than ever: 'Pasties And A G-String' was a parodic celebration of the best strip-joint in the universe where you 'getcha little sompin'/Thatcha can't get at home,' while 'Step Right Up' presented an hysterical exercise in barker's hyperbole. Among the album's other highlights were 'Small Change', the vivid narration of the shooting of a small-time crook, and 'The Piano Has Been Drinking (Not Me)', Waits' surreal paean to booze, an extended live version of which features on the compilation *Bounced Checks* (1982).

With *Foreign Affairs* (1977), Waits continued his investigations of city low-life. Once more it was a richly satisfying work. The title track and 'Burma Shave', the tale of two teenagers who die on the road to a place where 'dreams are growing wild', were the outstanding songs. 'Foreign Affair' neatly articulated the live-at-all-

costs, romantic philosophy of Waits' favourite characters: 'Most vagabonds I knowed don't ever want to find the culprit/That remains the object of their long relentless quest/The obsession's in the chasing and not the apprehending/The pursuit you see and never the arrest.'

For both *Blue Valentine* (1978) and *Heartattack And Vine* (1980) Waits moved into a more abrasive, electric sound, anchoring the melodies in the raunchy R&B of John Lee Hooker and Screamin' Jay Hawkins. Although some of the jazz intimacy and delicacy of his previous work was thereby sacrificed, these LPs showed that his songwriting gifts remained undiminished.

In 1980 the long-time loner got married. His wife, Kathleen, was a script analyst for 20th Century-Fox and their marriage signalled a move by Waits into the world of films, as he then began work on the music for Francis Ford Coppola's *One From The Heart* (1982). The director had become convinced of the dramatic potential of Waits' work when he heard the singer's smoky duet with Bette Midler 'I Never Talk To Strangers' (from *Foreign Affairs*). For the *One From The Heart* soundtrack Waits, sharing the microphone with Crystal Gayle, created perhaps his gentlest, most accessible recording – an LP of love songs that really say something about love – played with skill and commitment by a collection of top jazz musicians. Though the movie itself was not a great success, Waits was nominated for an Oscar for his music. He subsequently took an acting role in Coppola's *Rumblefish*.

Sounds fishy

In 1983 Waits, who had just signed to Island Records, released his most eccentric and exciting album for many years, *Swordfishtrombones* – 'Either a musical instrument that smells bad or a fish that makes a lot of noise,' he explained. The LP was a startling collage of sounds, variously involving marimbas, pipe organs, bagpipes, a 'Salvation Army' type band and raving R&B.

Waits continued his idiosyncratic path through the Eighties with a series of individual and highly acclaimed albums: *Rain Dogs* (1985), *Frank's Wild Years* (1987) and *Big Time* (1988). The last-named was also the title of a film in which he starred.

Waits' music demands the listener's total attention, a fact which has prevented him achieving much more than cult status, despite the almost uniform excellence of his work.

ALASTAIR DOUGALL

Tom Waits
Recommended Listening

Bounced Cheques (Elektra K 52316) (Includes: Tom Traubert's Blues, I Never Talk To Strangers, The Piano Has Been Drinking (Not Me), Jersey Girl, Diamonds On My Windshield, Burma Shave); *Swordfishtrombones* (Island ILPS 9762) (Includes: Underground, Dave The Butcher, Soldier's Things, Gin Soaked Boy, Just Another Sucker On The Vine, Shore Leave).

RICKIE LEE JONES

Street-wise singer with jazz in her soul

To compare Rickie Lee Jones with Janis Joplin, Bruce Springsteen, Tom Waits or Joni Mitchell, as reviewers have done so frequently, is as misleading as it is illuminating. Certainly Jones' use of street life as material for her songs has its echo in Springsteen and, particularly, Waits. Also, there are times when her music *sounds* like Mitchell's early-Seventies records (especially 1974's *Court And Spark*), but anyone familiar with both musicians would know instantly how spurious this parallel really is.

What really needs to be remembered about Rickie Lee Jones is her quite startling originality, one reason why her records have sent reviewers scurrying off in search of the nearest reference point. Jones' music is quintessentially American, with its roots in the Beat generation and beyond to Forties pop. Jones' songs are peopled with losers and those who live on the seamy underbelly of society. Nevertheless much of Jones' music has a slick West Coast gloss that is misleading; she was signed to Warner Brothers with the stipulation that Lenny Waronker, best known for his work with Randy Newman and Maria Muldaur, produce her debut album.

The first thing the public heard of Jones was the joyously infectious 'Chuck E's In Love', not surprisingly a hit on both sides of the Atlantic. Its upbeat, West Coast jazz-pop sounded perfect on the radio and led one to believe that Jones' music was relatively straightforward. However a careful listen to her subsequent album, *Rickie Lee Jones* (1979), revealed unsuspected depths in her work – a view strengthened by 1981's *Pirates* and her long overdue third album, *Girl At Her Volcano* (1983), the latter a ten-inch, partly live album of the kind once favoured by jazzers.

The boho dance

Jones' background reads like one of the characters in her songs. She was born in Chicago in 1955, but drifted all over America with her parents before winding up in Los Angeles in 1973. There was (failed) showbiz in the family – her father was an amateur jazz singer who had made a living as a waiter; her mother was a waitress. She once recalled her parents: 'They fought and didn't fight, drank and didn't drink, as much as anybody else.' At 14, so Jones tells it, she stole a car with her Italian boyfriend and ran away from home.

In Los Angeles, where she worked as a waitress, she hung out with a bohemian crowd that included Tom Waits, with whom she had a long romance, and Chuck E. Weiss, the 'Chuck E' of the aforementioned song; she is the blonde depicted on the cover of Waits' 1978 *Blue Valentine* LP. Apparently she has always preferred to be with males. The tomboy shows through clearly in Jones' songs.

In the mid-Seventies Jones started

Tom Scott, Chuck Findley and Ernie Watts. The players sounded like they had a ball on this finger-snappin', jazzy affair.

Songs like 'On Saturday Afternoons in 1963', 'Night Train' and the closing 'After Hours (Twelve Bars Past Goodnight) revealed a side to Jones that was a good deal softer than her street-wise image; in addition, 'Company' had all the hallmarks of a classic torch song. Her fondness for minor-key piano motifs doubtless explained the 'new Joni Mitchell' tag that certain critics used to describe Jones' music, a comparison that Jones has said she did not relish: 'She sings jazz but she's not jazz, she's not a jazz artist.' The inference was that Jones definitely was.

The price of fame

In retrospect, it is clear that her first album was not entirely representative of Rickie Lee Jones. It is thus not hard to understand why *Pirates* (1981) failed to repeat the commercial success of its predecessor. The public initially took Jones for something that she wasn't, as the less obviously commercial *Pirates* and *Girl At Her Volcano* were to show.

Only one song on the first LP, 'Coolsville', pointed the way to *Pirates*. Jones' wailing vocals and the song's unusual construction demonstrated the depth of Jones' originality. From the brilliant, dramatic opening of side one, track one, 'We Belong Together', *Pirates* did not miss an opportunity to be unpredictable, while the title song was typical of the emotional intensity Jones injected into this album.

Apparently depressed at the fate of *Pirates*, Jones was a long time releasing a follow-up. *Girl At Her Volcano* picked up where *Pirates* left off on Jones' innovative reworking of 'Walk Away Rene'. She also performed a dazzling re-arrangement of the Drifters' 'Under The Boardwalk'. Elsewhere the mood was low-key, conjuring up an after-hours jazz flavour, epitomised by Jones' understated rendering of Rodgers and Hart's 'My Funny Valentine'.

By this time Jones had uprooted from America to Paris, the way of many a boho before her. She commented: 'I had to leave the States for my own peace of mind. Fame is a poison, a venomous thing. I wasn't writing. I wasn't feeling any hope or joy. Physically I was falling to bits.'

Rickie Lee Jones is one of the few major American rock acts to have emerged in the late Seventies and after. It remains to be seen whether she will be accorded the respect she deserves, instead of being rashly written off as just another Joni Mitchell imitator.

1984's *The Magazine* garnered mixed reviews, and by early 1989 the world still waited for Jones' fifth album. STEVE CLARKE

Jones' raunchy, jazz-tinged style (left and above) rapidly gave the lie to the 'new Joni Mitchell' image initially fostered by Warner Brothers (below).

singing in Southern Californian bars. One of her early songs – 'Easy Money', a jazzy account of two hookers on the make – was subsequently covered by Lowell George on his solo album, *Thanks I'll Eat It Here* (1979). George's decision to feature the song convinced Warners to sign this unknown, rather eccentric songstress who had little in common with the type of female who had graced the American charts in the Seventies.

Rickie Lee Jones became the surprise smash of the season, and abruptly switched from playing bars to doing headline concerts at Carnegie Hall. For the album, Warners had paired Jones with the cream of Los Angeles' session men, including drummers Steve Gadd, Andy Newmark, Jeffrey Porcaro, bassist Willie Weeks, Dr John and Victor Feldman on keyboards, and a horn section featuring

Rickie Lee Jones
Recommended Listening

Rickie Lee Jones (Warner Brothers K56628)
(Includes: Chuck E's In Love, On Saturday
Afternoons In 1963, Night Train, Young Blood,
Easy Money, The Last Chance Texaco).

A critical assessment of Seventies rock lyrics

Words From The Wise?

THERE IS A WORLD of difference between Boudleaux Bryant's bathetic lament that 'Love is like a stove – it burns you when it's hot' (from 'Love Hurts') and the plangent blend of faith and fatalism in Tim Buckley's 'In the scarlet light of Valentine's/Our paper hearts are blind' (from 'Valentine Melody'). Thus had the importance and power of rock lyrics changed from the Fifties to the Sixties. To hear Tom Waits melodically snarling the lines 'It takes a lot of whiskey/To make these nightmares go away/And I cut my bleedin' heart out every nite/And I die a little more on each St Valentine's day' in 'Blue Valentines', is to see at once how the atmosphere had changed by the late Seventies. The shift is even more apparent in the work of a bloatedly pretentious writer like Peter Gabriel of Genesis who wrote in 'IT': 'It is chicken, it is eggs/It is in between your legs/It is walking on the moon/Leaving your cocoon.'

The major songwriters of the Sixties – not least among them Dylan, Lennon and McCartney, Jagger and Richards and Pete Townshend – had shown that rock songs could accommodate an enormous range of tone and topic. By the Seventies, in the wake of protest music and psychedelia, rock writers could confidently put pen to paper about anything that came to mind.

The ghost of Zimmerman
The trouble was that what came to mind was often garbled (and garrulous) tripe, represented at one end of the scale by the Archies' clichés – 'Sugar sugar/You are my candy girl' – to the rambling inanities of Queen, which were always cunningly disguised by the appeal of their melodies.

Behind such gigantic empty structures as Queen's, and such hilarious forms of seriousness as Genesis' *The Lamb Lies Down On Broadway* (1974), looms the ghost of Bob Dylan, flanked by the sheepish shades of Pink Floyd. Not only have their songs so often been made up of extended – and sometimes disjointed – metaphors that edge into surrealism, but when they have gone awry they have revealed how precariously and how rarely rock lyrics can actually sustain poetry.

Rock songs, good ones, more often approach a higher form of doggerel because, after all, they are *songs*: much of the finer shades of meaning is borne by subtleties in the musical structure. A useful example is 'A Case Of You', by one of rock's best lyricists, Joni Mitchell. The lines 'You said "Love is touching souls"/Surely you touched mine/'Cause part of you pours out of me/In these lines from time to time . . .' are precise and uncluttered but would amount to little more than sentimental verse were it not for the music, which marvellously expresses the pouring-out of the singer's longing.

A clever lyric calls for more than grand

gestures and phrases that cover lack of wit with an eiderdown of the unexpected. David Bowie, one of the biggest sellers of the Seventies, rarely rises to the epigrammatic pungency of his line from 'Diamond Dogs', 'When they pulled you out of the oxygen tent you asked for the latest parties', apparently because it is so much easier to conjure with vague atmospheric 'images' than it is to commit oneself to the exacting demands of meaning and communication.

Another mega-seller who quickly discovered that a passing mention of Shakespeare, kings, thighs and jesters was enough to convince an audience that profundities were crowding the air was Bernie Taupin, Elton John's sometime partner in song. Exactly what can 'the whippoorwill of freedom' (mentioned in 'Philadelphia Freedom'), possibly mean?

Not that the Seventies were entirely bereft of good songs. Sometimes they turned up in unexpected places. Against all the odds, Chinn and Chapman's 'The Race Is On' (written for Suzi Quatro) neatly detailed the anger, selfishness and dishonesty of a collapsing relationship: 'Will we ever be ready for what we're heading for . . ./Surprise, surprise, a few more lies – or do we simply call them alibis?' Rod Stewart proved adept at condensing whole novels into a few lines: 'Me and the boys thought we had it sussed/ Valentinos all of us/My Dad said we looked ridiculous/But boy we broke some hearts . . ./I could never win' (from 'I Was Only Joking'). He also showed a nice line in self mockery: 'Think of me and try not to laugh,' he says in 'You Wear It Well', straight on top of an honest compliment – 'Madame Onassis got nothing on you'.

Crawling from the wreckage

The Seventies saw the rise of only a handful of songwriters who could really compete with the old guard of the Sixties. Joni Mitchell came into her own during the decade, shedding her early hippie-comelately leanings for the delicate chronicling of her own 'search for love and struggle for higher achievement'. Most notable is the amazingly sustained cycle of songs on *Hejira* (1976), which blends the themes of false freedom and hopelessly circumscribed emotions through the metaphor of travel, never losing an opportunity to pun her way out of the pain: 'Maybe I've never really loved/I guess that is the truth/I've spent my whole life in clouds at icy altitudes/And looking down on everything/I crashed into his arms/Oh Amelia, it was just a false alarm' ('Amelia').

Pain and alienation were themes that

Top left: Johnny Rotten, scathing spokesman of the punk generation. Left: Joe Walsh added lyrical depth to the Eagles' music. Top right: Freddie Mercury's lyrics ranged from the pretentious to the inane, but were disguised by Queen's lush melodies. Right: Rod Stewart's words provided touches of gentle cynicism.

the escapist mythology of heavy metal or the din of punk was largely incapable of touching upon with any degree of subtlety. Not surprisingly, the best lyrics in the Seventies came from adult-oriented rock, out of the wry musing attendant on experience. In turn that meant that it was often the old guard, soldiering gamely on, who built their best work out of the ruins of the revolution they had helped make.

Blood and valentines

Dylan fell to earth with *Blood On The Tracks* (1974) and *Street-Legal* (1978), Pink Floyd released *Meddle* (1971) and *Dark Side Of The Moon* (1973), while Randy Newman still produced occasional gems like 'Texas Girl At The Funeral Of Her Father'. Long apprenticeships like that of Joe Walsh in the James Gang and his own Barnstorm contributed to some of the Eagles' better songs and some brilliant ones of his own – 'Help Me Through The Night', for instance, conveyed a shifting mixture (and assessment) of ideals and disillusion.

Of the genuine newcomers in the Seventies, Tom Waits and Bruce Springsteen deserve special mention. Waits has to be counted a major songwriter, if only for *Blue Valentine* (1978), set in the Chicano-riddled area of Hollywood Boulevard, with its mindless violence, low-rider cars, guns, knives and macho madness. Springsteen's lyrics – when they are audible – display a strong sense of irony and plot – witness the long, hot and hurting tale that is 'Racing In The Streets'.

But more often than not, persistent verbal dexterity in the Seventies wasn't to be found in rock at all, but in that haven of resignation and fatalism, country music. Here, wit represented one of the few ways of accommodating loneliness, heartbreak or death – and, perhaps most characteristically, the celebration of a frequently troublesome independence: 'Cowboys love smoky old poolrooms and clear mountain mornings/Little warm puppies and children and girls of the night,' was the treachery that Willie Nelson sang in 'Mamas, Don't Let Your Babies Grow Up To Be Cowboys'. Merle Haggard, meanwhile, laughed and raised one rude finger thus: 'There's two kinds of cherries/And two kinds of fairies/And two kinds of mothers I'm told/. . . There's good dogs and all kinds of cats/. . . But I stand right here where I'm at' ('My Own Kind Of Hat').

Given the ballad tradition that lies deep behind country music, perhaps one shouldn't be surprised at its characteristic way with words. And, given the mindless physical intoxication that lies at the roots of rock's appeal, perhaps the wonder is that the music could accommodate as many intelligent lyrics as it has. PETER BROOKESMITH

Some of the best rock lyrics of the Seventies came from American adult-oriented artists like Joni Mitchell (top), Tom Waits (centre) and Bruce Springsteen (right, with E Street Band member Roy Bittan).

Disco Fever

How a generation danced away the blues to an irresistible new beat

THE HISTORY OF black American music has been littered with instances of commercial exploitation by white acts and entrepreneurs. Either the major record companies leeched off black artists, creating subsidiary 'race' labels in order to isolate and milk that market to the full, or else they repackaged the music with 'acceptable' white faces upfront.

A curious corollary of this injustice was that for half a century black American music evolved naturally, missing most of the dilutions demanded for a larger market-place. A new cycle began in the Forties when energetic combos began playing rhythm and blues, the rock'n'roll music of the ghetto that was to dominate the next decade. In the Fifties many white artists, including Bill Haley and Elvis Presley, were suddenly credited with its invention and many of R&B's black originators moved on to develop other musical styles, notably soul.

In August 1969 *Billboard* magazine belatedly replaced the term R&B with soul, thereby recognising a new aesthetic born of a 20-year flirtation between gospel and blues. Soul spoke for the majority of the black population. It was safe from easy imitation and – unlike rock 'n'roll – mercifully free from discrimination on grounds of age.

Soul, like the blues before it, engendered a sense of community. Celebration and release on the dance floor had been the prime concern when Amos Milburn hammered out 'Chicken Shack Boogie' in 1949. The same spirit shaped such mid-Sixties classics as the Drifters' 'At The Club' and the Miracles' 'Going To A Go-Go', surviving to inspire the Trammps' 'Disco Inferno' in 1976.

Ooh la, la! Let's go dancing

When the French coined the word 'discothèque' to describe a club dependent on records for entertaining its patrons, they inadvertently supplied America with an upmarket replacement for the juke-joint, those crazy, hole-in-the-wall establishments of the South. Northern sophisticates had enjoyed a brief acquaintance with such places in the early Sixties when the Cameo-Parkway label had filled dance floors with devotees of such dances as the Twist and the Bird. The British beat invasion, coupled with the rise of rock, swept away New York's Peppermint Lounge and similar venues and it was only in the latter half of the decade that Americans investigated their soul heritage. By the close of the Sixties the discothèque or disco had rapidly attained national popularity, being supported by a racially mixed clientele.

A sizeable minority of white American teenagers had discovered soul, just as they had

Faded blue jeans were out (even expressly forbidden) and the sharp dresser made a comeback as the disco craze hit the US and Europe. One of the style's earliest stars was Gloria Gaynor (above), who managed to strike a small blow for the feminist cause singing the resolute lyrics of 'I Will Survive' in 1974.

rock'n'roll – particularly the easily-assimilated sounds emanating from Chicago or Detroit on labels like Chess, Okeh, Ric Tic and Motown. For the latter, teams of writers such as Lamont Dozier and Brian and Eddie Holland turned out countless invitations to dance. The same trio continued at Invictus, where hugely successful sides like Freda Payne's 'Band Of Gold' in 1970 helped set the tone for the disco decade. Any chance that the Memphis rennaissance on Stax might save the day for the heavier sound of Southern soul was scuppered when Isaac Hayes defected to Hollywood with his film score for *Shaft* late in 1971. He provided disco with much of its musical vocabulary, ranging from chattering guitars to florid string sections.

Meanwhile, at Motown, the inflated egos of Norman Whitfield and Paul Riser all but drowned the supreme vocal talents of the Temptations in overwrought arrangements. Snorting in Whitfield and Riser's wake came Barry White, Gene Page and Van McCoy, and soon it seemed as if an entire culture had mistaken technological overkill for sophistication. For the first time since Phil Spector, the producer was king – but on a far wider scale.

Soul destroying
The irony was that soul already possessed ample sophistication evinced in a frequently exquisite grasp of vocal dynamic, timbre and inflection. Worldly and controlled, soul exuded grace under pressure yet, like the blues, it was spurned by black youth because it mirrored a troubled world of migrants, poverty and urban dereliction. In the afterglow of the Civil Rights struggle, young blacks chose to embrace their birthright in the American Dream.

They were thus drawn to the silky blandishments of Philadelphia soul, which was the creation of composer-producers Kenny Gamble and Leon Huff. The Philly sound's well-oiled rhythm sections and lush orchestrations heralded the arrival of the first wave of disco. Within Gamble and Huff's slick format there appeared fine records from the O'Jays, Billy Paul, Lou Rawls and the Three Degrees, but the standard fell when New York producers and engineers like Meco Monardo, Tony Bongiovi and Tom Moulton weighed in with their facile approximations to the Philly sound.

Among the first successes was Gloria Gaynor's version of the Jackson Five number 'Never Can Say Goodbye', which reached Number 2 in the UK in December 1974. At Moulton's behest all the tracks on side one of her subsequent album merged into one continuous dance marathon. The effect was functional, faceless music that set a deathly precedent. Increasingly the practice was to overdub vocals, horns and strings in studios miles apart, leaving the producer and engineer to concentrate on the ubiquitous 'disco mix'. A fractional increase in the speed of the vocal track resulted in an edgier and more compelling sound.

Records were made, rather than performances duplicated, and for once marketing

Expensively groomed, Freda Payne (top) and Angela Bofill (left) figured large among the claimants to the title of Disco Queen in the Seventies and Eighties respectively.

departments spoke accurately of 'product'. If people could be persuaded to buy 12-inch singles, or twice the tedium at twice the price, so much the better. Mindful of the main chance, producers like Vincent Montana Jr, Van McCoy, Tony Sylvester, Bert DeCoteaux and Freddie Perren released a deluge of vinyl.

With the primacy of the vocal gone, only hard-funk bands resisted the flood – outfits like Kool and the Gang, the Ohio Players, Slave and Brass Construction with their roots in the durable music of James Brown, Sly Stone and the Isley Brothers. Even these underwent a subtle metamorphosis which took account of disco. Earth Wind and Fire sang vacuous lyrics but succeeded in maintaining a fresh, challenging sound. Some groups, like the Commodores and Switch, adopted a frankly romantic approach on occasion, while others, notably Parliament and Funkadelic, resorted to silliness illuminated by occasional flashes of wit.

Most *bona fide* jazzmen quailed visibly at the new trends. As early as 1970, Miles Davis had shown how jazz-rock fusion might be achieved without compromise when he unleashed his *Bitches Brew* album, but for lesser lights it proved impossible. Shrewd jazz musicians, such as saxophonist Grover Washington, chose to mine a vein of instrumental R&B stretching back through King Curtis to the Fifties. Others, like Herbie Hancock, adopted a panoply of vocoders and synthesisers in order to subsidise their true vocation, in his case the jazz group VSOP, with disco hits. Inevitably, by the late Seventies most had sold out to jazz-funk, a misnomer if ever there was one.

With the disciplines of soul discarded, the way was clear for all manner of imposters. The rediscovery of black dance by the media in the mid Seventies resulted in the usual promotion of imitators rather than founding figures. Although John Travolta sheepishly disowned the dance trophy at the end of *Saturday Night Fever* in 1977, his symbolic action didn't stop white groups like the Bee Gees eagerly jumping on the disco bandwagon. Where optimists saw the possibilities of racial integration and a higher level of exposure for black artists, those of a more cynical disposition, like August Darnell (of Kid Creole) and Nile Rodgers (of Chic), saw disco fever as subtly institutionalised racism. Certainly black musicians could

Above left: The jolly, high-camp antics and catchy dance tunes of the Village People helped make the gay scene acceptable to the mass pop audience in the mid Seventies. Above right: By the end of the decade, widespread disco-dancing competitions attempted to elevate dance-floor fun into an art form.

make more money, providing they were willing to prostitute their musical culture to mindless disco boogie and forego their right to play anything else.

All aboard the gravy train

European producers like Giorgio Moroder were quick to seize their moment. The Munich sound operated on the simple premise that Donna Summer's sexual sounds on *Love To Love You Baby* (1975) would sell heavily, especially if gift-wrapped in further vulgarisations of the brash sound patented by Norman Whitfield. Frank Farian, the Svengali behind Boney M, was similarly forthright. Boney M's brainless confections – songs such as 'Daddy Kool' and 'Ma Baker' – shot to success in 1976-77. The group's album sleeves compounded the felony by indulging a Teutonic taste for bondage and ladies of colour.

Fortunately the kind of vacuous disco purveyed by the Salsoul Orchestra, Disco Tex, Dan Hartman, Musique and Anita Ward gave way to a new consensus in the late Seventies. Kid Creole, Chic, Shalamar, Odyssey, Narada Michael Walden, Kashif, Michael Jackson and Luther Vandross represented a new breed with quicksilver sounds and a willingness to ring some changes. Along with a new generation of rappers like Grandmaster Flash and Indeep, they gave cause for cautious optimism. Furthermore, the collision between soul and disco resulted in several new stars, such as Deniece Williams, Randy Crawford, Angela Bofill and Brenda Russell, while revitalising the careers of established ones like Diana Ross and Aretha Franklin.

The time was not yet ripe for the final word on disco. Used with discretion, its style could enhance, as Talking Heads and David Bowie have shown. Disco had supplied harmless colour to Abba on one hand, and transformed calypso into soca on the other. As a vehicle for personal, lyrical expression, however, it was in the main woefully deficient. When Robert Johnson moaned 'Dead Shrimp Blues' in 1936, he caught his capricious woman in one devastating line: 'Everything I do babe, you got your mouth stuck out.' All Silver Convention could say about the human condition in 1976 was 'Fly, Robin, Fly'! What price progress?

CLIVE ANDERSON

CHILDREN of the WORLD

The Bee Gees: from down under to the disco

SINCE ENTERING POP MUSIC in the Fifties, the Bee Gees have had three careers on three continents, each more successful than its predecessor. The first was in Australia as child prodigies. In 1967, they came to Britain as suitable opposition to the Beatles. Finally in the mid Seventies they found themselves setting the pace for the disco boom and emerging as songwriters of note on the adult-oriented rock scene.

The career of the three Gibb brothers began inauspiciously enough in December 1956 at the Gaumont cinema in Chorlton-cum-Hardy, Manchester, where they

volunteered for the regular mime spot preceding the Saturday morning films. The boys were all set to mouth their lyrics when the presenter broke the record they had been rehearsing to. Thus they were forced into their vocal debut.

The trio were no strangers to music, however. Father Hugh Gibb was a band-leader and drummer who had worked the Northern Mecca circuit and had met their mother in 1940 at a Manchester ballroom. They had married in 1944 and moved to the Isle of Man after the war where there was work to be found playing for holiday-makers. It was here that the Bee Gee brothers were born – Barry on 1 September 1946, the twins Robin and Maurice on 22 December 1949.

The family left for Manchester in 1955, where youngest brother Andy was born;

that September Barry was given a trumpet by his father, followed by a £4 second-hand guitar that Christmas. The introduction to rock'n'roll came through sister Leslie, a fan of Bill Haley, Tommy Steele and Elvis.

Racing to success
In 1958 the Gibb family emigrated to Australia, settling in Brisbane, Queensland. Hugh Gibb became a travelling photographer and the youthful Barry made his first fumbling attempts as a song-writer. When the twins were nine and big brother Barry 12, they approached the local Redcliffe Speedway for a singing spot between races. They were engaged on the understanding that the only payment they would get would be whatever the crowd threw to them. Each weekend after that the brothers would return home from the race track with pockets weighed down by loose change.

This engagement led to their first serious break when an appreciative racing driver by the name of Bill Goode contacted Bill Gates, a local disc jockey. As a result they were asked to sing on radio and, for the first time, became known as the BGs (in honour of Bill Gates, Barry Gibb and Bill Goode). Later, when the name had stuck, it came simply to stand for the Brothers Gibb.

At this point they were performing the hits of the day to a mostly adult audience – singing Lonnie Donegan's 'My Old Man's A Dustman' and 'Does Your Chewing Gum Lose Its Flavour' – when their personal favourites were Ray Charles, Neil Sedaka and the Everly Brothers. This hotel and vaudeville work, supplemented by TV and radio appearances, soon put them in the position of being the family's major money earners. It became obvious to Hugh Gibb that the time was right for him to take over as manager and make their career a priority.

In 1962 the Bee Gees were brought to Sydney by Col Joye, an Australian pop star of the time, and his agent billed them locally with Chubby Checker and arranged a deal with Festival Records. They found moderate success with the singles 'Three Kisses Of Love', 'I Was A Lover And A Leader Of Men' and 'Wine And Women', but when the Beatles arrived they were virtually ignored.

When they had sailed to Australia in August 1958, the brothers had entertained on board as Barry and the Twins. In January 1967, aboard the *Fairsky*, they worked their passage back to Southampton as the Bee Gees, performing Beatle numbers in the ballroom to enthusiastic young Australians. Meanwhile, another Australian, Robert Stigwood, had casually picked up a tape the Bee Gees had sent to his co-director at Brian Epstein. Within a day of ̶ival, Stigwood had set up an audi- ̶hem at London's Saville Theatre. ̶ebruary 1967 the Bee Gees were ̶ NEMS on a five-year contract. ̶ after, they began writing for ̶ut album at Polydor Studios, and ̶ere in the well of a staircase, ̶vantage of the natural echo, that ̶posed what was to be their first ̶t, the plaintive, doom-laden bal- ̶ York Mining Disaster 1941'. This ̶le with tremulous vocals and ̶estra was to characterise most ̶ritish work. Australians Colin ̶(drums) and Vince Melouney ̶ere added to the band (with

Barry playing second guitar and Maurice on bass). Bill Shepherd organised the orchestra.

Stigwood officially launched the Bee Gees in April 1967, spending some £50,000 on promoting the album *Bee Gees First* and the single 'New York Mining Disaster 1941', calling the group 'the most significant talent since the Beatles'. The single fulfilled its promise by going to Number 12 and, after an inexplicable flop with 'To Love Somebody', 'Massachusetts', a response to the West Coast longings of flower-power, became their first UK Number 1 in October.

Inside the cucumber castle

The Bee Gees were never a serious challenge to the absolute supremacy of the Beatles during this period, however. They had little sense of style, while their sensitive, string-based sound was too safe to have the cutting edge necessary to compete. Although they toyed with the mellotron and produced the surrealistic type of song titles fitted to the psychedelic era, it was always obviously derivative and self-conscious. Striving perhaps for the poetry of 'Eleanor Rigby' or 'Penny Lane', they could produce only trite observations.

Despite the comparative lack of hysteria surrounding the trio and their music, they were well-liked; readers of *New Musical Express* voted the Bee Gees Best Group of 1967. Throughout the rest of the decade they scored regularly with UK Top Ten singles: 'World', 'Words', 'I Gotta Get A Message To You', 'First Of May' and 'Don't Forget To Remember', all of them safely within their ballad limitations. The one time they did try and step the rhythm up, with 'Jumbo', they flopped.

As the Sixties closed, the Bee Gees were heading for a break-up. The once inseparable brothers had each married: Robin to NEMS receptionist Molly in December 1968, Maurice to singing star Lulu in February 1969 and finally Barry to

a Scottish beauty queen in September 1970. At the same time there were the emotional problems resulting from such a concentrated period of success. Robin developed a taste for pills and decided on a solo career, Maurice perfected a London club lifestyle fuelled by alcohol and Barry became known as a marijuana smoker.

The Bee Gees effectively ceased to exist for a period of nearly two years from early 1969. In this period Robin scored a Number 2 solo hit with 'Saved By The Bell', while the remaining brothers, along with Peterson, made an album-cum-film titled *Cucumber Castle* (1970). Legal threats were batted between all and sundry, perhaps the most ridiculous charge being drummer Peterson's allegation that the Gibb brothers had no right to the name Bee Gees. The trio reformed late in 1970 to record *Two Years On*; then came *Trafalgar* (1971) and *Life In A Tin Can* (1973), both albums lacking the cohesiveness to pull the brothers out of their slump.

Between the single 'Run To Me', which reached Number 9 in the UK in 1972, and the disco successes of 1975, the Bee Gees were to remain hitless. The depth of their fall from greatness came home to them during a season at Batley Variety Club in Yorkshire, where they were singing their greatest hits to an uninterested audience of dinner eaters. This indignity led them to engage veteran Atlantic producer Arif Mardin to oversee their next album. Mardin had his roots in R&B, had produced greats like Aretha Franklin and was destined to turn their career around. The initial result, *Mr Natural* (1974), wasn't ground-breaking, but it was a necessary transitional step.

Now settled in America, the Bee Gees' follow-up was to set them up for the international superstardom that had eluded them in the Sixties. What Mardin did with *Main Course* (1975) was to connect them with the R&B sources they had always admired from a distance but never investi-

̶he Brothers Gibb in sultry
̶ft Maurice, Barry and Robin.
̶ee Gees perform for the
̶meras in the Sixties, with
̶roup members Colin Peterson
̶Vince Melouney (guitar).

gated. He convinced them that now was the time to go for something different in their music.

In Florida, the Bee Gees began to soak up chart music and to learn to think rhythmically. The idea for 'Jive Talkin'', the hit taken from the album, came from the sound of their car wheels running over a railroad track. They imitated the rhythm in the studio and then improvised lyrics.

It was on a track from this album, 'Nights On Broadway' (later a big hit single for Candi Staton), that Mardin first encouraged the falsetto vocals that would later become instantly recognisable. Barry had let the falsetto out spontaneously on a chorus and it was soon developed into an essential part of their new sound. Mardin also worked with Maurice, teaching him new bass runs.

Unknowingly, the Bee Gees had tapped into a dance music that was soon to be the staple diet of the night-club scene the world over. They thought of it as R&B, but it was the discothèques that were to provide the name – disco music. 'Jive Talkin'' with its bumpy railroad-track riff was perfect for the new indoor sport that was about to grant a reprieve to the ailing record industry.

Night Fever

Shortly after the success of *Main Course*, however, Stigwood negotiated a new distribution deal for RSO Records with Polydor and so could no longer use Arif Mardin, who was a staff producer for Atlantic. But, as fortune would have it, an engineer from Criteria Studios, Karl Richardson, was to prove an able successor. The new production combination also involved Albhy Galuten, another Criteria engineer and music-school graduate, who interpreted the Bee Gees' musical imaginings to session musicians and to Richardson on the mixing desk.

Their next LP, *Children Of The World* (1976), went platinum and yielded three hit singles, including 'You Should Be Dancing'. The second result was the *Saturday Night Fever* soundtrack, one of the best-selling albums of all time, that appeared in the following year.

Somewhat surprisingly, the Bee Gees' contributions to the soundtrack of the film (starring John Travolta) were written before seeing the movie script. The request for music had come during sessions at the Chateau d'Herouville in France.

Their next film venture sounded a dream on paper; the top group (Bee Gees) backing the top solo artist of the day (Peter Frampton) in a musical based on what is arguably the best pop album of all time (*Sgt Pepper's Lonely Hearts Club Band*). It was far from a dream on celluloid when it appeared in 1978, however – and it didn't help the Bee Gees to be reverting to Beatle tunes when their own career was in the ascendant.

Younger brother Andy achieved considerable success in his musical career, scoring three successive Number 1 hits in the US with 'I Just Want To Be Your Everything', '(Love Is) Thicker Than Water' (both 1977) and 'Shadow Dancing' (1978). In 1980, he teamed up with Olivia Newton-John for the single 'I Can't Help It' which reached Number 12 in the US.

The years following *Saturday Night Fever* saw only two new Bee Gees albums – *Spirits Having Flown* in 1979 and *Living*

Eyes in 1981 – but there was no lack of studio activity as they took to writing for and producing other artists. 1980 saw the Gibb-Galuten-Richardson production of *Guilty* for Barbra Streisand, following this two years later with *Heartbreaker*, an album written and produced for Dionne Warwick. Both projects topped the US album charts and yielded a number of successful singles.

In 1983 came *Staying Alive*, the long-awaited follow-up to *Saturday Night Fever*. Like its predecessor, it starred John Travolta and, as before, the Bee Gees were involved with the musical score. They contributed six songs (including the title track, which had also appeared on the *Fever* album), but the rest of the music was supplied by lesser-known artists including Sylvester Stallone's brother Frank.

In 1987, the trio re-emerged with a UK Top 5 album *ESP* and Number 1 single 'You Win Again'. It seemed the Bee Gees could never be entirely written off in chart terms.

STEVE TURNER

Above right: Robert Stigwood hugs his money-making discoveries; the younger Gibb brother, Andy (right), joins in the fun. Below: Bee Gees come alive.

Bee Gees
Recommended Listening

Spirits Having Flown (RSO SPLEP 48) (Includes: Tragedy, Search, Find, Too Much Heaven, Love You Inside Out, Stop (Think Again), Until); *Bee Gees Greatest* (RSO RSDX 001) (Includes: Night Fever, How Deep Is Your Love, Tragedy, Stayin' Alive, More Than A Woman, You Stepped Into My Life).

KOOL
& the
GANG

Funk'n'fun from Robert Bell and friends

JUSTIFIABLY REGARDED as one of the finest and most successful US soul outfits of the Eighties, Kool and the Gang were then enjoying their second period of prominence. The first had been as a good-time street-funk band in the early Seventies when, along with such acts as James Brown, War and the Ohio Players, they set the pace in black music. Having initially suffered at the hands of the disco boom, the Gang adapted successfully to end the decade on a second wave of success.

They began life as the Jazziacs in 1964, a group comprising four teenage New Jersey schoolfriends – Robert 'Kool' Bell, his brother Ronald Bell, Dennis Thomas and Robert Mickens. Although the majority of their gigs were confined to the neighbourhood, they sometimes got the chance to journey to New York to support some of the leading jazz artists of the day. Despite their obvious leanings towards jazz – John Coltrane, Freddie Hubbard and Miles Davis being among their influences – their music owed as much to dance-oriented music (in the days before 'disco' was a convenient tag) for its inspiration. Over the next five years, Kool and his friends acquired four more musicians to become a 'Gang' and signed to De-Lite Records at the beginning of 1969.

Soul anthem

Dispensing with a lead vocalist, the seven-man line-up – Kool (bass), Ronald Bell (tenor and soprano sax), Dennis 'Dee Tee' Thomas (alto sax, flute and congas), Robert 'Spike' Mickens (trumpet), Rick West (keyboards), Claydes 'Clay' Smith (guitar) and 'Funky' George Brown (drums and percussion) – quickly established themselves chartwise with their first single releases. 'Kool And The Gang' reached Number 59 in *Billboard*'s Hot Hundred in October 1969, while their second 45, imaginatively entitled 'The Gang's Back Again', hit the Hot Hundred in January of the following year. Two further singles in 1970, 'Let The Music Take Your Mind' and 'Funky Man', dented the pop charts and won over many fans to their fusion of rhythmic R&B and jazz, but the band seemed nevertheless fated to remain in the lower reaches of the popular listings.

The long-awaited break came in 1973 when 'Funky Stuff' crashed into the US Top Thirty; although it failed to make the pop charts in the UK, the song became something of an anthem for many soul music fans and laid the foundations for a commercial breakthrough later in the decade. The album on which 'Funky Stuff' appeared, *Wild And Peaceful* (1974), took off like a rocket and contained two further songs that were to become million-sellers

Inset: Robert 'Kool' Bell (left) and vocalist James 'JT' Taylor compare nicknames.
Left: The Gang on stage in exuberant mood.

when released as singles in 'Jungle Boogie' and 'Hollywood Swinging'. Both singles appeared in the US Top Ten at Numbers 4 and 6 respectively, earning gold discs along the way.

Although not packed with hit singles, the *Light Of Worlds* album released in 1974 remains one of the better Kool and the Gang albums. The atmospheric, synthesiser-led ballad 'Summer Madness' eventually found its way onto the soundtrack of *Rocky* (1976), while 'Street Corner Symphony' ranks alongside the Fatback Band's 'Street Dance' and 'Wikki Wakki' as one of the best funk tracks of that era. In contrast, 'Fruitman' represented a return to the tongue-in-cheek funk style of the year before.

Don Boyce, the man whose vocals had made 'Jungle Boogie' so popular, returned in 1975 to help out with *Spirit Of The Boogie*, an album that, surprisingly, was not a big hit. Neither was 'Caribbean Festival', a song that found the Gang flirting with reggae rhythms. Around this time Ronald Bell was also helping his younger brother Kevin get the Kay-Gees off the ground; they scored on the soul charts, 'Hustle Wit Every Muscle' getting their career off to a good start.

The next three years, however, found the Gang somewhat lacking in creativity – 1976's *Love And Understanding* album, half of which was recorded live at London's Rainbow Theatre, contained only one truly exceptional track in 'Come Together'; *Open Sesame* (1976) barely crept into the Top Sixty, despite the title track's appearance on 1977's *Saturday Night Fever* soundtrack (although it is alleged that the song's inclusion in the film prompted John Travolta to ask for something by the Bee Gees). Neither *The Force* (1977) nor *Everybody's Dancin'* (1979) contained much of note. After a meteoric climb to fame, the Gang's fortunes were at their lowest ebb: their rough and ready vocals and chunky rhythms set them aside from the popular disco mainstream, and a change of direction seemed long overdue.

The decision in 1979 to draft Eumir Deodato into the producer's chair for *Ladies Night* turned out to be a winner. To many, Deodato's only claim to fame had been his adaptation of the theme to Stanley Kubrick's film *2001* – 'Also Sprach Zarathustra', a transatlantic Top Ten hit in 1973 – but he had continued to turn out a host of classy jazz albums for a variety of labels. With a riff that owed much to Al Hudson and his Soul Partners, and vocals from new member James 'JT' Taylor, the 'Ladies Night' single hit Top Tens in charts the world over and gave the Gang their third gold 45 for sales in excess of one million copies.

Taylor offered a silky-smooth lead voice previously missing from the Gang's raucous ensemble chants, and the vocal backing changed to accommodate this – not too many vocal harmonies, nevertheless, but a glossy call-and-response that made their music as easy to listen to as it

was to dance to. 'Too Hot' quickly followed 'Ladies Night' into the US Top Ten; although original UK copies of 'Ladies Night' had 'Too Hot' on the B-side, the song made a brief appearance in its own right at Number 29.

The giddy heights achieved by *Ladies Night* were easily equalled by 1980's *Celebrate* – the title track, 'Celebration', gave Kool and the Gang their first platinum single and was chosen as the song to play to the hostages upon their return from captivity from the American Embassy in Iran; 'Jones Vs Jones', a bitter-sweet tale of divorce and disharmony that probably took Billy Paul's 'Me And Mrs Jones' to its logical conclusion, hit the Top Twenty, and 'Take It To The Top' became the third cut to leap into the UK singles charts.

The top draw

Although 'Ladies Night' et al bore little or no relation to the Gang's instrumental-based work of the early Seventies, it is easy to see why they were proving so popular the world over. With Deodato's expertise in the studio and the Gang's 15 years of experience, dance floors the world over were being set alight. By the time *Something Special* was released in 1981, Kool and the Gang had replaced the Commodores as the big black American draw. Three further hit singles – 'Steppin' Out', 'Get Down On It' (which peaked at Number 3 in the UK) and the metronomic 'Take My Heart (You Can Have It)', revived in 1983 by Robert Palmer, enabled *Something Special* to reach the album Top Ten in both the UK and the US.

The run continued into 1982 – *As One* also contained three UK hit singles, with 'Ooh La La La (Let's Go Dancin')' breaking into the Top Ten, 'Hi De Hi, Hi De Ho', aided no doubt by the BBC comedy programme 'Hi Di Hi', and 'Big Fun' completing the trio. The following year seemed an appropriate time for a retrospective glance at the group's career – as well as letting UK audiences hear what they had missed in the Seventies. *Twice As Kool* featured an excellent track listing drawing on all of their major hits from the mid Seventies on – and, with the help of TV advertising, it emerged as one of the biggest-selling albums of the year.

In the early Eighties, the new-look Kool and the Gang – no longer working with Deodato – broadened their horizons by writing and producing for reggae star Jimmy Cliff.

The hit sequence continued with a US/UK Number 2, 'Joanna' (1984), a US 2/UK 4 in 'Cherish' (1985) and four other US Top 10 hits. The 1988 defection of singer James Taylor for a solo career was the only problem.

GRAHAM BETTS

Kool and the Gang Recommended Listening

Twice As Kool: The Hits Of Kool And The Gang (De-Lite Records PROLP-2) (Includes: Ladies Night, Get Down On It, Celebration, Night People, Too Hot, Take It To The Top).

Burning up the dance floor with Donna Summer

IT WAS NOT UNTIL the late Seventies, when Donna Summer's work began to take on the aspect of adult-oriented rock, that she became a 'respectable' artist in the eyes of the rock establishment. Although this period of transition produced some of her finest moments, it also marked the end of her most influential involvement in the forming of international pop-music tastes. It had been Donna Summer's earlier liaison with the Munich-based production and arrangement team of Giorgio Moroder and Pete Bellotte that made her both a star and a crucial figure in the popularisation of disco music.

Summer love

One of a family of seven, Donna Summer was born in 1948 in Boston, Massachusetts, where, in the classic tradition of black American singers, she first sang publicly as a church-choir soloist at the age of 10. After moving to New York as a young adult, she obtained her first worthwhile professional break when she was cast in the musical *Hair*, which entailed her moving to Munich, West Germany. From 1967 to 1974 she remained in Europe, working as a singer in a variety of shows including *Godspell, Porgy And Bess* and *Show Boat*; elements of this background in conventional showbiz were to be apparent in many of her later activities.

In 1974, now with a young child to support, Summer answered an advertisement for a female backing singer. She got the job, thereby making contact with Moroder. They made an album together, a slight affair called *Lady Of The Night*, from which a single, 'The Hostage', sold well in France and Holland, although not in the major US and UK markets.

The following year, under the dual influence of Jane Birkin and Serge Gainsbourg's soft-porn best-seller 'Je T'Aime . . . Moi Non Plus' and the orchestral soul epics of Barry White, Norman Whitfield and Isaac Hayes, 'Love To Love You Baby' was released after an earlier single version had failed. Re-written as a 17-minute erotic epic, it took up a whole side of an LP of the same name. A single version reached Number 4 in the UK and Number 1 in the US, achieving similar acceptance all over Europe. The record's sumptuous catalogue of sexual, simulated sounds set against a sultry backing captured a lucrative, adult market.

The next album, 1976's *A Love Trilogy*, confirmed the Summer/Moroder/Bellotte musical identity in the public mind. The arrangers created a polished mesh of dense rhythmic pulses and spry string

Right: Donna Summer sings soul. Insets: Three shades of Summer . . . the devoted mother with daughter Mimi (left), the fairytale princess of 1977's Once Upon A Time *(centre) and the disco siren (right).*

HOT STUFF

embellishments to accompany her breathy explorations of love and sex – before, during and after. Once more, a whole side was devoted to a single extended track – this time, 'Try Me'. This successful formula was repeated on the album *Four Seasons Of Love*, released in Britain the same year. Consisting of four lengthy tracks, it yielded a minor Christmas hit with 'Winter Melody'.

Moroder, Bellotte and their Oasis company had paved the way for a plethora of European disco imitators. Donna Summer was generally regarded by critics as little more than the shop-window for a shrewd commercial operation. An idealised Broadway vision of female glamour she certainly was; but she often captured the melancholia, confusions and transience of contemporary courtship, striking a sympathetic chord not only with female teenagers and disco dancers, but also with an increasingly visible generation of gay men. Donna's initial image as the sexual voyeur's delight was being gradually eclipsed. She was, by now, the undisputed Disco Queen; glossy, 'girly', but sufficiently of the real world to be a genuine heroine.

Deep thrills

In 1977, as the disco market flooded with sterile, crass imitators, Summer decided on a change of approach. The *I Remember Yesterday* album was largely a collection of pastiches, and two of the hits it contained – the Forties-style title track and the Sixties-style 'Love's Unkind' (a UK Number 3 in December) – offered nothing more than nostalgia. She also recorded the theme tune of the film *The Deep* (1977), a half-hearted attempt to cash in on Steven Spielberg's *Jaws* (1975). All this suggested that she was becoming a new, bland family entertainer. However, *I Remember Yesterday* contained one real surprise in 'I Feel Love', a single that unleashed Moroder's 'Europercussion' sound – a backing track composed entirely of programmed synthesisers. The record made Number 1 in the UK in July 1977, marked Summer's final farewell to bedroom reveries and heralded the true arrival of the synthesiser in mainstream pop.

The same year saw further Donna Summer product, a grand conceptual project in double-album form – *Once Upon A Time* – which narrated a modern-day, fairy-tale quest for true love. The album contained some of Moroder's finest arrangements, notably the synthesised 'Act II', and also revealed Summer's capacity to express a song's sentiments. If she lacked the power of an Aretha Franklin or the slinkiness of a Diana Ross, she boasted a vocal *ache* that was all her own – showcased by the hit single 'I Love You'.

With characteristic business acumen, Oasis catered to the affluent American public's by-then established taste for live double albums by releasing the shabby *Live And More* in 1978. Its chart-topping status in the US proved conclusively that Donna Summer was now a consumer

2111

favourite for her albums as well as single releases.

This state of affairs can be good news for an artist financially, but often signals an artistic decline. Sadly, Donna Summer's subsequent output mostly served to confirm this rule. The great exception, however, was *Bad Girls* (1979), perhaps her finest recording. It was another thematic work, and another two-record set. Broadly based around the aspirations, experiences and (rather less plausibly) the appetites of street-corner hookers, two of its sides merged disco, rock and (for the first time in the traditional sense) soul to unstoppable effect. The assertive confidence of the opening 'Hot Stuff' track (an American chart-topping 45) was maintained throughout the LP, making *Bad Girls* undeniably *her* album.

The high standard of *Bad Girls* was not maintained, although single releases such

Above: Donna Summer – a disco dream of the Seventies in fur and feathers.

as an overblown rendition of 'MacArthur Park' and 'No More Tears (Enough Is Enough)', a shrill duet with Barbra Streisand, were predictably popular. *The Wanderer* (1980), released on the Geffen label and her last with her initial collaborators, *Donna Summer* (1982), produced by Quincy Jones, and *She Works Hard For The Money* (1983) were all patchy efforts, with occasional gems swamped by much that was clichéd and trite; all were blighted by routine MOR rock instrumentation.

This creative decline coincided with Summer's marriage to songwriter Bruce Sudano and their subsequent conversion to the 'born again' school of Christian fundamentalism. Although it might be unfair to link religion to Donna's musical output,

the inward-looking conservatism and sentimentality of most of her Eighties releases are elements that lie at the heart of the back-to-the-Bible movement.

Summer's empathy for working women of all kinds – given vivid expression on the title track of *She Works Hard For The Money* – has perhaps been her greatest attribute as a recording artist. Whatever themes and styles she pursues in her future recordings, her various greatest hits collections are worth anyone's hard-earned pay.   DAVE HILL

Donna Summer
Recommended Listening

Greatest Hits Volume 1 (Casablanca 9128032) (Includes: Love To Love You Baby, I Feel Love, Our Love, I Love You, Last Dance, I Remember Yesterday); *Greatest Hits Volume 2* (Casablanca 9128033) (Includes: MacArthur Park, Hot Stuff, Bad Girls, Dim All The Lights, No More Tears (Enough Is Enough), Sunset People).

C'est Chic!

Nile Rodgers (left) and Bernard Edwards, founders of the Chic Organization.

Good times guaranteed by the Chic Organization

THE MUSICAL PARTNERSHIP known as the Chic Organization Ltd was founded in 1977 by guitarist Nile Rodgers and bassist Bernard Edwards, two extremely gifted musicians who between them were to redefine the sound of disco, bringing craftsmanship and a stamp of individuality to a form of music not previously noted for either. In the years 1978-79, their own group Chic released a series of massive hits which were to establish them as the biggest-selling singles group in the history of Atlantic Records, while Rodgers and Edwards' reputation as composers, producers, arrangers and performers led to production/recording deals with Diana Ross, Debbie Harry and others. The warm and intelligent disco style pioneered by the Chic Organization was to have a far-reaching influence on popular music.

Allah in the Apple
Nile Rodgers was born in New York City and was raised in Greenwich Village and, later, Los Angeles. Having taken up the guitar during his early teens, Nile returned to New York where he worked his way through a number of bands before joining an electric-folk outfit called New World Rising in the mid Sixties. Nile's catholic taste in music later resulted in his joining a weird, left-field black outfit called Allah and the Knife-Wielding Punks. Meanwhile, Bernard Edwards, who was born in Greenville, North Carolina, had also moved to New York, where he became proficient at reeds and bass. Bernard took a

Among the acts produced by the Chic Organization have been Sister Sledge (above) and Sheila and B. Devotion (inset below). Bottom: Chic bump and grind.

day job at the local post office and met Nile through a friend who also worked there.

Together, Rodgers and Edwards joined a local group, the Big Apple Band, and won an audition to back New York City, a vocal act signed by noted producer/arranger Thom Bell. In 1973, New York City scored a Top Twenty hit on both sides of the Atlantic with 'I'm Doing Fine Now', and, along with the Big Apple Band, toured Britain and Europe that same year. Although New York City disbanded just

over a year later, Rodgers and Edwards kept the Big Apple Band together. Encouraged by Rob Drake, a New York club DJ, they began writing and recording demos of dance numbers that Drake played at his Night Owl Club and that started generating favourable reactions.

By June 1977, Rodgers and Edwards had renamed the group Chic and signed a worldwide recording deal with Atlantic. The initial Chic line-up featured ex-LaBelle drummer Tony Thompson, singer Norma Jean Wright and various session friends. The vocal front line was later fleshed out with the addition of singer Luci Martin, while Norma Jean (who quit to pursue a solo career) was replaced by Alfa Anderson, a former member of Luther and Raw Sugar.

Exuding an image of black sophistication, Chic launched their debut single 'Dance Dance Dance (Yowsah Yowsah Yowsah)' in November 1977. This sped up the British and American charts to reach Number 6 in both countries while the group's first album, *Chic*, was released early in 1978 and rapidly went gold. By midsummer, Chic had become a headline attraction throughout the American continent with dates as far south as Rio de Janeiro and Sao Paulo. 'Everybody Dance', their second 45, was only a modest hit in the US (although it reached Number 9 in the UK), but their next offering, 'Le Freak', hit the top of the American charts in January 1979 and sold over four million copies worldwide. The single's parent LP, *C'est Chic*, went on to sell two million copies in the US alone.

The secret of Chic's success lay in Rodgers and Edwards' almost uncanny

ability to find a persuasive and infectious riff, repeat it and harden each repeat with flamboyant bass runs peppered with caustic strings or urgent rock guitar – 'The most inventive guitar/bass coupling of the decade' declared *Melody Maker* at the time. The ballads, too, were graced with seductive arrangements and attention to fine detail.

Kings of the world

In 1979, Rodgers and Edwards were offered their first outside project when Atlantic asked them to assume artistic control of female vocal group Sister Sledge. The Philadelphian sisters had been signed to Atlantic in 1974 but, apart from a 1975 UK hit with 'Mama Never Told Me', had had no success. Pairing the group with Rodgers and Edwards proved to be a masterstroke, however. In April, Sister Sledge's 'He's The Greatest Dancer', written and produced by Nile and Bernard with musical backing provided by Chic, hit the Top Ten in both the US and the UK. The *We Are Family* album entered the charts the following month and an edited version of the title track, released as a single that summer, was another huge success. Meanwhile, Chic continued to score hits in their own right – 'I Want Your Love' reached Number 7 in the US, where 'Good Times' gave them a second chart-topper in July. Both of these singles also made the UK Top Five.

In August 1979, Chic's third album appeared. *Risqué* featured an elongated 'Good Times' and six other slices of immensely strong, modern dance-floor music – but, by previous standards, the LP sold modestly, as did 'My Forbidden Lover', another single lifted from the album. From here on, the Chic group moved into a commercial decline as Rodgers and Edwards

Above: Caustic strings added much to the Chic sound both on record and stage.

concentrated their creative energies on work for other artists.

In the winter of 1979-80, the partners revived the faltering career of Eurodisco act Sheila and B. Devotion (who had hit the UK charts the previous year with a tiresome disco version of 'Singin' In The Rain') by composing, producing and playing on a hit single, 'Spacer', and an excellent album. *King Of The World* was, arguably, the duo's strongest work to date; Edwards' sturdy bass riffs were intoxicating throughout, while Rodgers' guitar-work sparkled and the puzzling diction of French singer Sheila proved irresistible. Although the LP failed to chart in the US or UK, it was an enormous success in Europe and Australia.

Subsequent outside productions were less fruitful, however. In 1981, a collaboration with Blondie singer Debbie Harry resulted in the hugely disappointing (though commercially successful) *Koo Koo* album, a Rodgers and Edwards-produced Johnny Mathis album was shelved, and a proposed teaming with Aretha Franklin failed to get off the ground because, according to Nile, 'she wanted a disco-oriented record but we wanted to produce a pure R&B sound'. The partners' score for the 1982 film *Soup For One* was another disaster (although the soundtrack album contained an extra track not included in the film, Carly Simon's 'Why', which made the UK Top Ten as a single).

Meanwhile, Sister Sledge parted company with the duo, preferring to work with Narada Michael Walden, and Chic's own albums became increasingly lacklustre: *Real People* (1980), *Take It Off* (1981) and *Tongue In Chic* (1982) were all greeted

with critical indifference. Rodgers and Edwards' only real commercial success during the early Eighties was a production for superstar Diana Ross: *Diana* (1980), on which all songs were written, arranged, conducted and produced by the pair, sold three-and-a-half million copies and yielded the hit singles 'Upside Down', 'My Old Piano' and 'I'm Coming Out'.

1983 saw the creative team embarking on individual projects: Bernard Edwards released a solo album, *Glad To Be Here*, which met with mediocre reviews and few sales; Nile Rodgers' solo effort, *Adventures In The Land Of The Good Groove*, fared no better, although his co-production with David Bowie on Bowie's *Let's Dance* proved an enormous success.

Tuning in to Chic

In November 1983, a new Chic album emerged; on *Believer*, the duo managed to recapture at least some of the early magic and show that their talents had not vanished. By now the danceable Chic sound had infiltrated into such diverse bands as Talking Heads, Queen ('Another One Bites The Dust' was a direct lift of 'Good Times') and Culture Club, and it is for their overwhelming influence that Rodgers and Edwards will be best remembered. As Bernard Edwards has said: 'I listen to a lot of radio and there's at least 20 or 30 groups that have actually rewritten a Chic tune or something around a tune we wrote.'   DAVE WALTERS

Chic
Recommended Listening

C'est Chic (Atlantic K50565) (Includes: Chic Cheer, (Funny) Bone, Everybody Dance, Happy Man, At Last I Am Free, Savoir Faire); *Chic's Greatest Hits* (Atlantic K50686) (Includes: Le Freak, My Forbidden Lover, Good Times, My Feet Keep Dancing, I Want Your Love, Dance, Dance, Dance).

NATURAL HIGH

Lionel Richie took the Commodores to the top

IT WAS DURING the first week of February 1969 that the Commodores, then merely a group of young musicians fresh out of college, made their first recordings. The studio was New York's Groove Sound, the producer was Jerry Williams Jr (also known as Swamp Dogg) and the record label was Atlantic.

Most of the session consisted of versions of contemporary hits such as Johnnie Taylor's 'Who's Making Love', Sly Stone's 'Sing A Simple Song', the Intruders' 'Cowboys To Girls' and Alvin Cash's 'Keep On Dancing'. Atlantic issued only the last-named tune, a funky but anonymous instrumental, and it disappeared without trace.

By 1971, however, the same group had secured a new recording deal – this time with Motown – and an opening spot on the Jackson Five's Madison Square Garden concert in July. These two career mile-stones eventually led the Commodores to become one of the hottest properties in black music.

Between 1974 and 1981, the Commodores reached the Top Ten of *Billboard*'s soul charts with 14 releases, including six that went to the top. More significantly, nine of these soul hits also made the pop Top Ten, broadening the band's popularity and boosting album sales.

The Commodores were almost as popular abroad, thanks to extensive touring. Early acceptance in Africa (Nigeria, in particular) and Asia (Japan, the Philippines) was gradually followed by popularity elsewhere, and by the late Seventies the group's visits to Europe were generating standing-room-only audiences.

Into the Mystics

To hear singer Lionel Richie tell the story, however, the Commodores were formed (in 1967 in Tuskegee, Alabama) as much to meet girls as to make music and money. Being in a band, he said, would guarantee them the favourable attention of Tuskegee

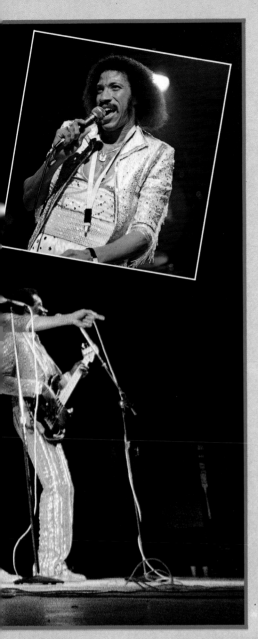

The Commodores (above) were one of Motown's most successful acts of the Seventies. Unlike their Sixties predecessors, who were purely vocal groups back by Motown house musicians, the Commodores played their own instruments. Singer and keyboardist Lionel Richie (inset above) later enjoyed a phenomenally successful solo career.

Institute's female campus members.

Richie, Thomas McClary (guitar) and William King (trumpet) originally played together as the Mystics before being joined by keyboard-player Milan Williams from another Tuskegee act, the Jays. With a couple of other musicians, Andre Callahan and Michael Gilbert, they became the Commodores and set their sights on professional opportunities in New York.

Those opportunities began to materialise when the group was spotted by Benny Ashburn, a public relations man and a former marketing executive with Pepsi-Cola. Having obtained a number of local night-club bookings for the Commodores,

Ashburn managed to secure the Jackson Five support gig through a neighbourhood acquaintance, Suzanne DePasse, who worked for Motown. By this time, Callahan and Gilbert had departed to be replaced by drummer Walter Orange and bassist Ronald LaPread.

Performing with the Jacksons in New York and elsewhere immediately gave the Commodores valuable experience and exposure, but the recording deal did not pay off so promptly. Part of the problem lay with the various writers and producers – Tom Baird, Jeffrey Bowen, Gloria Jones and Pam Sawyer – Motown assigned to the group. The lack of a regular producer made it difficult for the group to create an identifiable sound.

Platinum hooks
The breakthrough eventually came in 1974 with 'Machine Gun', a rapid-fire, synthesiser-driven instrumental produced by James Carmichael that reached Number 22 in the US and Number 20 in Britain. The Commodores followed it with several similar exercises in high-energy funk, including 'The Zoo (The Human Zoo)', 'I Feel Sanctified' and 'Slippery When Wet'.

James Carmichael, like Benny Ashburn, proved to be a key figure in the Commodores' creative evolution. He was highly versatile, and a better arranger than other producers with whom they had worked; this became important when the success of 'Sweet Love', the act's first Top Ten pop hit in the States, suggested that their crossover chances were best with ballads. Carmichael crafted mellow, soulful arrangements to the lyrics and music of Lionel Richie, resulting in a series of major hits: 'Just To Be Close To You' (1976), 'Easy' (1977), 'Three Times A Lady' (a transatlantic chart-topper in 1978) and 'Sail On' (1979).

Although Richie's romantic songs turned out to be the most commercial, the Commodores continued to deliver uptempo funk aimed predominantly at their black fans, and tunes such as 'Brick House' and 'Too Hot Ta Trot' were particularly popular in concert.

Each member contributed to the group's repertoire – and profited from it: in 1969, the six musicians, along with Ashburn, had formed the Commodores Entertainment Corporation (CEC) to handle their careers and income. In 1980, the company grossed more than 10 million dollars through interests in touring, recording, publishing, licensing, transportation, management and real estate.

The popularity of the Commodores generated substantial income for Motown, too, thereby ensuring its full and enthusiastic support of all the group's releases. In addition, two acts managed by CEC, Platinum Hook and Three Ounces of Love, recorded for the label.

The Commodores' fortunes began changing in 1980, however. Their tenth album, *Heroes*, failed to deliver a Top Ten hit single and, consequently, failed to match

the sales of its predecessors. And although the group's next LP, *In The Pocket* (1981), returned them to hitmaking form, it was apparent that their most valuable commodity, Lionel Richie, was increasingly preoccupied by solo projects: first with country-pop crooner Kenny Rogers, for whom he wrote and produced 'Lady', and then with the music for Franco Zeffirelli's movie *Endless Love*.

In August 1981, Richie became the first artist in US chart history to appear in the Top Ten as composer, performer and/or producer of three simultaneous hits: Kenny Rogers' 'I Don't Need You' (which he produced), the Commodores' 'Lady (You Bring Me Up)' (which he co-produced and on which he sang lead vocal), and the title track from *Endless Love* (which he wrote, produced, and performed in duet with Diana Ross).

For their part, other members of the Commodores also engaged in various solo projects. Ronald LaPread, who had previously worked with another young band from Tuskegee called Seventh Wonder, produced A Taste of Honey. Milan Williams handled country singer Stella Parton, sister of Dolly, while Thomas McClary got involved with Klique (producing their first major hit, 'Stop Doggin' Me Around') and Michael Henderson.

It was the media attention paid to Lionel Richie's solo achievements, however, that created the most stress within the group. In 1982, shortly after the death of Benny Ashburn, Richie left and put his career in the hands of Kenny Rogers' manager. A highly successful solo album, *Lionel Richie*, followed later that year, and his second LP, *Can't Slow Down* (1983), provided five UK Top Twenty singles, including 'All Night Long (All Night)' and the Number 1 hit 'Hello'.

Now we are 13
The remaining Commodores brought out the album *13* (1983). With Richie's sensuous ballads gone, the band went for a more energetic feel, with Walter Orange and Harold Hudson (one of the group's brass section) on vocals. In 1985 the title track from their LP *Nightshift* made the UK Top Five. It featured vocals by the band's new singer J. D. Nicholas, formerly of Heatwave.

'Lionel deserved to be the focal point,' commented McClary, 'but the general feeling is we are now more entertaining – the group has a chance to diversify and show what we can offer collectively.' With this positive attitude, and stacks of talent, the Commodores seemed set for continuing success in the Eighties.   ADAM WHITE

**The Commodores
Recommended Listening**

Zoom (Motown STMS 5061) (Includes: Squeeze The Fruit, Heaven Knows, Brick House, Won't You Come Dance With Me, Funny Feelings, Patch It Up); *Greatest Hits* (Motown STML 12100) (Includes: Three Times A Lady, Zoom, Slippery When Wet, Easy, Flying High, Just To Be Close To You).

THE MUNICH MACHINE

The mechanical sound of Eurodisco

THE EURODISCO PHENOMENON of the mid to late Seventies was the work of a handful of producers, based mainly in the West German city of Munich, who crafted a sound that sold millions of records all over the world, and took America by storm. Most of the artists that these producers made famous were actually British or American, although they had in many cases spent years working in Europe. The producers, who closely controlled their artists' material and sometimes the artists themselves, had a Euro-pop background.

Disco was born in Europe, in the France of the early Sixties when an enterprising Parisian restaurateur decided to provide recorded music for his customers. He then added a light show: *voilà, la discothèque!* The idea spread to England, and then the US. At the end of the Sixties the popularity of disco began to fade, but it revived in the early Seventies, boosted by the salsa-influenced American dance, the Hustle. Barry White's 1974 US Number 1 'Can't Get Enough Of Your Love, Babe' and Gloria Gaynor's 'Never Can Say Goodbye' of the same year helped re-establish disco, this time with a much more distinct soul-based sound.

Before Gloria Gaynor became the first Queen of Disco in her native America she had spent years performing in Europe, where British and American acts had dominated throughout the Sixties. At the turn of the decade, a small number of mainly Dutch groups enjoyed international success. EMI/Imperial producer Klaas Leyen was responsible for the Cats, while George Bouens wrote, produced and performed with the George Baker Selection. Their second million-seller, 'Paloma Blanca', owed much of its European success to the tremendous exposure it received in the discos of European holiday resorts during 1975.

Robert Van Leeuwen wrote, produced and played lead guitar for Shocking Blue. Their 'Venus' topped the American charts and sold 10 million copies worldwide in 1970. This sort of success showed that European material could sell globally, and encouraged others, like Italian writer and producer Giorgio Moroder, to try and produce English-language material for the world market.

Moroder, the most successful of the continental producers, was born in St Ulrich, South Tirol, where he studied at the local Academy of Fine Arts. He later travelled Europe as bass player in a band playing hotels and small clubs. In the early Seventies he wrote, produced and performed on a number of hit records in Germany, a country where soul was popular due to the US military presence and American forces network radio.

Moroder based his recording activities in Munich. Only a three-hour drive from his home in Northern Italy, it was the nearest city with modern recording facilities. In 1970 he met Englishman Pete Bellotte, who later enjoyed some success as part of the studio band Trax. They formed Say Yes Productions and licensed their product to Oasis Records, which was based in the same hotel complex as the Musicland studios they used.

Bellotte and Moroder enjoyed some success as songwriters, most notably with 'Son Of My Father' in 1972. In England, Chicory Tip took a cover version to Number 1, while Moroder's original was a minor hit in the States. Even then, the hook-line was played on a synthesiser, the instrument that was later to dominate Moroder's sound.

Erotic epic

It was the duo's historic partnership with Donna Summer, begun in 1974, that was to make such a lasting impact on the disco world. After producing some locally-released records, the Bellotte/Moroder/Summer partnership struck gold with the 17-minute epic 'Love To Love You Baby', an erotic litany set to a mesmeric disco beat. An edited single version swept to international chart success at the start of 1976, and laid the foundation for a career that eclipsed all other disco stars. In the US Donna Summer enjoyed four Number 1 singles and three Number 1 albums between 1978 and 1979.

Explaining their success in *Music Week* in April 1977, Moroder suggested that 'our style was a lot different from the black American style. We make it really commercial, and we found a way to make the bass sound more interesting, and to add little melody hooks to make it stand out from the run-of-the-mill heavy funk that was around at that time . . . We aim at a more laid-back disco sound, which not only makes the record danceable, but makes the dancer go out and buy it . . . I think that we invented the bass drum and bass sound that is a feature of the modern disco style, and we never break the dancing rhythm.

Opposite: Donna Summer (inset top) casts a glance at mentor and producer Giorgio Moroder. Above: When Frank Farian created a hit record in the studio, he created Boney M (inset) to promote it.

In this way I think we have innovated the whole disco scene.'

In an interview with *New Musical Express* 18 months later, Moroder defined their style. 'We take something from everything, then make it our own, although it is hard to analyse this exactly. There are obvious aspects we used from the Philadelphia sound.' Motown was clearly another major influence.

In the earlier *Music Week* interview, Pete Bellotte had outlined the way he and

Moroder worked. 'The process starts with a reference track on rhythm machine. Without it we could never keep things tight for a 17-minute disco cut. Using that as a guide, we bring in the bass and drums to do the rhythm section track, and then the arranger is called in to add things on top of that. However, most of the arranging is done in the mixing stage as a kind of post-arrangement process. Very little is pre-conceived . . . the only thing that is really thought out in advance is the bassline.'

Moroder produced other acts such as Roberta Kelly and recorded four solo albums of his own. He also enjoyed great success with films, winning an Oscar for his electronic score of *Midnight Express* (1978). As musical director of *American*

Michael Kunze (above) was the production brain behind the mid-Seventies hits of Silver Convention (inset).

Gigolo (1980), he produced Blondie's transatlantic Number 1 of the same year, 'Call Me'. His contribution to *Foxes* (1980) included Donna Summer's 'On The Radio', while his soundtrack to *Cat People* (1982) drew widespread critical acclaim.

While Moroder and Bellotte were creating Donna Summer's sound, Michael Kunze was independently making similar excursions with Silver Convention. Kunze, a successful German lyricist, started producing in the early Seventies, and scored a moderate hit in 1975 with Silver Convention's 'Save Me', initially on the Jupiter label. The repetitive, thumping follow-up, 'Fly Robin Fly', went to Number 1 in the States at the end of the year and sold a million, as did their biggest British hit, 'Get Up And Boogie', released in 1976.

There were other producers and artists at work who helped to create a 'European sound', notably French disco star Sheila and B. Devotion, while some of Abba's records, such as 'Dancing Queen' and 'Knowing Me Knowing You', helped to define the new European pop sensibility. One of the most successful acts in this field was Boney M, the brainchild of German producer Frank Farian.

As a solo singer, Farian had topped the German charts in 1976 with the million-selling ballad 'Rocky'. He then produced a

disco record, 'Baby, Do Ya Wanna Bump?', a studio creation made entirely by session men, which he credited to Boney M as simply a name to put on the record label. When it became a hit there were embarrassing requests for the act to appear on television, prompting Farian to create a group called Boney M to perform his music.

'Daddy Cool' was the first Boney M single that the group sang on themselves. A string of Eurodisco hits followed, although their impact in the US was limited. In 1978 they had two British Number 1 singles, including the massively successful 'Rivers Of Babylon'/'Brown Girl In The Ring', and a Number 1 album, *Night Flight To Venus*, which sold millions for the European-based Hansa Records. Two further UK chart-topping albums followed before the bubble burst.

Farian worked to a certain formula, first recording his backing tracks, usually in Munich, and then trying the tapes out at a disco, using public reaction to gauge the best cut before recording the vocals on top. In common with other Eurodisco producers, the syndrum, with its considerable range and pitch, was central to his sound,

as was the extensive use of synthesisers.

The so-called 'Munich Sound' became widely celebrated, with major bands such as the Rolling Stones and ELO using the Musicland studios, although – as Pete Bellotte pointed out – there was nothing particularly German about it. Rather, it was a meeting-point for talent drawn from all parts of Europe. Say Yes Productions, run by Bellotte (English) and Moroder (Italian), employed an Icelandic arranger and a team of session players (who recorded a couple of albums as the Munich Machine) drawn largely from Britain and other parts of Europe.

Germany calling

Although Moroder has commented that they might all have been successful earlier if they had been based in London or Los Angeles, the fact is that they were based in Munich which was where, in the mid Seventies, everything came together at the right time. It was German record companies – Oasis, Jupiter and Hansa – who put faith, time and money behind Eurodisco. With that support, and as a result of the work of producers like Giorgio Moroder, Pete Bellotte, Michael Kunze and Frank Farian, Eurodisco became a significant strand of international popular music in the late Seventies.   DEMITRI ARGYROPULO

Tunes of Glory

Pairing pop harmonies with a rock beat proved a huge money spinner in the Seventies

IN THE LATE SIXTIES and early Seventies, American bands like Grand Funk Railroad, Mountain and Blue Cheer showed that a noisy, basic and unsubtle musical approach – carried by crude guitar overkill – was no barrier to commercial success. Acts such as these appealed, essentially, to young teenagers, but by the mid Seventies, with the ascent of FM radio, it had become evident to record companies that it was within the 18- to 35-year-old market that the big bucks lay. Consequently, hard rock began to cater to more adult tastes while still attempting to hold the attention of younger rock fans. The traditional riff-based, sprawling attack of heavy metal was now blended with the formulas of pop – hooks, melodies and harmonies – thereby appealing to both camps.

The professionals
The most successful exponents of this new trend towards commercial hard rock were by no means newcomers to the rock world. The members of acts like Styx, REO Speedwagon, Foreigner, Journey and Toto were, for the most part, veteran players who were able to combine musical expertise and performing experience with a thorough knowledge of studio production techniques.

REO Speedwagon, for example, had formed in 1971 and built up a reputation on the arena-rock circuit playing support to acts such as Aerosmith and the James Gang. Throughout the Seventies they refined their style in the studio, blending sumptuous vocal harmonies, lush guitar arrangements and simple pop chord structures with their original straightforward hard-rock style. In 1980, they broke into the platinum league with their tenth album *Hi Infidelity* and a US chart-topping single, 'Keep On Loving You'.

Styx had been in existence even longer than REO Speedwagon – they formed in 1963 – but it was not until 1976, when they began to augment their heavy pseudo-classical, pomp-rock sound with deft melodic touches, that they began to shake off their cult image. Their 1977 album, *The Grand Illusion*, sold more than three million copies, bringing the group superstar status.

Anglo-American act Foreigner, meanwhile, were formed in New York in 1976 by English guitarist Mick Jones, who had begun his career during the British instrumental pop boom of the early Sixties before moving into session work, and multi-instrumentalist Ian McDonald, an original member of British progressive outfit King Crimson. Foreigner's debut album, released in 1977, was a somewhat unimaginative mixture of hard-rock roots and 'progressive' posturing, yet it proved to be highly effective FM fare and established the band as a powerful commercial force.

Journey's rock pedigree was an equally prestigious one: Gregg Rolie and Neal Schon had been with Santana while Aynsley Dunbar, a graduate of Britain's late-Sixties blues boom, was a session drummer with the highest credentials. Journey's sound, dominated by synthesiser and smooth guitar, was calculated and bland in the extreme, but the polish and attention to detail of their productions guaranteed success in both the US album and singles charts.

The survivors
In the wake of these FM rock successes came a host of imitators, bands like Russia, Touch, Loverboy and Survivor who followed the AOR formula with a depressing lack of fire or imagination. And yet the original crude energy of heavy metal still survived. Van Halen, though patchy on record, provided a perfect parody of the HM genre on stage with singer Dave Lee Roth's absurd stage antics and the squawking, over-the-top guitar work of Eddie Van Halen. Blue Oyster Cult, on the other hand, brought a rare intelligence to the form with music that combined ferocious riffs with wry sensitivity, while Pat Benatar, with her raunchy power-pop, became the female sex symbol of American rock'n'roll. Although American hard rock had developed a soft centre by the Eighties, there was still substance at the edges.

BYRON ST. TUGBY

Journey treat a fan-packed stadium to their brand of FM rock. The late Seventies saw many US hard-rock bands blending the riff-based attack of heavy metal with pop hooks and vocal harmonies. The results, although often bland, made for healthy sales.

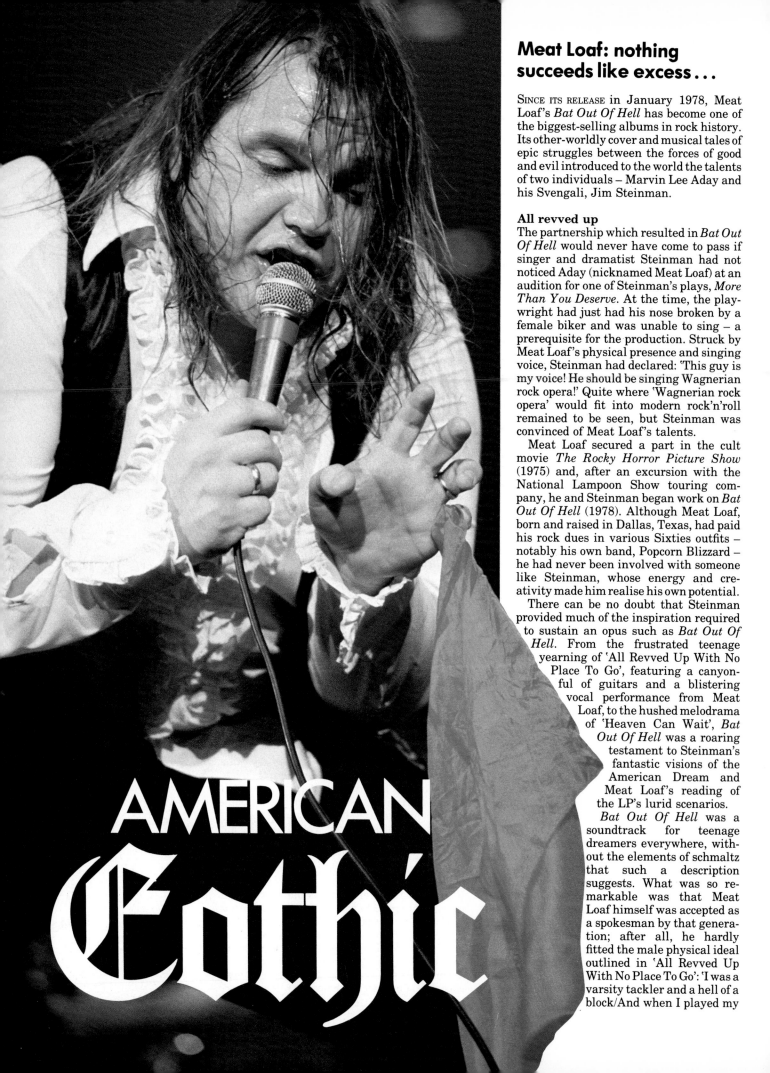

Meat Loaf: nothing succeeds like excess...

SINCE ITS RELEASE in January 1978, Meat Loaf's *Bat Out Of Hell* has become one of the biggest-selling albums in rock history. Its other-worldly cover and musical tales of epic struggles between the forces of good and evil introduced to the world the talents of two individuals – Marvin Lee Aday and his Svengali, Jim Steinman.

All revved up

The partnership which resulted in *Bat Out Of Hell* would never have come to pass if singer and dramatist Steinman had not noticed Aday (nicknamed Meat Loaf) at an audition for one of Steinman's plays, *More Than You Deserve*. At the time, the playwright had just had his nose broken by a female biker and was unable to sing – a prerequisite for the production. Struck by Meat Loaf's physical presence and singing voice, Steinman had declared: 'This guy is my voice! He should be singing Wagnerian rock opera!' Quite where 'Wagnerian rock opera' would fit into modern rock'n'roll remained to be seen, but Steinman was convinced of Meat Loaf's talents.

Meat Loaf secured a part in the cult movie *The Rocky Horror Picture Show* (1975) and, after an excursion with the National Lampoon Show touring company, he and Steinman began work on *Bat Out Of Hell* (1978). Although Meat Loaf, born and raised in Dallas, Texas, had paid his rock dues in various Sixties outfits – notably his own band, Popcorn Blizzard – he had never been involved with someone like Steinman, whose energy and creativity made him realise his own potential.

There can be no doubt that Steinman provided much of the inspiration required to sustain an opus such as *Bat Out Of Hell*. From the frustrated teenage yearning of 'All Revved Up With No Place To Go', featuring a canyonful of guitars and a blistering vocal performance from Meat Loaf, to the hushed melodrama of 'Heaven Can Wait', *Bat Out Of Hell* was a roaring testament to Steinman's fantastic visions of the American Dream and Meat Loaf's reading of the LP's lurid scenarios.

Bat Out Of Hell was a soundtrack for teenage dreamers everywhere, without the elements of schmaltz that such a description suggests. What was so remarkable was that Meat Loaf himself was accepted as a spokesman by that generation; after all, he hardly fitted the male physical ideal outlined in 'All Revved Up With No Place To Go': 'I was a varsity tackler and a hell of a block/And when I played my

AMERICAN Gothic

guitar I made the canyons rock/And every Saturday night I felt the fever grow/All revved up with no place to go.' Nonetheless, his deliberately seedy, slightly menacing persona struck a chord in his audience; empathy became adulation when he took his show on the road.

There was another element crucial to the success of *Bat Out Of Hell* – the production, which was masterminded by Todd Rundgren. His rigorous but thoughtful treatment of Steinman's music and the leeway he allowed Meat Loaf's vocal dramatics firmly etablished him as a top-rank producer.

For the next two years Meat Loaf concentrated on live performance, playing continual sell-out American tours while also managing to find the time to fit in work on various movies, the most publicised of which was *Roadie* (1980), a commercial failure that co-starred Debbie Harry of Blondie. The time was drawing near, however, when a follow-up to *Bat Out Of Hell* was required. The only other 'new' material that had appeared since its release was an album called *Stoney And Meat Loaf* (1979), but this consisted solely of pre-Steinman material and was of interest only to the most avid collector.

When Meat Loaf commenced work on his second album, the fatigue of constant touring caught up with him and manifested itself in voice problems. As the seriousness of his condition became evident – he had to undergo specialist therapy – material that was originally destined to appear on the album surfaced on Steinman's own solo album, *Bad For Good* (1981).

Although Meat Loaf was not involved with the record, *Bad For Good* was a logical extension of *Bat Out Of Hell*. The cover drawing depicted the hero from the cover of *Bat Out Of Hell*; instead of clinging to a motorbike, he was now clutching a girl – presumably won after some arduous battle with the forces of darkness. The LP was a resounding success and a single taken from it, 'Rock And Roll Dreams Come Through', was as strong and as stirring as anything on *Bat Out Of Hell*.

Hard to follow

After prolonged therapy, Meat Loaf rejoined Steinman and they set about making a new album, *Dead Ringer* (1981). Once again, Steinman wrote all the material and co-produced the album along with newly-recruited cohorts Jimmy Iovine (whose credits included work with Tom Petty and Bruce Springsteen) and Steven Galfas.

In the interim period, many doubts had been expressed by both fans and the rock media as to Meat Loaf's or Steinman's ability to follow *Bat Out Of Hell* with an

Left: Marvin Lee Aday – better known as Meat Loaf – sweats it out on stage. Right: Loaf gets into some meaty riffing. Inset above right: Jim Steinman, the musical brain behind Meat Loaf's throne. Inset far right: Mr Meat gets heavy.

album of the same calibre. There was a widespread feeling that *Bat Out Of Hell* was one of those rare occasions when artist, writer and producer had pooled their respective talents and come up with something so genuinely original as to be impossible to equal; the follow-up, *Dead Ringer*, was thus destined to be unfavourably compared with the first LP.

Under pressure

Although *Dead Ringer* lacked the insistent, imaginative bite of *Bat Out Of Hell*, it was clearly no epitaph. Top-notch musicians such as Roy Bittan and Max Weinberg from Bruce Springsteen's E Street Band, Liberty Devito from Billy Joel's group and Davey Johnstone from Elton John's band were drafted in to play on the album, while Meat Loaf's wife Lesley featured on the track 'Peel Out'. He also received vocal assistance from Ted Neeley (of *Jesus Christ Superstar* fame) and Rory Dodd, who had duetted with Steinman on 'Rock And Roll Dreams Come Through'.

With *Dead Ringer*, Steinman and Meat Loaf consciously or unconsciously steered clear of the epic subject-matter previously used and moved towards a more immediately accessible feel. The title track, a duet with the vivacious Cher, was released and became a massive hit. In the early Eighties the promotional video had come into its own as a means of selling a record, and the film of 'Dead Ringer' had all the ingredients necessary to sell the song – the most

Below: Meat Loaf greets singer Karla Devito (left) and Roadie co-star Debbie Harry. Bottom: Karla serenades him.

alluring of which was Cher, in a minuscule leather outfit, continuing a line of female vocal partners that had begun with Ellen Foley on *Bat Out Of Hell*.

Apparently cured of his throat problem, Meat Loaf took to the boards again. His stage act, brought to the UK for the first time in 1982, was a visual enactment of his songs. The highlight of the show was 'Paradise By The Dashboard Light', from *Bat Out Of Hell*, which was pure rock'n'roll vaudeville.

Meat Loaf bumbled around the set, the epitome of angst-ridden adolescence while a leather-clad girl singer, often resembling Cher in the 'Dead Ringer' video, portrayed the forbidden object of every teenager's new-found lust. The theatrical elements in the performance of every song established Meat Loaf as a firm favourite on the international rock circuit, a fact underlined by a series of sell-out tours in the UK in 1982 and 1983.

Bye-bye sci-fi

There was considerably less fuss made over the arrival of Meat Loaf's third album, *Midnight At The Lost And Found*, released in April 1983. By then, the music industry had grown almost complacent about his awesome debut – and, having swallowed its disappointment over *Dead Ringer*, expected little of interest. However, *Midnight At The Lost And Found* represented Meat Loaf's biggest departure yet from his 1978 debut. Steinman was not involved with the album at all; it was produced by veteran Tom Dowd, the man behind the controls of several of Lynyrd Skynyrd's albums and many of Rod Stewart's successes.

Gone were all traces of the sci-fi covers; instead only a rather unflattering black-and-white photograph of Meat Loaf graced the LP's sleeve. *Dead Ringer* had had the same *sound* as *Bat Out Of Hell* – and the same bombastic, monolithic production – but *Midnight At The Lost And Found* was a more traditional hard-rock album.

Jim Steinman wrote two tracks for Meat Loaf's 1984 album *Bad Attitude,* which reached Number 5 in the UK album charts. A single from it, 'Modern Girl' made the UK Top Twenty.

Though the cleverly titled *Hits Out Of Hell* compilation of former glories made Number 2 in Britain in 1985, the following year's dalliance with German disco producer Frank Farian for *Blind Before I Stop* was a mistake. It was clear that *Bat Out Of Hell*—still his only US chart album—would remain Meat Loaf's finest moment.

JAY WILLIAMS

Meatloaf
Recommended Listening
Bat Out Of Hell (Epic EPC 82419) (Includes: Bat Out Of Hell, Heaven Can Wait, All Revved Up With No Place To Go, Two Out Of Three Ain't Bad, Paradise By The Dashboard Light, For Crying Out Loud); *Dead Ringer* (Epic EPC 83645) (Includes: Peel Out, I'll Kill You If You Don't Come Back, Read 'Em And Weep, Nocturnal Pleasure, Dead Ringer For Love, More Than You Deserve).

AGENTS of FORTUNE

The well-kept secrets of Blue Oyster Cult

ALTHOUGH THEY NEVER sold records in the enormous quantities of some of their hard-rock contemporaries, Blue Oyster Cult were remarkable for bringing a rare intelligence to heavy metal, a genre more usually noted for its base predictability.

The band was formed in Long Island, New York, in the late Sixties by Eric Bloom (guitar, vocals), Allen Lanier (keyboards, guitar), Donald Roeser (also known as Buck Dharma – lead guitar, vocals), Joe Bouchard (bass, vocals) and Albert Bouchard (drums, vocals). Originally, the group was called Soft White

Above: Eric Bloom holds down a chord on his legendary 'stun guitar'.

Underbelly, later becoming the Stalk-Forest Group and recording two albums for Elektra, neither of which was released. It was not until late 1971 when, as Blue Oyster Cult, the band signed to Columbia that their fortunes began to change.

An important element in Blue Oyster Cult's development was the vision of the band's two Svengali figures: Sandy Pearlman and Murray Krugman. They conceived an approach to heavy rock which was based on the two UK bands they most admired, the Yardbirds and Black Sabbath, fusing the Yardbirds' blues-based guitar pyrotechnics with Sabbath's dense occult riffing to form a rock'n'roll mutant of awesome power. Pearlman and Krugman produced or co-produced the group's first seven albums and Pearlman regularly contributed song lyrics which reflected his demented obsessions.

Tyranny and mutation

By the time the band's first LP *Blue Oyster Cult* appeared in January 1972, a distinctive sound had already been forged and, with the possible exception of a slightly thin production, it remains one of the most remarkable debut efforts of all time. From the opening power surge of 'Transmaniacon MC', Blue Oyster Cult whipped up a frenzy of inexorable hard rock. The set contained a clutch of songs which were to retain a place in their live act for years to come: 'Stairway To The Stars', 'Before The Kiss, A Redcap', 'Cities On Flame With Rock And Roll'.

It is possible to discern a refined melodic sensibility on the album, particularly in 'Then Came The Last Days Of May', Donald Roeser's chilling tale of a dope deal going horribly wrong. That track provided him with the ideal opportunity to display his credentials as both ace songwriter and nascent guitar hero. While the loud but powerful music defied easy HM categorisation, the lyrics simply defied belief in presenting a heady brew of astronomy, ancient myth, pop mythology, black humour and plain madness.

This period also saw the first Blue Oyster Cult concerts in the US, and the group swiftly established themselves as a live force to be reckoned with, capable of pleasing the average fan in the same way they pleased critics. The focal figure on stage was Eric Bloom, attired in tight black leather and mirrored shades, snarling out the words and pausing occasionally to crash out monster chords on his legendary 'stun guitar', an enormous black, over-amped monstrosity. Over the stage hung an outsize replica of the Blue Oyster Cult logo, the ancient Greek symbol of Kronos (Saturn). Buck Dharma was very much the foil to Bloom's black leather nightmare, a small, dapper figure in a white suit who would step forward to solo with frantic power or chiming clarity. Behind these two, Allen Lanier contributed keyboard colourings or third guitar on the rowdier numbers, while the Bouchard brothers kept the rhythm section nailed down tight.

Below: Blue Oyster Cult go guitar crazy, from left Eric Bloom, Allen Lanier, Buck Dharma, Joe Bouchard and Albert Bouchard.

Above: R U Ready 2 Rock? – the Cult take Paris by storm, 1975. Right: The dapper figure of lead guitarist Buck Dharma steps into the spotlight.

In order to take full advantage of the success of these early concerts, Columbia released a strictly limited edition 12-inch EP in October 1972 entitled *Live Bootleg*. It contained 'Cities On Flame' and 'Workshop Of The Telescopes' from the first LP, together with 'The Red And The Black' (a taster from the second album) and 'Buck's Boogie' (which would resurface on the first official live set). In February 1973, the second LP *Tyranny And Mutation* was released in the US to a favourable critical reception. The album was divided into 'black' and 'red' sides, the former espousing a 'play and be damned' philosophy and including another crop of embryonic stage favourites in 'OD'd On Life Itself', 'Hot Rails To Hell' and the epic '7 Screaming Diz-Busters'. The second side concerned itself with weird beasts and paranormal happenings summed up in titles like 'Mistress Of The Salmon Salt' and 'Baby Ice Dog', the latter co-written by Patti Smith, longtime girlfriend of Lanier.

By 1974, a policy of constant touring in America had brought the band to the status of a major headlining act. In April of that year *Secret Treaties* was released, again to mass critical approval. The album's themes included supernatural Nazi plots, sado-masochism and general mayhem, and among the songs were two showstopping anthems in 'Me 262' and 'Astronomy'. In February 1975, the band attempted to capture the power of their stage set with a live double LP, *On Your Feet Or On Your Knees*; however, this fell some way short of pleasing the group and it is not hard to see why, for among a scattering of gems (in particular 'Last Days Of May'), there resided a great deal of dross such as the bloated guitar workouts 'Maserati GT' and 'Buck's Boogie'. To make matters worse, the album also included a thoroughly uninspired version of Steppenwolf's 'Born To Be Wild'.

Agents of fortune

At the end of 1975, Blue Oyster Cult finally arrived in the UK for their first tour, culminating with a sell-out show at Hammersmith Odeon. The London audience was stunned by the raw power of the band, the flashes of laser trickery and a winning way with stagecraft: the last number saw all five members of the group down at the front of the stage, all playing guitars – heavy metal taken to the extreme and parodied simultaneously.

Songwriting chores in BOC had always been spread around democratically and this process was taken one stage further for the next LP, *Agents Of Fortune* (1976), with each group member laying down individual tracks on a 4-track tape recorder and then presenting the finished product for band approval. The result, perhaps inevitably, was somewhat patchy, but the LP contained one indubitable ace in '(Don't Fear) The Reaper', which was released as a single to give the band a Number 12 hit in the US, Number 16 in the UK. This in turn gave the LP a boost and it rapidly became the group's most successful album. Patti Smith was again in evidence, both singing and composing, and with tracks of the quality of 'ETI' and 'This Ain't The Summer Of Love' the album fully justified its sales. A newly-developed 100,000-dollar laser show clinched the popularity of their live shows.

The appearance of BOC's sixth LP *Spectres* (November 1977) was heralded by the release of a single, 'R U Ready 2 Rock'. The LP presented a more melodic side of the band with an impressive trio of ghostly 'love' songs – 'Death Valley Nights', 'I Love The Night' and 'Nosferatu'.

Building fires

After a hectic period of touring, which again included UK dates, another live album was released in September 1978 entitled *Some Enchanted Evening*. This was a spirited workout, far superior to its live predecessor, and was particularly notable for a version of 'We Gotta Get Out Of This Place' recorded in the Animals' backyard in Newcastle. The following year, Tom Werman took over LP production duties from Pearlman and the resulting *Mirrors* was a major disappointment. For the first time, the Cult seemed to be floundering for want of direction and only 'Dr Music', an everyday tale of sado-masochism with vocal assistance from Ellen Foley and Genya Ravan, lived up to the group's usual high standards.

1980 brought a rapid return to form, however, with the June release of *Cultosaurus Erectus*, which was a conscious move back towards metal mania. The album was produced by Martin Birch, who had recently completed work on the Black Sabbath comeback album, *Heaven And Hell*, and the Sabbath connection was underlined when the two bands went on tour together billed as 'Black and Blue'.

1981's *Fire Of Unknown Origin* featured collaborations with Patti Smith, Michael Moorcock and rock critic R. Meltzer, with Martin Birch again producing. The highlight of the set was the mildly tastless 'Joan Crawford (Has Risen From The Grave)' but, on the whole, it was a lacklustre effort. 1982's live double LP *ETI* was an engaging romp through BOC classics, but fans had to wait until 1984 for a new studio LP, *The Revolution By Night*.

After 1983's *The Revolution By Night* and 1985's *Club Ninja*, the group members re-formed after solo projects in 1988 for *Imaginos*, a concept album in the mould of their early work. Arguably the most intelligent group in heavy metal, the Cult had been sorely missed. PETER CLARK

**Blue Oyster Cult
Recommended Listening**

Blue Oyster Cult (CBS 64904) (Includes: Transmaniacon MC, Stairway To The Stars, Before The Kiss, A Redcap, Redeemed, Workshop Of The Telescopes); *On Your Feet Or On Your Knees* (CBS 88116) (Includes; Harvester Of Eyes, Last Days Of May, 7 Screaming Diz-Busters, Cities On Flame, Hot Rails To Hell, Me 262).

THE GRAND ILLUSION

Styx: pop, pomp and pantomime

Top: Hicks from the Styx, from left Chuck Panozzo, Dennis DeYoung, John Panozzo and James Young. Above: Can you hear me at the back? – James Young as Mr Roboto, a character who featured on Kilroy Was Here. *Opposite: Styx's* Paradise Theater.

From the end of the Seventies, American adult-oriented rock music was dominated by a triumvirate of easy-listening rock bands – Journey, Foreigner and Styx. With their meticulous combination of pop and pomp, Styx blended music and theatre to create their brand of suburban escapism, earning themselves a long string of platinum-selling albums and hit singles.

The Styx foundations were laid as long ago as 1963 in Chicago, Illinois, when twin brothers Chuck and John Panozzo, on bass and drums respectively, began jamming with keyboardist/vocalist Dennis De Young. For five years their efforts were confined to the rehearsal room, until they were joined by guitarists James Young and John Curulewski in 1968. Calling themselves the Tradewinds, they began playing around the Chicago area.

In 1970 they changed their name to Styx, signed with the locally-based Wooden Nickel label, and released their first album, *Styx I*. As a debut it showed considerable promise, though the ideas were in the main poorly executed. Their second LP, *Styx II* (1973), was an improvement (and eventually yielded their first US hit single, 'Lady', in 1975), but in common with subsequent albums on Wooden Nickel, *The Serpent Is Rising* (1973) and *Man Of Miracles* (1974), it lacked depth.

1975 saw a change of label to A&M, and that year's album, *Equinox*, marked a creative watershed in Styx's career. Such classic songs as 'Midnight Ride', 'Born For Adventure' and the mini-epic 'Suite Madame Blue', were still looked upon as one of their most accomplished tracks.

The replacement of guitarist John Curulewski by the charismatic Tommy Shaw in 1975 gave the band another fillip. Shaw's commitment and energy onstage provided a new foil for vocalist Dennis De Young, while his superior guitar abilities and vocal harmonising enhanced their recorded work, as evidenced by 1976's *Crystal Ball* album.

Paradise lost

But it wasn't until 1977's *The Grand Illusion* that Styx made the breakthrough to mass recognition in the US. With this album, they finally hit on just the right mixture of syrupy vocal harmonies, pompous lyrics and ersatz rock'n'roll to beguile the great middle-American public into buying the album in quantities that quickly earned it platinum status. Tracks such as 'Miss America', 'Superstars', and 'Castle Walls' were to remain Styx favourites, while 'Come Sail Away', the single from the album, was a Top Ten hit.

The success of *The Grand Illusion* signalled Styx's elevation to the US stadium circuit, where they staged their typically baroque performances complete with massive light show and much formula gesturing in the rock'n'roll tradition.

With seamless professionalism, they continued to put out an album a year for the next three years. *Pieces Of Eight* (1978)

featured a slight softening of vocal style
and less emphasis on the keyboards, while
Cornerstone (1979) seemed to betray a lack
of direction, highlighting their tendency
towards blandness. Both albums went
platinum, and 'Babe', taken from *Cornerstone*, was a US Number 1 in 1979, and their
first UK hit, reaching Number 6 in 1980.

Their tenth album, *Paradise Theater*
(1980), represented a new, clearer direction for Styx. It was a concept album built
around the story of the Paradise Theater in
Chicago, which writer De Young used as a
rather clumsy metaphor to describe
America's decline in the late Seventies.
Originally 'built for perpetuity' in the
Thirties, the Paradise Theater fell into
disuse and was eventually torn down in

1958. Two singles, 'The Best Of Times' and
'Too Much Time On My Hands', both
reached the US Top Ten in early 1981.

1983's *Kilroy Was Here* continued with
the concept approach. Based on another De
Young idea, it told the story of Kilroy, the
'last rocker' at large in the US of the near
future when rock music had been banned,
and all rock'n'roll musicians locked up.
Styx made an 11-minute film of the 'story'
with members of the band acting the different parts. It was directed by Brian
Gibson, who had directed *Breaking Glass*
(1980). This was shown as a prelude to
their live appearances, for which the
various band-members continued to play
their film parts. The whole became woven
together as part-film show, part-concert
and part-theatre; a kind of multi-media
rock'n'roll pantomime.

Caught In The Act—Live (1984) reached
only Number 31 in the US after the
Number 1 success of *Paradise Theater* and
the Number 3 of *Kilroy*. And when
DeYoung and Young released solo albums
in 1984 it was widely assumed the Styx
story had ended.   CHRIS COLLINGWOOD

Styx
Recommended Listening

Rock Galaxy (RCA Records CL 43215) (Includes:
Lady, You Need Love, I'm Gonna Make You Feel It,
Best Thing, Right Away, Father OSA); *Kilroy Was
Here* (A&M Records AMLX 63734) (Includes: Mr
Roboto, Don't Let It End, Heavy Metal Poisoning,
Double Life, Cold War, High Time).

*Below: The guitars of Young (left) and
Tommy Shaw provide crucial elements
of the Styx sound.*

Going Dutch with the showmen of US rock

SINCE THE GREAT rock festivals of the late Sixties and early Seventies and the subsequent advent of arena rock, concerts in the United States have increasingly taken on the air of dazzling, money-spinning circuses. In response to the demands of this growing stadium circuit, a new breed of 'power and spectacle' heavy-rock band emerged in the late Seventies. In the forefront of this movement were US hard-rockers Van Halen, who combined a broadside of on-stage visual effects with their highly accomplished and aggressive style of playing.

The Van Halen brothers, Eddie (born 26 January 1957) and Alex (born 8 May 1955) started life in Nijmegen, Holland, and began studying classical piano at an early age at the insistence of their musically-minded father. In their teens, however, they changed to guitar and drums respectively. The family moved to California in 1968, where the brothers attended Pasadena High School and met singer Dave Lee Roth (born 10 October 1955 in Indiana).

The trio recruited a bassist and in 1974 began playing modest, low-key gigs under the name Mammoth. The initial bass player was replaced by Michael Anthony and, after further exhaustive gigging on the local circuit, they came to the attention of Kiss bassist Gene Simmons. He introduced them to producer Ted Templeman, who not only signed them to Warner Brothers in 1977 but also went on to produce all their albums.

Ready for Eddie

Re-christened Van Halen, the band recorded their first album, *Van Halen* (1978). It was an inspired debut for such a young band, highlighting in particular the guitar artistry of Eddie Van Halen. His astounding playing technique and inventive use of tremelo effects on tracks like 'Ain't Talkin' About Love' and 'Runnin' With The Devil' prompted singer Dave Lee Roth to comment: 'Eddie Van Halen is the first guitar hero of the Eighties; all the other guitar heroes are dead.'

A sweeping statement perhaps, but Eddie Van Halen's playing was consistently and widely admired – not only by fans, but by other guitarists too. In 1983 *Guitar Heroes* magazine asked practically every major rock guitarist to name their favourite player – Eddie Van Halen came out on top by a mile.

By the end of 1978, constant live work had earned Van Halen an impressive reputation, and Black Sabbath chose them as support on their American tour that year – only to be resoundingly upstaged by them. The second album, *Van Halen II* (1979), was again dominated by high-energy rock, although there were more subtle inclusions such as 'Spanish Fly' (an acoustic instrumental) and 'Dance The Night Away', a US Top Twenty single. On tracks

such as 'Somebody Get Me A Doctor', however, Van Halen reverted to the characteristic guitar histrionics, which they performed with an extraordinary technical facility.

The band's 1979 world tour was their first sustained exposure to consistently large audiences and confirmed their status as a top stadium act – so much so that nine months of 1980 were also given over to touring, and by 1982 they were able to gross 10 million dollars from the curiously-named Hide Your Sheep tour.

Van Halen failed to continue their all-conquering progress, however, with their

third album. *Women And Children First* (1980) was a hastily recorded affair that failed to realise the promise of the preceding releases. One track, 'Chains', was a notable exception, but otherwise the album was a self-indulgent ramble that fell short of their consistently excellent

Inset below: All tanked up and ready to roll – Van Halen prepare to assault the senses. Inset bottom: On-stage mayhem with balloons and bubbly – Eddie gets a soaking. Inset right: Eddie Van Halen strikes up his best guitar-hero pose. Below: Vocalist Dave Lee Roth.

live work. Fortunately, the balance was redressed by their fourth LP *Fair Warning* (1981), which was a welcome return to their original high-powered heavy rock and as strong a statement as anything since *Van Halen*.

Covering tracks

Diver Down, the band's 1982 album release, comprised 12 tracks, four of which were covers. These included unremarkable versions of Roy Orbison's '(Oh) Pretty Woman' and Martha and the Vandellas' 'Dancing In The Street', both of which reached the US Top Forty when released as singles. Although previous albums had incorporated one or two cover tracks – a version of the Kinks' 'You Really Got Me' from *Van Halen* was their first US hit single – four covers on one album seemed to betray a rather cavalier approach to recording. Only glimmers of their original rock'n'roll spirit shone through on 'Hang 'Em High' and 'The Full Bug'.

The main criticism levelled against Van Halen is that they achieved too much too soon. Their debut album, recorded when they were still hungry, showed how menacing and incisive their music could be, and although *Women And Children First* was their only truly disappointing album, they consistently failed to produce the material they were fully capable of.

On stage, however, they were brash and brilliant, careering through a chain of modern rock'n'roll anthems. Van Halen supplied visual entertainment allied with consummate technical skill. JAY WILLIAMS

ROCK·IN·EXILE

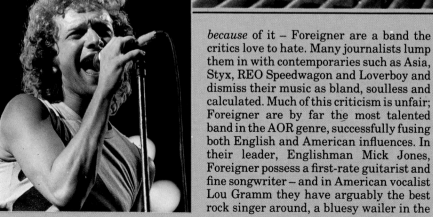

The triumphant travels of Foreigner

FOREIGNER ARE ROCK'S equivalent of that old show-business cliché 'the overnight success story'. With the release of their debut album in March 1977, this Anglo-American group leapt from obscurity to stardom. *Foreigner* sold a staggering five million copies, receiving saturation airplay and catapulting the group on to the money-spinning, stadium-rock circuit.

But despite this success – or perhaps *because* of it – Foreigner are a band the critics love to hate. Many journalists lump them in with contemporaries such as Asia, Styx, REO Speedwagon and Loverboy and dismiss their music as bland, soulless and calculated. Much of this criticism is unfair; Foreigner are by far the most talented band in the AOR genre, successfully fusing both English and American influences. In their leader, Englishman Mick Jones, Foreigner possess a first-rate guitarist and fine songwriter – and in American vocalist Lou Gramm they have arguably the best rock singer around, a bluesy wailer in the

Inset top: Foreigner's first edition, from left Lou Gramm, Al Greenwood, Mick Jones, Ian McDonald (standing), Dennis Elliott and Ed Gagliardi. Above: The band pace the boards in America. Below left: Singer Lou Gramm gives it some emotion.

full-blooded style of Free-period Paul Rodgers and Led Zeppelin's Robert Plant.

Disque blues
Mick Jones formed Foreigner in New York in 1976 after years of dues-paying in various bands, either obscure or only near-successful. At the age of 18 he gave up a career in surveying to travel to France as '24th guitar player' with instrumental band Nero and the Gladiators. The group dissolved while still in France but Jones chose to remain on the continent, pursuing a career as songwriter and session man for various French artists. Eventually he teamed up with 'the French Elvis', Johnny Halliday, leading his backing band. Halliday and Jones often visited London and New York to record, with Jimmy Page, Steve Marriott, Peter Frampton and producer Glyn Johns often helping out on the sessions.

Going West
In the early Seventies a dissatisfied Jones returned to London, initially for studio work with George Harrison, Peter Frampton and others. With ex-Spooky Tooth keyboardist/vocalist Gary Wright, Jones formed the unsuccessful Wonderwheel; a year later, on the advice of Island Records boss Chris Blackwell, the pair reformed Spooky Tooth. This English blues/rock band had enjoyed moderate popularity in the late Sixties, with former members including Luther Grosvenor (who went on to Mott the Hoople), Greg Ridley (Humble Pie) and Mike Kellie (the Only Ones).

The new-look Spooky Tooth concentrated on the American market and released three further, moderately successful albums, splitting in 1974 when Wright opted for a solo career. Jones then worked briefly as an A&R man for an English record company before landing a job as second guitarist in the Leslie West Band, spending the next nine months plastering American audiences with heavy-rock licks. When West's group folded, Jones returned to New York where, supported by manager Bud Prager (whose clients included Mountain and West, Bruce and Laing), he wrote songs, formulated plans for a new group and paid the rent with session work.

The seeds for Foreigner were sown when Jones contacted another expatriate Englishman, multi-instrumentalist Ian McDonald, and suggested forming a band. McDonald had been a founder member of the influential British group, King Crimson, whom he left after the successful LP *In The Court Of The Crimson King* (1969). During subsequent years he dabbled in a solo career, played on numerous sessions and produced various off-beat acts such as Ireland's Fruup and America's Fireballet. Having laid the foundations, Jones and McDonald enlisted two Americans, former Storm keyboardist Al Greenwood and bassist Ed Gagliardi. The rhythm section was completed by English drummer Dennis Elliott, a noted session player who had met Mick Jones at the recording of an Ian Hunter solo album.

The final recruit was a native New Yorker, vocalist Lou Gramm. Gramm co-founded and sang with hard-rock band Black Sheep and his display of vocal bravado on the group's two mid-Seventies albums convinced Jones that he was the man for Foreigner. Gramm was enlisted to the band after an audition in which he tackled songs like 'Feels Like The First Time'. The auditions were recorded – and eventually secured the band a worldwide deal with Atlantic Records.

After over a year of preparation, *Foreigner* was released in March 1977. Co-produced by Jones, McDonald and Gary Lyons, it yielded the US hits 'Feels Like The First Time', 'Long, Long Way From Home' and a worldwide smash, 'Cold As Ice'. Before the release of the album, *Double Vision*, in June 1978, Foreigner built upon their ecstatic American reception with a world tour, picking up gold and platinum awards from Europe, Japan, the Far East and Australia. *Double Vision* equalled the massive sales of their first LP and brought further US hit singles in 'Hot Blooded', 'Double Vision' and 'Blue Morning, Blue Day'.

The third album, *Head Games*, followed in September 1979, and was preceded by the replacement of Gagliardi by another Briton, Rick Wills. Wills' long list of credits included stints with Peter Frampton, Pink Floyd's Dave Gilmour, Roxy Music and the re-united Small Faces. *Head Games* continued the band's policy of switching producers with the presence of Roy Thomas Baker (Queen, the Cars). But despite multi-platinum sales and the inclusion of a Foreigner classic ('Dirty White Boy'), Jones later described the album as 'a disappointment' and, amid bitter recriminations, sacked McDonald and Greenwood. 'Things had become a little blasé and predictable,' Jones told reporters.

Guest stars
The fourth Foreigner album, *4*, emerged in July 1981 after a year of intensive rehearsal and recording and was co-produced by Jones and Robert John 'Mutt' Lange (whose credits included AC/DC, the Boomtown Rats and City Boy). Despite being reduced to a four-piece, Foreigner's attack was maintained with guest appearances by ace Motown saxophonist Junior Walker, guitarist Hugh McCracken and synthesiser whizz-kid Thomas Dolby, resulting in the band's strongest album to date. Highlights included 'Urgent', the stage favourite 'Juke Box Hero' and the ballad 'Waiting For A Girl Like You', a worldwide success that reached Number 2 in the US and Number 8 in the UK. Foreigner supported *4* with a year-long world tour, releasing a greatest hits album, *Records*, in late 1982. Their fifth LP, *Agent Provocateur*, was released in early 1985.

Thanks to Jones' commercial acumen and undoubted instrumental and song-writing talents, Foreigner remained one step ahead of their rivals. Their concentration on slick studio production coupled with a willingness to undergo gruelling tours has undoubtedly paid dividends in the form of vast record sales and packed concerts.

CHRIS MALCOLM

Foreigner
Recommended Listening
4 (Atlantic K50356) (Includes: Woman In Black, Urgent, Juke Box Hero, Waiting For A Girl Like You, Don't Let Go, Night Life); *Records* (Atlantic 78.0999-1) (Includes: Cold As Ice, Dirty White Boy, Hot Blooded, Feels Like The First Time, Head Games, Double Vision).

Hard rock's woman for all seasons?

THE ACCOMPLISHMENTS OF women in rock in the late Seventies and early Eighties have been well documented. But in terms of success, Pat Benatar towered above them all, a colossus in Spandex, out-selling, out-drawing and out-Grammying all competition.

Pat Benatar was middle America's rock'n'roll woman of the Eighties, mirroring all that was safe and acceptable, both music-ally and socially. She once said in an interview, 'I'm not very avant-garde or leftist, and I'm not really a tough girl. I see myself as singing mainstream Eighties rock 'n'roll.' And so teenage girls (and boys) flock to baseball stadiums to see her perform, punctuating their applause with clenched fists and buying her albums by the million because she is just like them.

Born in Brooklyn in 1953, Pat Andrzejewski grew up in Lindenhurst, New York, a middle-class New York City suburb. She recalls having 'a happy childhood, a real Catholic upbringing – cheerleader, the beach, Gidget.' Her father was a sheet metal worker and her mother a singer who was going to join the chorus of the Metropolitan Opera but abandoned her career when she became pregnant with Pat. Both her mother and grandmother loved opera and Pat began singing at nine with an eye to a career in serious music, despite her love for the Beatles and other British invasion bands. 'I always sang art songs and opera,' she remembers. 'I studied with a great teacher, training to go to Juilliard (America's premier music conservatory), and then I got bored with the idea.'

Fortune teller

So, after high-school graduation, Pat enrolled in the State University of New York at Stony Brook to study health education. She dropped her studies after two years and at 19 married her high-school sweetheart, Dennis Benatar, and moved with him to Richmond, Virginia, where he was stationed at the local army base.

Benatar worked as a bank teller for the first two years of her stay in Richmond, a job that led to her first fantasies of fortune, if not fame. Explaining why she started her singing career, Benatar recalled: 'I sat in that teller's cage every day, looked at the money and thought: "I know there's a way for me to have this without going to jail." I didn't want to sing, but I always knew that if I did it well enough, it could work. So I quit the job on an impulse and became a singing waitress.' Benatar quickly realised that the Richmond Holiday Inn lounge circuit was not the road to a recording contract and so she and her husband moved back to New York in 1975.

At an open audition at Catch A Rising

Left and opposite: Pat Benatar – a colossus in Spandex. Benatar succeeded in combining mighty vocals with a sexy image to make a mint.

Star, an Upper East Side comedian's show-case and cabaret, Benatar's three octave rendition of Judy Garland's 'Rockabye Your Baby With A Dixie Melody' caught the attention of club owner Rick Newman. Although it was 3.45 am, he was so impressed that he booked her into a regular spot at the club and a year later became her manager, a position he still held in the Eighties.

Newman was able to persuade Chrysalis Records chairmen Terry Ellis and Chris Wright to see Benatar's act and in 1978 they signed her to their label. She quickly assembled a band, including a guitarist from Cleveland named Neil Geraldo who was brought in to assist on the first LP. Geraldo stayed with the band, becoming Benatar's musical director and her lover.

In The Heat Of The Night was released in 1979. Produced in part by Blondie and Knack veteran Michael Chapman and his associate Peter Coleman, it went gold and produced two US hit singles, 'Heartbreak-er' and 'We Live For Love'. Press reaction was positive at first. Benatar was one of the first women to evoke Robert Plant and Ro-ger Daltrey as her inspiration, employ a heavy-rock band to back her up, and dress sexy on stage. But instead of the remote sensuality of Debbie Harry or the eccentric androgyny of Patti Smith, her sexiness was suburban shopping mall assertion. As she put it herself: 'A lot of women singers today seem to be saying: "if you love me and then hurt me, I'll die." I say: "If you love me, then hurt me, I'll kick your ass."'

Shedding her image
In 1980, Benatar released her follow-up album, *Crimes Of Passion,* which sold more than three million copies and yielded her first Top Ten single, 'Hit Me With Your Best Shot'. *Crimes Of Passion* was produced by Keith Olsen, known for his work with the Grateful Dead, and continued in the mainstream heavy-rock vein of the de-but. Although Benatar contributed more songs to the LP, including her bombastic epic against child abuse, 'Hell Is For Chil-dren', it was a style that she began to find increasingly confining.

On her 1980 tour, as opening act for the Doobie Brothers, Benatar began to feel embarrassed by her sexpot image. She took to wearing a jacket to cover her revealing leotards, refusing to take it off even when, at Omaha's Rosenblatt Stadium, the temperature soared past 95 degrees and she was dizzy with the heat. Benatar ascribed her embarrassment to media pressure. 'The thing I'm most reluctant ab-out is all the hoopla made,' she explained. 'I'm not going to stop doing it . . . If I was a man, none of this would be happening. It's just part of my personality. But when peo-ple make such a big thing of it, you become inhibited about it . . . you become a parody of yourself.'

Further stresses took their toll during the recording of 1981's *Precious Time* album, bringing Benatar to the verge of a breakdown. She argued with producer Olsen, broke up temporarily with Geraldo and began to wonder if it was all worth-while. She felt pressured especially to re-peat the formula of *Crimes Of Passion,* which had won her a Grammy for Best Female Vocalist. She described this period as 'hellish', saying: 'You wait your whole life for this and when it comes it's not what you expected . . . It stopped being fun. It became a job, a job I didn't want to do.' Nevertheless, *Precious Time* sold two million copies, and in a small but significant change of image, she asserted a new inde-pendence by cutting her hair and appearing on stage in trousers instead of tights.

1982 was a better year for Benatar. Having termin-ated her marriage, she and Geraldo were reconciled and in February were married on the Hawaiian Island of Maui.

Guitarist Scott St Clair Sheets left the band and was replaced by keyboardist Charlie Giordano who gave Benatar a cris-per, more lively sound. For her fourth LP, *Get Nervous,* featuring Benatar in a strait-jacket on the cover, Geraldo and Peter Col-eman's joint production proved to be more sympathetic to Benatar's idea of highly-pronounced vocals than Olsen's had been.

Above: Benatar and Geraldo (left) with the band. Right: Pat's best shot.

Get Nervous received good reviews and her 1983 tour was successful and provided a live LP, *Live From Earth*. In late 1984 Pat released the album *Tropico*. Pat gave birth to a baby girl in February 1985 in New York, just before the release of the single 'Love Is A Battlefield', co-written by Mike Chapman. The hits LP *Best Shots* (1986) went Top Ten after the disappointing *Seven The Hard Way* (1985), but *Wide Awake In Dreamland* (1988) was better.

Domestic bliss
Benatar has stated that she wants to settle down, have children and be 'the nicest old lady you ever saw', and she and Geraldo were frequently featured in national magazines billing and cooing about their new-found domestic bliss. But a very different picture of Pat Benatar – black tights, spiked heels, head thrown back, and microphone offered to the heavens – stands as a telling portrait of American women in music in the Eighties.   DEBBIE GELLER

Pat Benatar
Recommended Listening
In The Heat Of The Night (Chrysalis CHR 1236)
(Includes: No You Don't, Rated X, My Clone Sleeps Alone, So Sincere, In The Heat Of The Night, If You Think You Know How To Love Me); *Live From Earth* (Chrysalis CHR 1451) (Includes: Fire And Ice, Hit Me With Your Best Shot, Heartbreaker, Promises In The Dark, Hell Is For Children).

TURN IT UP!

How PA systems broke the sound barrier

THE MODERN CONCERT PA (public address) system can no longer be considered as simply a means of sound reinforcement. It has become a creative tool in its own right, and the sound engineer in charge of it will often bear a responsibility equal to that of any band member. This was not always so, however.

By the beginning of the Sixties, the electric guitar had become *the* instrument of modern music. With amplified guitars came a greater need for amplified vocals. The early PA systems were simply an extension of guitar systems: they used the same valve amplifiers to drive speakers primarily designed for instrument amplification. But these were less than suitable for vocal amplification, as their 'peaky' response aggravated feedback problems. To make matters worse, low budgets meant that most groups were less than fussy regarding their choice of microphones; although higher-quality models were available, few groups considered the extra expense worthwhile and so anything that would make a noise was plugged in regardless.

Above: Jimi Hendrix lays into his Marshall stack. Right: Charlie Watkins, pioneer of solid-state PA systems.

Marshall's law

The most popular British amplifier of the Fifties and Sixties was the Vox AC30, a simple but effective 30-watt valve amp favoured by the Shadows and later the Beatles. In 1965 Vox made a significant step forward with the introduction of their 100-watt, TC300 amplifier. This boasted bass, treble and 'presence' controls on each channel and Selmer and WEM soon had similar products on the market. The overall quality was still very poor, however, and these systems were soon to be dwarfed by the introduction of a new guitar amplifier by a man whose name remained at the forefront of modern instrument amplification in the Eighties: Jim Marshall. Marshall's legendary 100-watt guitar

Left: The Vox pop of the moptops. Below: Deep Purple listen to themselves through monitor 'wedges' placed on the stage edge.

amplifier was capable of creating previously unheard-of sound levels and suddenly it was back to square one: you couldn't hear the vocals.

It was obvious that a new PA system, enabling vocals to be audible above the guitar sound, would have to be developed for rock. The major problem was that valve technology in the mid Sixties suffered from electronic instability at higher power levels, or when two amplifiers were used in parallel with each other, leading to feedback and distortion.

Around 1966, RCA introduced the music industry to the delights of transformerless, solid-state circuitry by designing a circuit for a transistor amplifier. All the major manufacturers experimented with this new format, but they all came up with the same answer: transistorised amplification did not produce the warmth or depth of sound of valve amps. Furthermore, its

distortion was harsh and unpleasant – unlike the smooth, creamy nature of the valve equivalent.

Yet although the valve had advantages over the transistor for guitar amplification, the cleaner sound of the solid-state devices was ideal for PA applications. Equipment manufacturers at the time – with the exception of Charlie Watkins of WEM (Watkins Electric Music) – all seemed to miss this point, but it was one that Watkins was quick to exploit.

The slave trade

Watkins brought together two new concepts in sound reinforcement, both of which basically sprang from the advantages of this new stable transistor technology. First he separated the mixer from the power amplifier with the introduction of a small, five-input console, the Audiomaster.

Second, because transistor amps could be coupled together without the instability problems experienced with valve circuits, it made it possible to build a large PA system from a number of smaller units, and this gave rise to the modular or 'slave' system still used in the Eighties. The line output from the Audiomaster was connected to the input of the first 'slave' power amp; this had a parallel socket to allow the signal to be linked to a second slave, and from there to a third slave and so on.

In 1967, at the Windsor Jazz and Blues Festival, Watkins unveiled the world's first ever 1000-watt PA system. The appearance of the system's banks of speakers earned it the title of the 'Wall of Sound'. It was truly a revolution in sound reinforcement – a system of remarkable power and clarity – and soon every top band in the country was using WEM equipment. Several Audiomasters could be

Mixing the Music

The main PA mixer is generally centrally positioned somewhere in the mid-stalls so that the engineer can hear the balance of the sound as one of the audience. Signals from the stage are connected to the mixer via a single multicore cable which carries all the separate signals down possibly dozens of individual cables.

Any instrument with an acoustic output – guitar amps, drums, etc – will have a microphone placed closely to it. Certain modern microphones are designed to take the massive sound pressure levels involved with rock music, and they are also built to be sensitive only to sound arriving from directly in front of them: this 'unidirectional' characteristic helps stop the sound of other instruments 'spilling' into them. Purely electronic instruments, such as synthesisers, will generally be connected directly to the mixer from their line outputs. Having reached the desk, each signal can be individually processed with onboard equalisation (sophisticated tone controls) and auxiliary equipment, all of which can enhance or completely change its character.

By the late Seventies, new technology had led to highly sophisticated mixing consoles.

'Compressors' are used to maintain a constant signal level from any source prone to excessive fluctuation such as a bass guitar or vocals. 'Gates' and 'expanders' are used to reduce the effect of any spilling between microphones, while a multitude of effects units are used to introduce artificial reverb, echo and a whole variety of other tricks such as pitch changing, flanging and chorusing.

2139

linked together to provide more channels, and it became common practice to mike everything up through the PA rather than using the system exclusively for vocals.

The next significant development in the PA's evolution came in the Seventies with the American approach of using horn-loaded speaker systems (originally designed for the cinema) which were compact yet loud for the power involved. Designing a system to fill a large area so that the sound quality is consistent from the front row to the back demands a lot more than just knowing how to pile a mass of columns on top of each other. Some of the answers lie in the judicious use of horn-loading to control the throw and dispersion angles of each unit. Gradually the 'bins and horns' approach took the place of the column for all larger-scale applications.

But with all these developments in PA technology, another problem had presented itself – although the audience now had no difficulty in hearing the vocals and acoustic instruments, the general increase in sound levels meant that the band members themselves often found it hard to make out what was going on. This problem was solved by the introduction of 'foldback' systems – monitor speakers that were

Above: Setting up the PA for a Genesis concert – a massive task. Below: Van Halen blast away through their vast system.

placed on stage to allow the performers to hear a balanced representation of what each band member was playing and/or singing. The most popular type of purpose-built monitor speaker stood on the floor facing the artist and was generally referred to as a 'wedge' because of its shape.

Large and powerful PA systems marked the start of a continuing power game played between major rock acts of the Seventies. For many bands, the visual impact of a massive sound and lighting rig was an integral part of their stage show, and systems of 25-40,000 watts became the norm for major venues and festivals.

In the late Seventies and early Eighties, the wealth of the multi-track recording industry gave birth to a whole new world of signal-processing equipment. Little by little this new technology was applied to the live situation until a state-of-the-art live mixing console and auxiliary processing equipment rack became comparable in its sophistication to a top professional studio installation; in fact the equipment was often interchangeable. Live sound reproduction in the Eighties was better than it had ever been.   JIM BETTERIDGE

Children of the Revolution

Punk's splinter groups were caught between art and agitation

By THE END of 1978, punk rock seemed to have run out of steam. The biggest bands were either on the verge of breaking up or taking well-earned rests following heavy touring and recording schedules. It rapidly became clear that the future of punk rock lay in diversity and a greater degree of political orientation. After all, what had initially been termed 'punk' had in many cases simply been energetic boogie played by pub-rockers with the foresight to get a new haircut.

Revolution rock

Political ideas had rarely been expressed in song by the early punk bands – the main exception being the Clash. However, lyrics with some political content became a prerequisite for subsequent punk groups. Two of the most popular 'ideologically sound' bands in 1979 were Crass and the Ruts.

Crass' gigs at London's Conway Hall rapidly became the meeting place for people of similar anarchic ideals. The group's uncompromising, clumsy but exciting performances, both live and on record, set a trend for this strain of rock by according the lyrics more importance than the music. The Ruts were one of the last bands to combine pertinent lyrics with tuneful melodies; their hopes of major exposure were cruelly dashed, however, by the tragic death – from a heroin overdose – of lead singer Malcolm Owen in May 1980.

Both these bands had largely peaceful fans, many of whom would soon find themselves in open confrontation with the mindless followers of Sham 69. This band was fronted by Jimmy Pursey who, somewhat idealistically, encouraged skinheads to attend his group's gigs. Unable to control the resulting violence, he reluctantly disbanded the group.

The only punk bands that continued to develop in 1980 were heavily influenced by Crass and attempted to appeal to a 'politically aware' audience. Several – such as Vice Squad, Discharge, the Exploited, Chron Gen and Anti Pasti – became punk favourites around the time of the Apocalypse Now tour. These groups heralded the revival of interest in punk, but in the main the music they played was a tedious repetition of a style that had been fully exploited three years before. These outfits, with the exception of Discharge (the only *genuinely* political band of the bunch) rapidly disappeared; nevertheless, they had created a sizeable following of fans determined to continue picking over punk rock's carcass.

The only British music paper to continue covering punk to any great extent was *Sounds*, the cause being championed by writer Garry Bushell. Week by week, *Sounds* earnestly publicised the behaviour of bands like the Exploited, who 'entertained' fans with such incitements to violence as 'Kill A Mod'. Punk

had degenerated into nothing more than a musical soundtrack for an evening's head-breaking – a sordid state of affairs that was to continue throughout the early Eighties.

Along with the so-called 'new punk' of the above groups, *Sounds* introduced another movement – Oi! This was initially hailed as a genuinely working-class music, but was disgraced by the overt racism of its principal practitioners – notably the Four Skins. The group's presence sparked off the ugly scenes of the Southall riot in July 1981, when skinhead fans of the band battled with the local Asian community. British punk in the Eighties had come to involve every imaginable kind of youth sub-cult – some able to relate to one another, some violently hostile. While those bands that had been influenced by Crass-produced songs of unadulterated, pointed fury, the Oi! brigade pounded out football-terrace chants of unrepentant, unpleasant stupidity.

Ball of confusion

The possibility that a worthwhile, concerted movement might emerge from the thrashing excitement of late-Seventies punk rock had not been aided by the back-biting and bitching of the British music press. This helped to create an atmosphere of directionless uncertainty, reflected by the brief duration of many groups and the cliquish attitudes of their fans.

A more constructive side to punk was demonstrated by the groups influenced by the literacy, musical scope and avant-garde leanings of Siouxsie and the Banshees and Joy Division, such as Bauhaus, Sex Gang Children, Death Cult, the Mob, Alien Sex Fiend, Dead Man's Shadow and – best of all – Echo and the Bunnymen, Killing Joke and the Cure. While these bands displayed a number of good musical ideas and images, few appeared likely to achieve much more than cult status in the early Eighties.   MICK MERCER

Above: The Hambrough Tavern in Southall, London, goes up in flames in July 1981. It was set ablaze during the rioting that followed an appearance by Oi! band the Four Skins.

ROCK '78

1978 saw the first wave of UK punk collapse with the demise of the Sex Pistols and the decline of its ideals into drunken aggression and political violence. Bands like Sham 69 found it impossible to play because of the violent following they unwillingly attracted. But despite this tendency, many punk bands united in an impressive show of opposition to racism, and the year saw many major benefits for Rock Against Racism and the Anti-Nazi League take place in Britain.

Although several 'new-wave' acts like Blondie were beginning to make an impact on the charts, they were eclipsed – on both sides of the Atlantic – by established acts like Abba and born-again disco messiahs the Bee Gees; old favourites like Bob Dylan and David Bowie, meanwhile, undertook massively successful world tours.

January

2 Bob Dylan's ex-wife Sara pleads not guilty to charges of punching a teacher while attempting to take custody of her children.

14 The Sex Pistols play their last ever gig at Winterland, San Francisco: 'Ever had the feeling you've been had?' Rotten sneers at the audience.

27 Jefferson Starship singer Grace Slick is arrested for drunken driving after appearing as a guest judge at an amateur talent contest, where she swore at contestants, sang through their performances and pushed them around.

28 Rumours start that the Sex Pistols have split up.

February

11 Jamaican vocal duo Althea and Donna have a UK Number 1 hit with 'Uptown Top Ranking', while the Bee Gees' 'Stayin' Alive' is at Number 1 in the US.

20 Meat Loaf's 'Bat Out Of Hell' begins its three-year run in the US charts.

28 Bob Dylan's concert at the Budokan concert hall in Tokyo is recorded and later released as the LP, 'Bob Dylan At Budokan'.

March

4 Abba are Number 1 in the UK with 'Take A Chance On Me'.

11 'I'm just a person,' says Bob Dylan after being called 'the God of folk song' by Japanese fans.

29 Genesis start a world tour in the US.

30 Topper Headon and Paul Simonon of the Clash are charged with criminal damage after shooting six racing pigeons. Siouxsie Sioux is thrown out of a Soho, London, pub for wearing a T-shirt with an indecent picture on the front.

April

8 Tom Robinson announces that he is seriously considering representing Britain at an International Convention of Young Communists in Cuba.

17 Sandy Denny, ex-Fairport Convention singer, goes into a coma after falling down a flight of stairs; she dies four days later.

29 Covent Garden's Roxy Club is forced to close after residents protest about fighting and hooliganism.

30 Tom Robinson Band lead the Anti-Nazi League Carnival from Trafalgar Square to Victoria Park in Hackney, London, where, along with X-Ray Spex, Steel Pulse and the Clash, they play to some 15,000 people.

May

3 *The Last Waltz*, a film of the Band's farewell performance at Winterland two years earlier, opens at several Bay Area theatres in San Francisco.

13 Tubes singer Fee Waybill falls off stage and breaks his leg at Leicester's De Montfort Hall while acting out their punk parody 'Johnny Bugger'.

24 *Melody Maker* writer Allan Jones is punched in the mouth by Black Sabbath's Tony Iommi over an article he wrote four years previously.

June

10 The Who's Pete Townshend offers to pay for 2000 copies of the Skunks' first single after hearing them at London's Vortex Club.

14 Bob Dylan and Eric Clapton rub shoulders with Sid Vicious and Nancy Spungen at a Robert Gordon and Link Wray gig at the Music Machine in Camden, London.

17 German fans riot and set fire to the Lorelei Amphitheatre after Jefferson Airplane failed to appear because Grace Slick had severe stomach cramps.

18 A London Bohemian Love-In at the Roundhouse provides a bizarre union of punks and hippies, with Nik Turner and his band Sphynx, Tanz Der Youth, Steve Took's Horns, John Cooper Clarke, Patrik

Top: The Who's eccentric and extrovert drummer Keith Moon (above) dies of an overdose of drugs prescribed to cure his alcoholism. Left: Jimmy Pursey joins the Clash on stage at an Anti-Nazi League Carnival. Right: Sid and Nancy.

Fitzgerald, Roger Ruskin Spear, Michael Moorcock and Bob Calvert.

July
4   Joe Strummer is arrested at a gig at the Glasgow Apollo after trying to stop the bouncers manhandling members of the audience. Paul Simonon goes to his rescue and is also arrested. Both are later fined.

13/15   Graham Parker and the Rumour, the Fall, the Buzzcocks and Steel Pulse play a Rock Against Racism Festival in Alexandra Park, Manchester.
Capital Radio ban the Sex Pistols' new single, 'The Biggest Blow', which features vocals by train robber Ronnie Biggs, claiming it is 'a glorification of evil'.

August
5   Pete Meaden – the Who's first manager and a major influence on the London Mod scene in the Sixties – dies of barbiturate poisoning.

7   Les Perrin, leading PR man for the Stones, John Lennon, George Harrison and Frank Sinatra, dies at the age of 57.

19   Bryan Ferry reforms Roxy Music.

September
7   Who drummer Keith Moon is found dead in his Mayfair flat.

8   Johnny Rotten's new band Public Image Limited release their first single, 'Public Image'.

24   Elvis Costello, Aswad and Misty play for Rock Against Racism at Brockwell Park, Brixton. Sham 69 pull out, fearing that their presence will provoke violence.

October
7   Chet Helms puts on a 'Tribal Stomp' at the University of California. The bands appearing include Paul Butterfield, Country Joe, Big Brother and the Holding Company, Canned Heat plus poets, dancers and a light show. 'I'm high without acid,' he said afterwards.

9   French singer-songwriter Jacques Brel dies of a blood clot, aged 48.

12   Sid Vicious is charged with murdering his girlfriend Nancy Spungen.

23   Sid Vicious slashes his wrists with a razor blade and a broken light bulb while out on bail.

28   The Clash sack their manager Bernie Rhodes, who immediately sues the band for money he claims they owe him.

November
11   Midlands police investigate 'the sickest stunt ever staged by a punk-rock group' after the Birmingham based Anti-Social offer £15,000 to anyone willing to commit suicide on stage.

12   Johnny Rotten's lawyer applies to have the Sex Pistols' legal partnership wound up, and seeks an order preventing the use of the name Sex Pistols on any product not involving Rotten.

December
3   Elvis Costello and the Attractions lock themselves in their dressing room in Sydney after fans – who felt cheated because the band played for only an hour – pelted them with seats, yelling 'Elvis loves money' and 'Costello is a capitalist'.

8   Sid Vicious is slung into Rykers Island Jail, New York, after allegedly hitting Todd Smith – Patti's brother – with a bottle at Hurrah's disco.

16   Kenney Jones is named as the new Who drummer.

25/26   Public Image Limited play their first gigs at London's Rainbow. Promoters remove all 1800 stall seats.

CHRIS SCHÜLER, JENNY DAWSON

BORSTAL BREAKOUT

Sham 69's bold bid for freedom

THE STORY OF Sham 69 is the story of a broken dream. Their garrulous singer Jimmy Pursey saw himself as a spokesman for working-class youngsters; he hoped to bring them together, and encourage them to forget their differences: 'If the kids are united they will never be defeated,' he sang.

'The kids', however, had other ideas. The more frequently Pursey issued his appeals for unity, justice and tolerance, the more regularly they turned his gigs into battle-fields. The fights escalated into riots, and Pursey left the stage in tears at the Reading Festival in August 1978. One year later, it was all over for Sham 69: scared off by their violent reputation, no venue would book them.

Born and raised in Hersham, Surrey, Pursey ran away from home several times. At the age of 16, he embarked on a variety of jobs – everything from selling fruit on a barrow in the East End to working at Wimbledon greyhound track.

He started his musical career miming to records in pub discos and, in 1976, inspired by the excitement and possibilities of punk, decided to form his own band. The first Sham line-up was something of a false start, achieving little more than a series of gatecrashed university support gigs where 'no one took any notice of us'. In June 1977, Pursey broke up that band because 'they finally said they didn't believe in the songs', returning in the autumn with bassist Albie Maskall, drummer Mark 'Doidie' Cain and guitarist Dave Parsons. A three-track single, 'I Don't Wanna'/'Ulster'/'Red London', was released on Miles Copeland's Step Forward label in October that year.

A 'best mate'

By now, Sham 69 were building up a formidable army of fans, lured by the football-chant songs, the brazen punk roar of the music and the intense, hyperactive figure of Pursey himself. Yet despite this spectacle, Jimmy Pursey tried to project the personality of a 'best mate' rather than that of a rock star: 'I don't want people walking away saying "I spoke to Jimmy Pursey – he's a star". I want them to say, like: "Oh yeah, I spoke to Jimmy, he's alright, he's a good bloke".

'Something inside me tells me I should be getting up on stage and being a voicebox for those people, relaying back what I've felt from somebody else. It's like they're giving me the inspiration to write a song. I have to speak out for the people that inspire me.'

By the end of 1977, Sham 69 had signed a record deal with Polydor and changed their line-up again. Maskall left and was re-

Jimmy Pursey (top far left) and his band Sham 69 (top left) – from left Dave Parsons, Pursey, Albie Maskall and Mark Cain – were plagued by violence at their gigs (left and far left).

placed by bassist Dave 'Kermit' Treganna. A single, 'Borstal Breakout' (one of the great Sham classics), backed with 'Hey Little Rich Boy', was released in January 1978, to be followed by the band's first and most popular album, *Tell Us The Truth*, the next month.

It was at that time that Jimmy Pursey described the audience he wanted to reach: 'A punk is a kid in Glasgow, Liverpool, London, Southampton who lives in a grimy industrial estate, wears an old anorak, dirty jeans, pumps, goes out at night, has a game of football on the green, throws a couple of bricks through a window for a bit of cheek. They're the punks, they're the kids that this was supposed to get over to.'

Consistently complaining about uniforms as adopted by the young people who wore them to identify with certain cults and factions, Pursey tried, in his familiar breathless and excitable way, to plead for individuality among the people in the crowds who came to see him. Predictably, his rantings fell on deaf ears.

That's Life

Another album, *That's Life*, arrived in the shops in October 1978 and sold well enough for Sham to be awarded a silver disc. At the ceremony, a typically unimpressed Pursey stamped the disc under his feet as a protest at Polydor's treatment of the Angelic Upstarts – a band he had signed to his own JP custom label and who were later dumped by Polydor.

Despite recording a third and final album, *Hersham Boys* (1979) – a more light-hearted affair than its predecessors – Sham 69 were on their last legs. Disheartened by the growing scenes of violence at their gigs and dissatisfied with the group's direction, Pursey decided to wind up the band after an abortive project with former Sex Pistols Steve Jones and Paul Cook. 'I didn't want to make records and sell them for the sake of the record company. The other people in the band . . . wanted to go to America and I didn't. They wanted to do all the things that bands do and I didn't. I wanted to write about things that were heavy duty to them, and they wanted to write about other things.'

Dave Treganna went on to join Stiv Bators' Lords of the New Church, while Pursey made two solo LPs, *Imagination Camouflage* (1980) and *Alien Orphan* (1981). And so Sham 69 faded into history. Pursey, who reformed the group in 1988, remained hopeful. 'People say, "Punks and skinheads are always going to be like they are". If I believed that, I might as well kill myself now. I still believe the kids will be brought together when they understand themselves, and that's when they understand everybody else.' CAROL CLERK

Sham 69
Recommended Listening

That's Life (Polydor Deluxe POLD 5010) (Includes: Leave Me Alone, Who Gives A Damn, Hurry Up Harry, That's Life, Angels With Dirty Faces, Evil Way).

On the march with the Tom Robinson Band

TOM ROBINSON'S MUSIC in 1978 was often described as the 'thoughtful end of the new wave', and Robinson, throughout his career, certainly saw his role as a musician as something far more serious than simply being an 'entertainer'. He was an ardent campaigner for all manner of radical political movements, frequently commenting in his lyrics on current political issues. He was also perfectly frank about his homosexuality; however, he was not at all coquettish or camp in the accepted showbiz tradition, but a candid, direct personality who made his homosexual preferences abundantly clear in interview and song.

A 'problem youth'
Whereas that other would-be radical of the new wave, Jimmy Pursey of Sham 69, sang glibly about a 'Borstal Breakout', it is interesting to note that the altogether more mild-mannered Robinson had actually spent seven years in a 'corrective institution' – a readjustment centre in Kent for 'problem youths' to which he was sent at the age of 16. Another inmate was guitarist Danny Kustow, and the two of them played in a group together as early as 1971. However, the pair parted company, and in 1973 Robinson moved to London where he formed Café Society. Originally an acoustic trio, Café Society made one LP, *Café Society* (1975), on Ray Davies' Konk

label, before expanding in 1976 to a five-piece electric band.

During this period Robinson first took up the bass guitar. It was also at this time that he first came across punk, when he saw the Stranglers playing to 'an audience of maybe five people at the Hope and Anchor' and then the Sex Pistols at the 100 Club. 'I couldn't relate to it on any musical terms,' he later commented – but what he did relate to was the *impact* of these bands' music and the boldness of their ideas. He had already written several songs that went beyond the Sixties-style whimsy of Café Society; inspired by the message of punk, Robinson left to form his own Tom Robinson Band. He did a few gigs with a preliminary line-up at the end of 1976 before settling on a unit comprising himself on bass and vocals, Dolphin Taylor on drums, Mark Ambler on keyboards and his old friend Danny Kustow on guitar.

The Robinson band spent the first half of 1977 gigging around the London pubs,

Tom Robinson (left) played for many political causes, including Gay Pride Week (above). Above right: TRB at the Marquee.

building up a strong grass-roots following. Musically they were offering nothing new – Kustow's guitar-playing in particular had more in common with old-style heavy rock than the new buzzsaw energy of his contemporaries. But where they scored was in the passion of their delivery, their youthful commitment and the fact that Robinson was unafraid to bellow out his 'Glad To Be Gay' anthem in West London pubs run by hard-faced Irish landlords generally less than sympathetic to the gay movement. TRB gigs became a cross between a political rally and a vaudeville show, with song-sheets, news-letters and bulletins bearing the clenched fist symbol being passed among the audience. EMI signed TRB in the autumn of 1977, and '2-4-6-8 Motorway', released in October, rapidly rose to Number 5 in the UK charts.

Coming out
It is ironic that the single that launched TRB into the big league should have been a completely agreeable, life-on-the-road slice of boogie. EMI were wary of their new signing's socio-political stance and Robinson at first went along with the company's overtly commercial approach. However TRB's follow-up, a live EP called *Rising Free* (released in February 1978), laid the band's cards firmly on the table. It included 'Don't Take No For An Answer', 'Martin',

'Right On Sister' and the celebrated 'Glad To Be Gay'. These four powerful songs underlined the group's commitment to equal rights for all – especially gays. Despite its forthright, agit-prop message, *Rising Free* still made Number 18 in the UK charts.

TRB's first album, *Power In The Darkness*, duly appeared in May 1978, but behind the scenes all was not well with the group. Mark Ambler, still only 17 years old, had become increasingly erratic in his behaviour and in April he was ousted from the band. Then, although the LP sold well, reaching Number 4 in the UK, Robinson fell foul of many of the pitfalls that attend success in the music business: 'I think what really happened is that we all got too big for our boots,' he commented with candour in a BBC radio interview with DJ Peter Powell. Ambler was finally replaced by Ian Parker on keyboards, but then at the end of 1978 drummer Dolphin Taylor left the band.

Robinson, Kustow and Parker recruited session drummer Preston Heyman to complete the recording of a second LP, *TRB 2* (1979) – by Robinson's own admission a thoroughly unsatisfactory collection of songs. 'I think I was trying to write the sort of songs that were expected of me – but it was becoming *Socialist Worker* set to music.' As the rock press turned against them, the band's morale fell further; after a patchy six-week tour of America TRB broke up in July 1979.

Robinson's seeming failure as a group leader caused a crisis of confidence and he suffered a nervous breakdown. He undertook his next project, Sector 27, on the understanding that he would not play the role of principal performer. Comprising Jo Burt (bass, vocals), Stevie Blanchard (guitar), Derek Quinton (drums) and Robinson (this time on guitar and vocals), Sector 27 tried to begin life as a co-operative, four-piece group playing all-new material, and aimed to build up a following on its own merits as a band; but inevitably gigs were sold on the basis of Robinson's name. Sector 27 released various singles and an album, *Sector 27* (1980), but by the summer of 1981 Robinson decided to leave. The band carried on without him, eventually becoming a duo of Burt and Blanchard calling themselves BB.

The best is yet to come

In January 1982, Robinson moved to Hamburg, West Germany, where he recorded an album, *North By Northwest*, with percussionist Steve Laurie and producer Richard Mazda. The album signalled a new maturity in Robinson's approach, which led the *New Musical Express* to comment that he 'no longer preaches the reassuringly right-on line to the converted, but rather reveals himself as a victim of incurable romanticism . . . his best yet'. While garnering this critical praise, Robinson also confirmed his status as the darling of the alternative circuit by releasing *Cabaret '79*, a live recording of a show which he had put on three years earlier at the Collegiate Theatre, London, as part of Gay Pride week.

Robinson's renaissance was complete when, in the summer of 1983, he unexpectedly scored his biggest UK hit since 'Motorway' with the poignant 'War Baby'. He had by this time dispensed with the notion of maintaining a band with fixed personnel, preferring 'to have a very loose group . . . anything between three and 12 members depending on the occasion'. Danny Kustow, who had joined ex-Jam drummer Rick Buckler's Time UK, played on 'War Baby', which reached Number 6 on Robinson's own Panic label.

Despite concentrating on the alternative end of the rock circuit, Robinson was tempted to reform the TRB for a heady, nostalgic 1987 fling before resuming a low-key solo career. A man of tenacity and integrity, he had answered those commentators who had written him off as a spent force. Having survived the extremes of success and dejection, Robinson still had much to offer as a recording artist in the Eighties.   DAVID SINCLAIR

Tom Robinson Band
Recommended Listening

Power In The Darkness (EMI EMS 1066681) (Includes: Up Against The Wall, Too Good To Be True, Long Hot Summer, You Gotta Survive, Power In The Darkness, The Winter of '79); *TRB 2* (EMI EMS 1652151) (Includes: All Right All Night, Black Angel, Let My People Be, Law And Order, Bully For You, Blue Murder).

Psychedelia and psychosis from punk's high priestess

THE FACE is a chiselled mask, all cheek bones and black eyeliner, like an Egyptian tomb-painting. The voice, a cruel, hollow shriek, swoops gleefully on the lyric: 'Be a carcass, be a dead pork/Limblessly in love'. Love – or rather the 'moon-in-June' variety of love that infests the pop charts – lies bleeding as punk's most charismatic female performer stalks the stage. It is the winter of 1977-78: Siouxsie and the Banshees have a large cult following and a fearsome 'underground' reputation. Some-one has spray-painted 'Sign The Banshees – Do It Now' on the walls of 15 London record companies. But none of them will touch the band.

Bouquet of barbed wire

Susan Janet Dallion was born on 27 May 1957, and grew up in the South London suburb of Chislehurst. At this point fact becomes entwined with the carefully con-structed Banshee mystique: she allegedly attempted suicide at the age of six and was later ostracised at school for being a 'witch'. Her father died an alcoholic when she was 14, and she is reported to have laid a barbed-wire wreath on his grave.

She met Steve Bailey at a Sex Pistols gig in 1975. Two years older than Sue, he shared her musical interests. In addition to glam-rock – Bowie, Roxy Music, T. Rex – they both had a passion for American bands like the Velvet Underground, the New York Dolls and the Stooges. With their friends Bill Broad (later Billy Idol), Simon, Debbie and Sue Lucas (Cat-woman), they attended every Pistols gig in 1976. The 'Bromley Contingent', as they were called, became famous as Sex Pistols camp followers, posing for photographs with the band and even joining them on stage at times.

Sue and Steve soon decided to stage a musical event of their own. With Sid Vicious on drums and Marco Pirroni (who eventually joined Adam and the Ants) on guitar, Suzie and the Banshees made their debut at the 100 Club Punk Festival in September 1976 on the same bill as the Sex Pistols, the Clash and the Subway Sect. Apart from Marco, none of them had ever touched an instrument before. The result was 20 minutes of musical mayhem called 'The Lord's Prayer'. Steve Havoc, as Bailey then called himself, played a rudimentary E-string drone on a borrowed bass guitar, Sid thumped his kit and Marco's guitar fed back excruciatingly, while Suzie intoned the prayer and bawled snatches of any song that came into her head – 'Twist And Shout', 'Knocking On Heaven's Door', 'Rebel Rebel'. 'God, it was awful,' said one A&R man present.

That December, 'Punk Shocker' Siouxsie – she had now adopted the idiosyncratic spelling – found herself on the front page of the *Daily Mirror* after appearing with the Sex Pistols on the occasion of their

notorious Bill Grundy interview on Thames TV's 'Today'. By now, she and Steve were rehearsing seriously, but the Banshees' line-up remained unstable. Malcolm McLaren's assistant Nils Stevenson had taken over from Marco, but he soon became their manager, and P. T. Fenton took over on guitar. However, his playing was considered too 'rock'n'roll' (a Banshees hate-word) and he was replaced in June 1977 by John McKay, whose spare, eerie style was far removed from mainstream rock traditions.

With Kenny Morris on drums, the band started performing in earnest in the spring of 1977. Their material, which included cover versions of T. Rex's '20th Century Boy' and the theme from the TV series 'Captain Scarlet', along with original songs like 'Psychic', 'Scrapheap', 'Make Up To Break Up', 'Love In A Void' and 'Bad Shape' – was delivered at breakneck speed; Siouxsie's voice was shrill and thin, but the beginnings of the characteristic Banshees sound could be heard. Every gig would end with 'The Lord's Prayer', which was performed differently each time. Siouxsie and Steve – who eventually settled on the surname Severin, after a character in the Velvet Underground song 'Venus In Furs' – were developing into a strong writing team. They kept cuttings and swapped ideas from their notebooks – anything with a touch of the bizarre or sinister was grist to their mill.

The band gigged steadily throughout 1977 and the first half of 1978, building a large and fanatical following. But despite an appearance on Granada TV's 'So It Goes' in November 1977 and a widely bootlegged session for the 'John Peel Show' on BBC Radio One, the Banshees remained without a record contract.

Scream of the Banshee

It wasn't only their fervent artistic independence that scared off the record companies. The Banshees had attracted considerable public notoriety because of Siouxsie's penchant for posing in bondage garments and a swastika armband. The bondage gear, she claimed, was 'to show that erogenous zones are overrated and tits are no big deal,' while the swastika was 'a symbol of shock ... it was intended as nothing more'. Although the Banshees subsequently wrote to the *Melody Maker* protesting that 'We're not Nazis and we're getting pissed off for being shunned because of misquotes,' the image of Siouxsie as some kind of erotic Rhinemaiden was to plague the band for years.

On 9 June 1979, the Banshees finally signed to Polydor, who guaranteed the band a considerable degree of artistic control. When the Banshees objected to the company's choice of producer, Bruce Albertine, he was replaced by their own

Two faces of a Banshee: Siouxsie's strange and sinister stage presence (right) and rich, bizarre images (opposite) reflected the Banshees' changing music.

choice, Steve Lillywhite. Their first single, released that August, revealed the band's twin roots in glam-pop and the outer fringes of experimental music. The A-side, 'Hong Kong Garden', was an infectious number with a catchy 'oriental' guitar riff and brooding lyrics about imperialism, prostitution and drug trafficking, while the B-side, 'Voices', was a bizarre and haunting dream-soundtrack. The single reached Number 7 in the UK charts.

Siouxsie and the Banshees' debut LP, ominously titled *The Scream*, was released that October to ecstatic reviews and reached Number 25 in the album charts. On songs like 'Jigsaw Feeling', 'Mirage' and 'Suburban Relapse', Siouxsie delivered lyrics that explored the depths of neurosis and paranoia. Side one ended with one of their live favourites, a ferocious version of the Beatles' 'Helter Skelter' which began with a screech of guitar feedback over a death-knell bass before creaking into action like a rusty engine of torture.

The following year, they consolidated their position with two singles, 'The Staircase (Mystery)' and 'Playground Twist', and another album, *Join Hands*. This was an even more sombre affair than the first, but with the exception of a few tracks – like the intense dervish-dance of 'Icon' – it lacked the strength and sharpness of its predecessor. The lyrics were full of gothic imagery – skulls, coronets, catacombs and gallows – that reflected a move away from the harsh modernism of *The Scream* towards the barbaric splendour of their later albums.

Tales from the crypt
But tensions were developing within the group; the band's 'serious' intellectuals, Morris and McKay, felt that too many compromises were being made. Consistently outvoted by Siouxsie, Steve and Nils, they became increasingly frustrated. On 7 September 1979, the band arrived in Aberdeen at the beginning of the *Join Hands* tour. During an autograph session at a record shop, McKay and Morris had a public row with the rest of the band and stormed out.

Robert Smith, of support act the Cure, was drafted in as a temporary replacement for McKay. The new drummer was Budgie (real name Peter Clarke, born in St Helens, Lancashire, on 21 August 1957), formerly of Big In Japan and the Slits. With Smith playing two sets a night, one with the Cure and one with the Banshees, the tour resumed.

But before the Banshees could complete all the dates, Siouxsie collapsed with hepatitis. During her convalescence, she worked on new songs and learned to play the guitar. By the time she had recovered,

Above left: The line-up that recorded The Scream, *from left Kenny Morris, Steve Severin, Siouxsie and John McKay. Left: Siouxsie with Budgie (drums) and John McGeoch (guitar). Above far left: Robert Smith fronts his band the Cure.*

Robert Smith had returned to his own band; when the Banshees' next single, 'Happy House', appeared in March 1980, it featured Magazine's guitarist John McGeoch in a guest capacity. He also contributed some jangling, acoustic 12-string playing to their next single, 'Christine' – a distinctly psychedelic-sounding song, based on the true story of a woman with 22 different personalities.

With help from John McGeoch and ex-Sex Pistol Steve Jones, the Banshees completed their third LP, *Kaleidoscope* (1980), which showed them moving away from their punk origins towards their own peculiar blend of Eighties psychedelia.

Despite the relative failure of the 1980 single 'Israel', John McGeoch decided to join the band as a full-time member in January 1981. Steve Severin, meanwhile, produced two singles and an LP for the Scottish band Altered Images. Later that year, he played guitar with Lydia Lunch at a one-off concert at the Venue in London, an excruciating performance in the tradition of 'The Lord's Prayer' which was recorded on a 12-inch EP, *The Agony Is The Ecstacy*.

That summer, a new Banshees single, 'Spellbound', and an album, *JuJu*, were released. Among their strongest records, they combined the brooding menace of their earlier work with a driving energy and the swirling patterns of McGeoch's guitar. Particularly effective tracks on the LP were 'Into The Light', 'Head Cut' and 'Halloween'.

After the album's release, the band embarked on a massive world tour which, they announced, would be their last. Siouxsie and Budgie then set up their own band-within-a-band, the Creatures, and produced a 5-track EP, *Wild Things*, a sparse but effective record of drums and vocals only. In November 1981, a Siouxsie and the Banshees compilation album, *Once Upon A Time: The Singles,* was released.

For all its atmospheric power, *JuJu* had been a consolidation of the Banshees' musical strengths rather than a development of them. The first sign that their music was moving in exciting new directions came in April 1982, with the release of 'Fireworks'. This single – featuring a string section arranged by Virginia Astley, formerly of the Ravishing Beauties – had a rich, sensuous quality far removed from the bleakness of their early works.

These developments were temporarily halted when Siouxsie lost her voice during a tour of Scandinavia. Doctors advised her to abstain from singing for six months, then take lessons to learn how to project her voice properly, or risk ruining it permanently. Ignoring their advice, she played at the Elephant Fayre in Cornwall that summer and completed a new LP.

A track from the album, 'Slowdive', appeared in August, but did badly in the charts despite its relentless dance-floor stomp. *A Kiss In The Dreamhouse* (1982) followed a month later: its sumptuous, gold-embossed sleeve reflected the rich

exoticism of its music, which covered a wide variety of musical styles, ranging from the hushed, atmospheric 'Obsession' and the closed-circuit tape loop of 'Circle' to the trilling mandolin sounds of 'Melt!' and the late-night jazz of 'Cocoon'.

Pillars of the establishment
Shortly after the album's release, John McGeoch was mysteriously sacked. His replacement was none other than Robert Smith, who now decided to join the Banshees while continuing his career as singer/songwriter/guitarist with the Cure. Siouxsie and Budgie reactivated the Creatures, and had two hit singles. 'Miss The Girl' – their own composition – and an unlikely cover of Fifties jazz singer Mel Tormé's 'Right Now'. A trip to Hawaii produced an LP, *Feast*, recorded in local studios with local musicians. Steve Severin, meanwhile, contributed to Marc and the Mambas' LP *Torment And Toreros* (1983) and got together with Robert Smith and singer Jeanette Landray in a recording project called the Glove. This produced a single, 'Like An Animal', and an album, *Blue Sunshine* (1983).

The next Banshees single, released in September 1983, was further evidence of their fascination with psychedelia and late-period Beatles – a somewhat insipid cover of John Lennon's 'Dear Prudence' from *The Beatles* (1968). This was an unexpected hit – the biggest the Banshees had ever had – reaching Number 3 in the UK charts. Two gigs at a packed Royal Albert Hall were recorded on a live double LP, *Nocturne* (1983). For many fans, the Banshees had become a travesty of themselves. The bite of their lyrics had given way to Hammer schlock, the eerie elegance of the music to over-produced, arty self-indulgence.

The dismal 1984 LP *Hyaena* seemed to bear out this judgement; only 'Dazzle', also released as a single, stood out. Robert Smith hated the LP and left the band; his replacement was John Valentine Carruthers, formerly of Clock DVA. *The Thorn*, an EP of four of their old songs in classical arrangements by the Chandos Players, was followed by a lengthy silence. At the end of 1985, the Banshees made tentative moves towards recording some new songs.

Whatever their future, the Banshees' achievement was substantial. They influenced a wide range of performers, from Joy Division and the Cure through Echo and the Bunnymen to Toyah and Soft Cell. Siouxsie and the Banshees defined a whole area of sound, mood and feeling, and made it instantly recognisable as their own.

CHRIS SCHÜLER

> **Siouxsie and the Banshees**
> **Recommended Listening**
>
> *The Scream* (Polydor POLD 5009) (Includes: Jigsaw Feeling, Carcass, Helter Skelter, Metal Postcard, Mirage, Suburban Relapse); *Once Upon A Time: The Singles* (Polydor POLS 1056) (Includes: Hong Kong Garden, Playground Twist, Happy House, Christine, Israel, Spellbound).

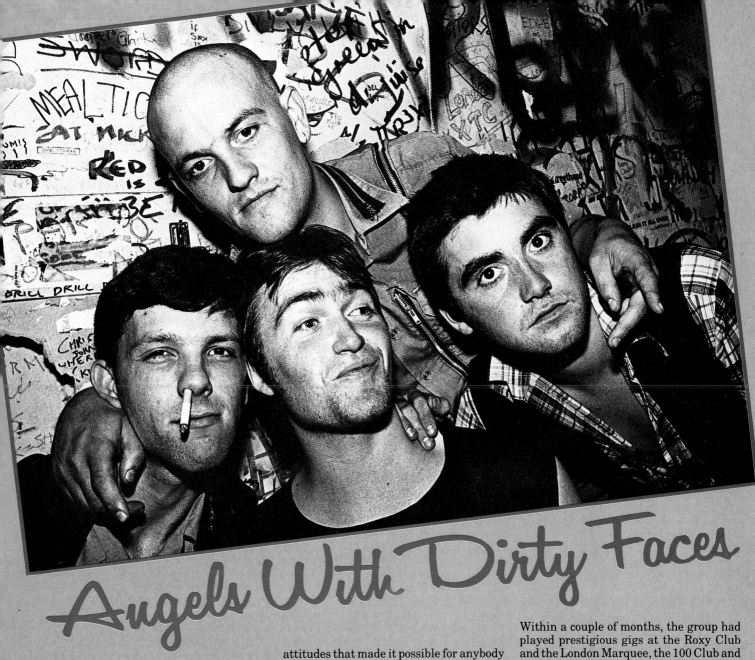

Angels With Dirty Faces

Three of the bands that kept punk alive

THE GENERATION of punk bands that sprang up after the first outburst had died away faced a changed music scene. Groups like the UK Subs, the Angelic Upstarts and the Cockney Rejects were aware that the original shock value of punk had long passed: the revolution was over, the course of music had been irrevocably altered and it was now their job to keep the momentum going. All three bands used the powerful energy of punk to create exciting and new styles of their own. They went about it in different ways, but their separate routes took them all to BBC-TV's 'Top Of The Pops' and brought a whole series of line-up changes, disappointments, problems and triumphs.

From their very beginnings, the Subs, Upstarts and Rejects made every effort to uphold the important principles of punk. They were the personification of the new

attitudes that made it possible for anybody and everybody to pick up a guitar and play it, to go to a gig and know that the group wanted to be at one with – rather than above – their audience. While earlier punk figures had become household names thanks to the national press, the punk bands of the later period were drinking in the pubs with their fans like any other 'normal' working people. As UK Subs vocalist and founder member Charlie Harper put it: 'Anybody can be a UK Sub'.

Those were the days

Harper recalls the pandemonium of 1978 with immense affection: 'There was a great sort of feeling in the atmosphere generally. Everyone was trying to work for something, everyone was joining bands and opening clubs, they were becoming DJs and starting independent labels and fanzines. People actually lived the music – they were involved.'

The UK Subs were formed in 1977, finding their identity in the autumn that year with the arrival of guitarist Nicky Garratt, who was to become Harper's co-writer.

Within a couple of months, the group had played prestigious gigs at the Roxy Club and the London Marquee, the 100 Club and the Vortex, as well as smaller shows at any pub that would have them.

'These gigs of ours tied in with the whole punk attitude of doing things for yourself,' Harper recalled. 'People were so hungry for music. We used to put on our own punk nights and get friends who had bands on the bill with us. Every band would bring 50, maybe 100 people.'

In the winter of 1978 their first single, 'CID', came out on City Records. It didn't chart, but their next single 'Stranglehold' made the UK Top Thirty and brought them a management deal early in 1979. This launched the Subs on a successful run of singles – 'Tomorrow's Girls', the *She's Not There* EP, 'Warhead' and 'Teenage' – that would win them a whole string of 'Top Of The Pops' appearances.

In September 1979 the UK Subs consolidated their fortunes with the release of their first album, *Another Kind Of Blues*, on Gem Records. Although the album has grown to sound almost subdued with the passing of time, the Subs' live sound was full of speed, volume and aggression, with

Charlie Harper bellowing like a rampant escapee from an asylum. Lyrically, the Subs' concerns ranged from the dole queue and the nuclear threat to the more usual rock subject-matter of love and sex.

From the atmospheric leanings of the *Brand New Age* album (1980) through the more directly experimental *Diminished Responsibility* (1981) and *Endangered Species* (1982) to the ambitious *Flood Of Lies* (1983) with its 'positive punk' overtones, the UK Subs widened their abilities and effectiveness without losing the powerful thrust that had always been at the heart of their music. Nor did they lose their sense of responsibility to the fans – their claim that 'anybody can be a UK Sub'.

The conflicts within this set of attitudes eventually led to the end of the long-term Harper-Garratt partnership. Charlie, with his 'man of the people' stance and his love for the pub and club circuit, insisted that the band continue to play small clubs alongside the larger venues they could now fill. Nicky Garratt was afraid that the UK Subs would become *too* accessible and lose sections of their following. This was indeed what started to happen, and Charlie struck out on his own in 1983 to rebuild the group.

Canning Town rejects

The Cockney Rejects – another London band – had no such reservations about fame and fortune. As vocalist Jefferson (previously Stinky) Turner said: 'I want to go to America and be a big star, have a

Above left: An early line-up of the Angelic Upstarts. Right: Upstart Mensi throttles a savage microphone with his bare hands. Above right: The Cockney Rejects, from left Vince Riordan, Jefferson 'Stinky' Turner and Micky Geggus.

house and a swimming pool.' Despite such grandiose ambitions, they quite happily continued hanging around the old haunts in their Canning Town homeland.

'Our music has always been about ourselves,' commented bassist Vince Riordan in 1981. 'Our lives always revolved round a big shithouse of a place called East London. We sang about violence because it was all we ever knew. People class us a lot of yobs which we were to start off with, but we've grown up now.'

Their first record, the *Flares And Slippers* EP, appeared on the independent Small Wonder Records in June 1979: the band's line-up then consisted of Stinky Turner (vocals), Micky Geggus (guitar), Chris Murrel (bass) and Paul Harvey (drums), but the next month saw a change in the rhythm section with Vince Riordan and Andy Scott coming in on bass and drums respectively.

The Rejects built up a large following that included many skinheads attracted by their football-terrace type music, which incorporated singalong chants and choruses and a thumping beat. They steadily acquired a reputation for violence at their gigs. 'I suppose you could blame us for being the instigators,' Micky admitted. 'We would incite trouble from the stage now and again and we'd jump in. Then we realised we were wrong. Our position in the music world was more important to us – we had everything to lose.'

But this realisation came too late for the Cockney Rejects. Very few venues would book them because of their early notoriety and their later association with Oi! – a movement they claim to have created but later disowned when its inherent violence led to a riot at Southall's Hambrough Tavern in 1981.

Getting heavy

As the Rejects carried on in the face of all opposition, they moved away from their old format, which had taken them to 'Top Of The Pops' with 'The Greatest Cockney Rip-Off' in April 1980 and 'I'm Forever Blowing Bubbles' the following May. Released in July 1981, *The Power And The Glory* was a hard-edged album but impressively melodic and a great deal more thoughtful than any of their three jokingly-titled *Greatest Hits* volumes. The damage had been done, however, and it was clear that the Rejects could no longer function in the punk format. As a result they met up with ex-UFO man Pete Way and renewed their earlier associations with heavy metal, releasing an album, *The Wild Ones*, in 1982 and working on plans for a new career that had little to do with their beginnings.

Fiercely political, determined to stand up for working-class people and to rage about their problems, Sunderland's Angelic Upstarts combined a strong sense of melody and a unique flair for choruses with some of the angriest lyrics to be heard anywhere. Equally likely to burst into thick Geordie recitations, soulful ballads or rocking anthems, singer Mensi delivered

Below: The UK Subs, from left Pete Davies (drums), Charlie Harper (vocals), Nicky Garratt (guitar) and Paul Slagg (bass). Above: Chief Sub Harper bellows away.

one tirade after another, yelling about everything from police brutality to the injustices of Conservative Britain: 'We're always going to sing about things that are relevant – we don't put our heads in sacks.'

Like the Cockney Rejects, the Angelic Upstarts first appeared on the small independent label Small Wonder, releasing singles like 'The Murder Of Liddle Towers', a raw, angry protest song about a man who died from injuries sustained while he was being arrested. They later signed to Warner Brothers and had hit singles with 'I'm An Upstart' and 'Teenage Warning' (both 1979).

These three groups were typical of the staunchly down-to-earth approach of the later punk bands. Although critics had long since pronounced punk dead, they carried on regardless of fashion, drawing considerable audiences and making a number of hit singles. Charlie Harper of the UK Subs summed it up when he said: 'I'll still be playing down the local pub once or twice a week in 20 years' time if I'm still here. An' that'll be good enough for me.'

CAROL CLERK

Angelic Upstarts
Recommended Listening

Angel Dust (The Collected Highs 1978-1983) (Anagram GRAM 007) (Includes: The Murder Of Liddle Towers, Police Oppression, I'm An Upstart, England, Never Say Die, Solidarity).

Cockney Rejects
Recommended Listening

Greatest Hits: Vol 1 (EMI ZONO 101) (Includes: Headbanger, Fighting In The Streets, Shitter, New Song, East End, Where The Hell Is Babylon?).

UK Subs
Recommended Listening

Recorded 1979-1981 (Abstract INT 145.066) (Includes: Warhead, Stranglehold, Scum Of The Earth, Emotional Blackmail, Keep On Running).

Independents' Day

The rise of the little label in UK rock

THE RECORD INDUSTRY in the Seventies was dominated by five major companies: EMI, CBS, Kinney Communications (who owned WEA), RCA and the German multinational Polydor/Phonogram. With their commitment to profit and chart success and their control over a band's image and, in some cases, their music, they were profoundly unappealing to the new wave of anti-establishment punk bands.

To many more, they were simply inaccessible. The majors all ran up massive overheads on recording, advertising campaigns, promotion and entertainment. By 1975, the British Phonographic Industry – the business' trade association – calculated that the average single had to sell 27,285 copies to recoup these costs. There was no place in this system for bands of more limited appeal, who could have made a respectable living by spending less extravagantly. And since the abolition of a statutory retail price in the late Sixties, most records were sold cheaply through bulk outlets like F. W. Woolworth and W. H. Smith, stores which only stocked albums in the Top Fifty.

In response to this situation, a whole new wave of independent labels sprang up

Manchester band the Fall (right) enjoyed a long and successful career on Rough Trade with their unique blend of snarled satire and abrasive music. Below: A selection of independent labels.

2155

to cater for new bands who demanded a degree of creative autonomy and often appealed to a smaller group of listeners.

There had always been independents of one sort or another, particularly in the US where labels like Sun and Atlantic were just a part of a lively tradition that continued through the Sixties; in the Seventies, Sire and Beserkley were influential in the growth of the American new wave. In the UK, meanwhile, Stiff and Chiswick sprang from the ashes of the pub-rock movement.

These labels proved that records could be released successfully for far lower overheads than the majors allowed for. Only one record in 20 released by major companies covered its costs – the rest sold very little. But Stiff and Chiswick, releasing records by the Count Bishops, Nick Lowe and the Damned, sold nearly 15,000 copies of virtually every single they released. Using eye-catching picture bags and witty, well-placed advertising, and by carefully placing their records in specialist shops, they managed to publicise their product while avoiding the expensive methods of the majors.

This was a more attractive option for the smaller bands and, by the end of 1977, a vast number of small independents had sprung up in the UK; New Hormones in Manchester released the Buzzcocks' first record, the *Spiral Scratch* EP, at the beginning of 1977 and provided an outlet for other local bands like Ludus; The Label's roster included the punk band Eater; Deptford Fun City was home for Squeeze and Mark P's Alternative Television; Cherry Red provided a UK outlet for American punks the Dead Kennedys and the Runaways; even Eighties supergroup the Police had their first single, 1977's 'Fall Out', released on an independent, Illegal.

Normal service

Many of these labels were little more than a name under which a band or an individual put out their self-produced records. The Desperate Bicycles recorded their EP *The Medium Is The Tedium* in 1977 for a total cost of just a few hundred pounds. At this level of cost, a record only had to sell about 1500 copies to break even, which was easily possible by then through the network of independent distributors like Lightning Records and Rough Trade.

Some of these 'own label' projects later developed into larger operations, like Mute. Formed in 1978 by Daniel Miller, the label's original release was a one-off single, 'Warm Leatherette'/'TVOD', by Miller himself under the name the Normal. The song was later covered by disco star Grace Jones, bringing in further funds, and the label went on to become an outlet for the highly successful electro-pop

Left: X-Mal Deutschland vocalist Anja. Relatively unknown in their native Germany, the band found success on the UK indie 4AD. Above left: Rough Trade hitmakers Stiff Little Fingers.

bands Depeche Mode and Yazoo.

This small-scale independent activity was made possible by a network of independent shops and distributors. By 1977, most large towns – and many smaller ones – had an independent record shop. They also served as meeting places and information exchanges, distributing home-made cassettes and fanzines.

Gold Fingers

Rough Trade was opened as an independent record shop in West London by Geoff Travis in 1976. It began distributing records by mail order early in 1977, and by the end of the year it had established a wholesale business. Since they kept receiving tapes from groups who could not get a record deal, it seemed logical to start a label themselves. Their first single was 'Paris Maquis', by the French punk band Metal Urbain, but the label really took off after the release of their first LP, *Inflammable Material* by the Northern Irish punk band Stiff Little Fingers, in February 1979 – by July, the album had gone gold.

This success enabled Rough Trade – an employee-managed co-operative – to build up a range of services for its artists: a publishing company, Rough Trade Music, an independent press and promotional service and a booking and tour management agency. Their roster grew to include Robert Wyatt, Red Crayola, Pere Ubu, the Fall, the Raincoats and Scritti Politti, but they continued to act as distributors for other less established names.

The late Seventies were undoubtedly the heyday for independent labels in the UK, but the climate was changing. The majors had been seriously shaken by this unexpected development: one CBS executive is reported to have arrived at a board meeting brandishing a handful of independent singles and demanding to know 'why haven't we got these bands?' Their response was to tempt away many of the bands who had made their name on indie labels with lucrative offers: Rough Trade's own most successful band, Stiff Little Fingers, signed to Chrysalis, where their career began to go downhill. Another tactic was to establish 'cosmetic' labels – often recruiting staff from the independents, who found it hard to refuse the offer of job security and a living wage. WEA set up Korova, which signed Echo and the Bunnymen, Polydor created Fiction, while Phonogram set up Back Door. These labels offered bands at least some kind of control over their product.

With the decline of punk, the indie boom began to falter. Bands were less concerned with creative control, aiming only at 'Top Of The Pops' once again. The music press – with the exception of *Sounds* and *ZigZag* – withdrew its support; reviewers adopted a cynical tone towards independent records, and *New Musical Express* dropped the listings of home-made cassettes that had provided such a valuable information service. Indies were suddenly unfashionable.

Several of the smaller companies went

Top: The Cocteau Twins. With the aid of extensive airplay on John Peel's radio show, the Scottish duo's second LP Head Over Heels *shot straight to the top of the indie charts in 1983. Centre: Tracy Thorne – one third of the Marine Girls, solo performer and reluctant star of the new jazzy acoustic pop music. Above: Alison Statton of Weekend.*

under: Small Wonder, which had successfully launched the careers of punk bands like the Angelic Upstarts, folded in 1981. Rough Trade and the other major indies were forced to become more selective in their releases, and it became harder for unknown bands to get their records distributed. In 1981, Rough Trade decided to concentrate on pushing their most commercial bands, Scritti Politti and Aztec Camera, and in the summer of 1982, Scritti Politti's debut album *Songs To Remember* reached Number 12 in the UK charts.

Quiet Giants

In 1982, Rough Trade streamlined the independent distribution by setting up the Cartel. This was a group of regional companies – Backs in Norwich, Fast Product in Edinburgh, Probe in Liverpool, Red Rhino in York and Revolver in Bristol – all of which had started as small shops. These outlets serviced the indie shops in their region, while Rough Trade continued to act as a central clearing house.

Despite the recession, there was still a healthy, if somewhat reduced, independent scene in the early Eighties. Rough Trade had come up with an exciting new band in the form of Young Marble Giants from Cardiff. This quiet and subtle pop group had recorded one excellent single, 'Final Day' and an album, *Colossal Youth* (1980) before they split. Their singer Alison Statton went on to front Weekend, a band very much in the new strain of jazzy, acoustic pop that was being encouraged by Cherry Red A&R man Michael Alway. After joining Cherry Red in 1980, he built up a new roster of acts like Eyeless in Gaza, Thomas Leer, Felt, Tracey Thorne, Ben Watt and the Marine Girls.

Together with the Beggar's Banquet subsidiary 4AD, whose discoveries included Modern English, the German band X-Mal Deutschland and the strange, swirling hypnotic music of the Cocteau Twins, Cherry Red represented one of the most exciting strands in the UK music scene in 1983; although no longer the fashionable cause they were in the punk heyday, the independent labels still had a vital role to fulfil.   PHYLLIS TYNE

The Politics of Punk

Musical manifestos and a radical message

FROM ITS BEGINNINGS in the Fifties, rock music offered the promise of rebellion. In an age of strict morality, racial segregation and political conformism, it lauded sex, adopted the mannerisms of black R&B and projected a defiant individualism. Yet rock was more a *symbol* of rebellion then the act itself – many of rock's early heroes, like Elvis Presley, were profoundly conservative, God-fearing Americans. It was only with the hippie era that the supposed rebelliousness of rock music became part of an entire lifestyle founded on opposition to the status quo. But success and its rewards saw such a stance abandoned.

When punk came along in the mid Seventies, its heroes were thus able to rebel not just against the establishment at large but against the rock establishment – the previous generation's rebels. 'Just the sight of one of their album covers makes me sick,' the Clash's Joe Strummer said about Led Zeppelin, while Sex Pistol Johnny Rotten sported a Pink Floyd T-shirt he had defaced with the words 'I hate'.

The fight against racism

Fuel was added to the fire in 1976 when David Bowie and Eric Clapton expressed fascist and racist sentiments in public. Coming at a time of increased activity in Britain by fascist groups like the National Front and the British Movement, these incidents led to the formation of Rock Against Racism. This organisation, dedicated to combating racism among young rock audiences, staged many benefits to raise money for anti-racist campaigns.

Rock Against Racism also produced a lively fanzine, *Temporary Hoarding*, which successfully adapted punk graphics to convey a political message. One of their covers juxtaposed the faces of Bowie and Clapton with that of Hitler, beneath the headline 'Love Music, Hate Racism'. Many prominent musicians played for RAR, and its success inspired many similar campaigns, from Rock Against Sexism in the UK to Rock Gegen Rechts (Rock Against The Right) in West Germany.

Rock Against Racism had close links with another anti-racist organisation, the Anti-Nazi League. Although this was aimed at a wider section of the public than just young rock audiences, there was considerable overlap between the two groups, and one of the ANL's biggest successes was a rally in Victoria Park, Hackney, East London, on 30 April 1978, at which the Clash, the Tom Robinson Band and X-Ray Spex played. In spite of allegations that they were merely front organisations for the Trotskyite Socialist Workers Party,

RAR and the ANL undoubtedly succeeded in combining rock music, striking graphics and a flair for organising demonstrations and carnivals to make rock audiences aware of anti-fascist and left-wing ideas.

Among the bands who played for RAR and the ANL were several whose songs were explicitly political. Apart from the Clash, with their macho 'urban guerrilla' stance, there was the Tom Robinson Band – who suffered, perhaps, from an excess of rhetoric – and the Gang of Four, from Leeds, whose début LP *Entertainment* (1979) welded fierce Marxist polemic to an angry blend of punk and funk.

One of the most successful political commentators in the music world at that time was Elvis Costello. 'Night Rally', from the LP *This Year's Model* (1978), was a chilling evocation of a clandestine fascist meeting, while his 1979 UK Number 2 single 'Oliver's Army' attacked the use of mercenaries. One of the simplest, catchiest political messages was contained in the Beat's 1980 single 'Stand Down Margaret' – a plea with which leftists, the unemployed and CND supporters alike could identify.

With the growth of the peace movement in the Eighties, the focus for political music-making shifted to groups like No Nukes Music and CND. Many groups such as the Beat, Madness, Orange Juice and the Jam – whose 1980 Number 1 single 'Going Underground' dealt with the nuclear threat – lent their services. The same year, two other anti-nuclear songs made the UK charts: Orchestral Maneouvres in the Dark had a Number 8 hit with 'Enola Gay' (the name of the aircraft that dropped the bomb on Hiroshima) and Kate Bush reached Number 16 with 'Breathing' (about an unborn child in the womb at the time the bomb drops). Glastonbury Fayre, a regular fixture in the festival calendar since the early Seventies, became a CND fund-raising event; in 1983, the bill included Curtis Mayfield, the Fun Boy Three (who burned the US flag on stage) and the visiting Nigerian band King Sunny Adé and his African Beats.

One area that the hippie 'revolution' had totally failed to address was that of sexism. Apart from a few exceptions like Grace Slick and Janis Joplin, women singers were associated with 'pretty' commercial pop. While punk hardly reversed this state of affairs, it did see the emergence of more women musicians like the Adverts' Gaye Advert and Tina Weymouth of Talking Heads, and more all-women bands like the Raincoats, the Slits and the Mo-Dettes. It also made sexual politics a popular topic for lyrics, with mixed-sex bands like the Delta Five and the Au Pairs writing some cutting songs about relations between the sexes.

Tom Robinson emerged in the late

Seventies as an energetic campaigner for gay rights; the subject of homosexuality had previously only been drawn upon by the likes of David Bowie to provide a titillating whiff of decadence. The singalong tune of Robinson's anthem 'Glad To Be Gay' (1978) could not conceal a sense of bitterness and injustice: 'Lie to your workmates, lie to your folks/Put down the queens, tell anti-queer jokes/Gay Lib's ridiculous, join their laughter/The buggers are legal now – what more are they after?'

Sales tactics

While many bands and organisations of the period showed considerable flair for campaigning and commentary, few seemed able to extend their political commitment into the economics of what they did. Without control of production and distribution, the most radical statements could be marketed and assimilated as just another commodity. 'The Revolutionaries Are On CBS' was an advertising slogan in the Sixties, and with the Clash signed to that label, and Tom Robinson and the Gang of Four on EMI, the situation in the late Seventies seemed little different.

A few small independents, like Recommended Records, whose roster included German experimentalists Faust, Slapp Happy and former Henry Cow members like Lindsey Cooper, offered an alternative, but lacked the broad appeal of the younger bands. A more successful attempt to bridge this gap was made by the Midlands-based 2-Tone label. Drawing on reggae's tradition of political comment and the furious energy of punk, Coventry band the Specials formed their own label, which they licensed to Chrysalis, retaining control over releases and artwork while availing themselves of the distribution facilities of a major label.

2-Tone's most conspicuous success came in the summer of 1981, when the Specials headlined an open-air concert in their home town to raise money for the Coventry Committee Against Racism, which had been set up after a series of vicious racial attacks in the city. Their single 'Ghost Town', a chilling picture of unemployment and urban decay, had reached Number 1 in the UK charts a few weeks earlier.

The growth of extreme right-wing movements like the National Front (top right) prompted the formation of Rock Against Racism to oppose them (right).

Although 2-Tone continued to release a series of excellent political singles from the Special AKA (the remnants of the now-defunct Specials and label-mates the Body-snatchers) as the Eighties continued, the label's fortunes declined as the record industry swung back towards safe, uncontroversial pop. The groups that survived the changes in pop fashion were those who – true to the spirit of punk autonomy – chose to work entirely outside the constraints of the commercial music business.

The most successful of these were the anarchist band Crass. Releasing records on their own label, with no advertising or radio airplay but gigging constantly on the benefit circuit, Crass built up a vast following in the late Seventies and early Eighties, their records regularly appearing at the top of the independent charts and even making inroads into the commercial chart. Taking their cue from the Sex Pistols, the former anarchist hippies cut their hair and despatched communiqués from their Epping commune in the form of punk singles like 'Big A Little A'.

Even Crass's most extreme musical ventures – excruciating collages of discordant sounds like 'Reality Asylum' and 'Nagasaki Nightmare' – failed to alienate their growing punk following, while a series of inspired stunts kept them in the public eye. The Royal Wedding in 1981 was celebrated by a special flexi-disc, which they somehow persuaded a girls' teenage magazine into giving away as a free gift. Its decidedly unromantic view of marriage brought them headlines in the *News Of The World*. The Falklands conflict of 1982 provoked the single 'How Does It Feel (To Be Mother Of 1000 Dead?)', which breached the House of Commons' rules of privilege by using a taped broadcast of a parliamentary debate. If the Sex Pistols had introduced the word anarchy to punk, Crass made it the movement's dominant political ideology.

Out of the kitchen
Perhaps the most exciting political band of the early Eighties, however, were the Poison Girls. They started out supporting Crass and releasing records on the Crass label, but after their excellent LP *Chappaquiddick Bridge* (1980) they decided to go it alone, although they later signed to the small independent label Illuminated. Fronted by Vi Subversa, a housewife in her forties, the Poison Girls broke all the rules about how pop groups – even anti-establishment ones – were supposed to look and act. While Crass remained aloof and even sinister on stage, the Poison Girls were warm and approachable. Their music, too, was more accessible, ranging from stomping numbers like 'State Control And Rock And Roll' to beautiful ballads like 'I'm Not Too Proud' and strange, ethereal songs like 'Cinnamon Garden'.

Simply by being who she was, Vi Subversa offered a far more profound challenge to the rock establishment than, say, the Clash or the Gang of Four ever could.

While the age of a jazz or soul performer has always been irrelevant, rock has traditionally derived its identity from the idea of 'youth' and its problems.

The idea of generational conflict has served to distract rock's 'rebels' from the more fundamental inequalities of race, class and gender. Rock may have caused the self-appointed guardians of public morals a few sleepless nights, but it has succeeded in changing little. Until rock could rid itself of the idea that a young, strutting, white male – be he Elvis Presley or Joe Strummer – was somehow 'rebellious', it seemed that it would never realise its full potential as a popular music capable of effecting serious social change.

CHRIS SCHÜLER

Below: 'Big Brother' adorns the cover of this Poison Girls single. Below right: Profits from the Beat's 'Stand Down Margaret' went to the Anti-Nuclear Campaign. Bottom: Music against the bomb.

No Nukes Music 14 Peto Place, London NW1

2160

U.S. HIT SINGLES

1984

JANUARY

7 SAY, SAY, SAY *Paul McCartney and Michael Jackson*
14 SAY, SAY, SAY *Paul McCartney and Michael Jackson*
21 OWNER OF A LONELY HEART *Yes*
28 OWNER OF A LONELY HEART *Yes*

FEBRUARY

4 KARMA CHAMELEON *Culture Club*
11 KARMA CHAMELEON *Culture Club*
18 KARMA CHAMELEON *Culture Club*
25 JUMP *Van Halen*

MARCH

3 JUMP *Van Halen*
10 JUMP *Van Halen*
17 JUMP *Van Halen*
24 JUMP *Van Halen*
31 FOOTLOOSE *Kenny Loggins*

APRIL

7 FOOTLOOSE *Kenny Loggins*
14 FOOTLOOSE *Kenny Loggins*
21 AGAINST ALL ODDS (TAKE A LOOK AT ME NOW)
   Phil Collins
28 AGAINST ALL ODDS (TAKE A LOOK AT ME NOW)
   Phil Collins

MAY

5 AGAINST ALL ODDS (TAKE A LOOK AT ME NOW)
   Phil Collins
12 HELLO *Lionel Richie*
19 HELLO *Lionel Richie*
26 LET'S HEAR IT FOR THE BOY *Deniece Williams*

JUNE

2 LET'S HEAR IT FOR THE BOY *Deniece Williams*
9 TIME AFTER TIME *Cyndi Lauper*
16 TIME AFTER TIME *Cyndi Lauper*
23 THE REFLEX *Duran Duran*
30 THE REFLEX *Duran Duran*

JULY

7 WHEN DOVES CRY *Prince*
14 WHEN DOVES CRY *Prince*
21 WHEN DOVES CRY *Prince*
28 WHEN DOVES CRY *Prince*

AUGUST

4 WHEN DOVES CRY *Prince*
11 GHOSTBUSTERS *Ray Parker Jr*
18 GHOSTBUSTERS *Ray Parker Jr*
25 GHOSTBUSTERS Ray Parker Jr

SEPTEMBER

1 WHAT'S LOVE GOT TO DO WITH IT *Tina Turner*
8 WHAT'S LOVE GOT TO DO WITH IT *Tina Turner*
15 WHAT'S LOVE GOT TO DO WITH IT *Tina Turner*
22 MISSING YOU *John Waite*
29 LET'S GO CRAZY *Prince*

OCTOBER

6 LET'S GO CRAZY *Prince*
13 I JUST CALLED TO SAY I LOVE YOU *Stevie Wonder*
20 I JUST CALLED TO SAY I LOVE YOU *Stevie Wonder*
27 I JUST CALLED TO SAY I LOVE YOU *Stevie Wonder*

NOVEMBER

3 CARIBBEAN QUEEN (NO MORE LOVE ON THE RUN)
   Billy Ocean
10 CARIBBEAN QUEEN (NO MORE LOVE ON THE RUN)
   Billy Ocean
17 WAKE ME UP BEFORE YOU GO GO *Wham!*
24 WAKE ME UP BEFORE YOU GO GO *Wham!*

DECEMBER

1 WAKE ME UP BEFORE YOU GO GO *Wham!*
8 OUT OF TOUCH *Daryl Hall and John Oates*
15 OUT OF TOUCH *Daryl Hall and John Oates*
22 LIKE A VIRGIN *Madonna*
29 LIKE A VIRGIN *Madonna*

1985

JANUARY

5 LIKE A VIRGIN   *Madonna*
12 LIKE A VIRGIN   *Madonna*
19 LIKE A VIRGIN   *Madonna*
26 LIKE A VIRGIN   *Madonna*

FEBRUARY

2 I WANT TO KNOW WHAT LOVE IS   *Foreigner*
9 I WANT TO KNOW WHAT LOVE IS   *Foreigner*
16 CARELESS WHISPER   *George Michael*
23 CARELESS WHISPER   *George Michael*

MARCH

2 CARELESS WHISPER   *George Michael*
9 CAN'T FIGHT THIS FEELING   *REO Speedwagon*
16 CAN'T FIGHT THIS FEELING   *REO Speedwagon*
23 CAN'T FIGHT THIS FEELING   *REO Speedwagon*
30 ONE MORE NIGHT   *Phil Collins*

APRIL

6 ONE MORE NIGHT   *Phil Collins*
13 WE ARE THE WORLD   *USA for Africa*
20 WE ARE THE WORLD   *USA for Africa*
27 WE ARE THE WORLD   *USA for Africa*

MAY

4 WE ARE THE WORLD   *USA for Africa*
11 CRAZY FOR YOU   *Madonna*
18 DON'T YOU (FORGET ABOUT ME)   *Simple Minds*
25 EVERYTHING SHE WANTS   *Wham!*

JUNE

1 EVERYTHING SHE WANTS   *Wham!*
8 EVERYBODY WANTS TO RULE THE WORLD
   Tears for Fears
15 EVERYBODY WANTS TO RULE THE WORLD
   Tears for Fears
22 HEAVEN   *Bryan Adams*
29 HEAVEN   *Bryan Adams*

JULY

6 SUSSUDIO   *Phil Collins*
13 A VIEW TO KILL   *Duran Duran*
20 A VIEW TO KILL   *Duran Duran*
27 EVERY TIME YOU GO AWAY   *Paul Young*

AUGUST

3 SHOUT   *Tears for Fears*
10 SHOUT   *Tears for Fears*
17 SHOUT   *Tears for Fears*
24 POWER OF LOVE   *Huey Lewis and the News*
31 POWER OF LOVE   *Huey Lewis and the News*

SEPTEMBER

7 ST. ELMO'S FIRE (MAN IN MOTION)   *John Parr*
14 ST. ELMO'S FIRE (MAN IN MOTION)   *John Parr*
21 MONEY FOR NOTHING   *Dire Straits*
28 MONEY FOR NOTHING   *Dire Straits*

OCTOBER

5 MONEY FOR NOTHING   *Dire Straits*
12 OH SHEILA   *Ready for the World*
19 TAKE ON ME   *A-Ha*
26 SAVING ALL MY LOVE FOR YOU   *Whitney Houston*

NOVEMBER

2 PART-TIME LOVER   *Stevie Wonder*
9 MIAMI VICE THEME   *Jan Hammer*
16 WE BUILT THIS CITY   *Starship*
23 WE BUILT THIS CITY   *Starship*
30 SEPARATE LIVES   *Phil Collins and Marilyn Martin*

DECEMBER

7 BROKEN WINGS   *Mr Mister*
14 BROKEN WINGS   *Mr Mister*
21 SAY YOU, SAY ME   *Lionel Richie*
28 SAY YOU, SAY ME   *Lionel Richie*

U.K. HIT SINGLES

1984

JANUARY

7	ONLY YOU	*Flying Pickets*
14	PIPES OF PEACE	*Paul McCartney*
21	PIPES OF PEACE	*Paul McCartney*
28	RELAX	*Frankie Goes to Hollywood*

FEBRUARY

4	RELAX	*Frankie Goes to Hollywood*
11	RELAX	*Frankie Goes to Hollywood*
18	RELAX	*Frankie Goes to Hollywood*
25	RELAX	*Frankie Goes to Hollywood*

MARCH

3	99 RED BALLOONS	*Nena*
10	99 RED BALLOONS	*Nena*
17	99 RED BALLOONS	*Nena*
24	HELLO	*Lionel Richie*
31	HELLO	*Lionel Richie*

APRIL

7	HELLO	*Lionel Richie*
14	HELLO	*Lionel Richie*
21	HELLO	*Lionel Richie*
28	HELLO	*Lionel Richie*

MAY

5	THE REFLEX	*Duran Duran*
12	THE REFLEX	*Duran Duran*
19	THE REFLEX	*Duran Duran*
26	THE REFLEX	*Duran Duran*

JUNE

2	WAKE ME UP BEFORE YOU GO GO	*Wham!*
9	WAKE ME UP BEFORE YOU GO GO	*Wham!*
19	TWO TRIBES	*Frankie Goes to Hollywood*
23	TWO TRIBES	*Frankie Goes to Hollywood*
30	TWO TRIBES	*Frankie Goes to Hollywood*

JULY

7	TWO TRIBES	*Frankie Goes to Hollywood*
14	TWO TRIBES	*Frankie Goes to Hollywood*
21	TWO TRIBES	*Frankie Goes to Hollywood*
28	TWO TRIBES	*Frankie Goes to Hollywood*

AUGUST

4	TWO TRIBES	*Frankie Goes to Hollywood*
11	TWO TRIBES	*Frankie Goes to Hollywood*
18	CARELESS WHISPER	*George Michael*
25	CARELESS WHISPER	*George Michael*

SEPTEMBER

1	CARELESS WHISPER	*George Michael*
8	I JUST CALLED TO SAY I LOVE YOU	*Stevie Wonder*
15	I JUST CALLED TO SAY I LOVE YOU	*Stevie Wonder*
22	I JUST CALLED TO SAY I LOVE YOU	*Stevie Wonder*
29	I JUST CALLED TO SAY I LOVE YOU	*Stevie Wonder*

OCTOBER

6	I JUST CALLED TO SAY I LOVE YOU	*Stevie Wonder*
13	I JUST CALLED TO SAY I LOVE YOU	*Stevie Wonder*
20	FREEDOM	*Wham!*
27	FREEDOM	*Wham!*

NOVEMBER

3	FREEDOM	*Wham!*
10	I FEEL FOR YOU	*Chaka Khan*
17	I FEEL FOR YOU	*Chaka Khan*
24	I FEEL FOR YOU	*Chaka Khan*

DECEMBER

1	I SHOULD HAVE KNOWN BETTER	*Jim Diamond*
8	THE POWER OF LOVE	*Frankie Goes to Hollywood*
15	DO THEY KNOW IT'S CHRISTMAS	*Band Aid*
22	DO THEY KNOW IT'S CHRISTMAS	*Band Aid*
29	DO THEY KNOW IT'S CHRISTMAS	*Band Aid*

1985

JANUARY

5 DO THEY KNOW IT'S CHRISTMAS *Band Aid*
12 DO THEY KNOW IT'S CHRISTMAS *Band Aid*
19 I WANT TO KNOW WHAT LOVE IS *Foreigner*
26 I WANT TO KNOW WHAT LOVE IS *Foreigner*

FEBRUARY

2 I KNOW HIM SO WELL *Elaine Paige and Barbara Dickson*
9 I KNOW HIM SO WELL *Elaine Paige and Barbara Dickson*
16 I KNOW HIM SO WELL *Elaine Paige and Barbara Dickson*
23 I KNOW HIM SO WELL *Elaine Paige and Barbara Dickson*

MARCH

2 I KNOW HIM SO WELL *Elaine Paige and Barbara Dickson*
9 YOU SPIN ME ROUND (LIKE A RECORD)
   Dead or Alive
16 YOU SPIN ME ROUND (LIKE A RECORD)
   Dead or Alive
23 EASY LOVER *Philip Bailey and Phil Collins*
30 EASY LOVER *Philip Bailey and Phil Collins*

APRIL

6 EASY LOVER *Philip Bailey and Phil Collins*
13 EASY LOVER *Philip Bailey and Phil Collins*
20 WE ARE THE WORLD *USA for Africa*
27 WE ARE THE WORLD *USA for Africa*

MAY

4 MOVE CLOSER *Phyllis Nelson*
11 19 *Paul Hardcastle*
18 19 *Paul Hardcastle*
25 19 *Paul Hardcastle*

JUNE

1 19 *Paul Hardcastle*
8 19 *Paul Hardcastle*
15 YOU'LL NEVER WALK ALONE *The Crowd*
22 YOU'LL NEVER WALK ALONE *The Crowd*
29 FRANKIE *Sister Sledge*

JULY

6 FRANKIE *Sister Sledge*
13 FRANKIE *Sister Sledge*
20 FRANKIE *Sister Sledge*
27 THERE MUST BE AN ANGEL (PLAYING WITH
   MY HEART) *Eurythmics*

AUGUST

3 INTO THE GROOVE *Madonna*
10 INTO THE GROOVE *Madonna*
17 INTO THE GROOVE *Madonna*
24 INTO THE GROOVE *Madonna*
31 I GOT YOU BABE *UB40 and Chrissie Hynde*

SEPTEMBER

7 DANCING IN THE STREET *David Bowie and Mick Jagger*
14 DANCING IN THE STREET *David Bowie and Mick Jagger*
21 DANCING IN THE STREET *David Bowie and Mick Jagger*
28 DANCING IN THE STREET *David Bowie and Mick Jagger*

OCTOBER

5 IF I WAS *Midge Ure*
12 THE POWER OF LOVE *Jennifer Rush*
19 THE POWER OF LOVE *Jennifer Rush*
26 THE POWER OF LOVE *Jennifer Rush*

NOVEMBER

2 THE POWER OF LOVE *Jennifer Rush*
9 THE POWER OF LOVE *Jennifer Rush*
16 A GOOD HEART *Feargal Sharkey*
23 A GOOD HEART *Feargal Sharkey*
30 I'M YOUR MAN *Wham!*

DECEMBER

7 I'M YOUR MAN *Wham!*
14 SAVING ALL MY LOVE FOR YOU *Whitney Houston*
21 SAVING ALL MY LOVE FOR YOU *Whitney Houston*
28 MERRY CHRISTMAS EVERYONE *Shakin' Stevens*